Roberto De Zerbi

92 Build Up, Passing Combinations and Attacking Positional Practices Direct from De Zerbi's Training Sessions

Published by

Roberto De Zerbi

92 Build Up, Passing Combinations and Attacking Positional Practices Direct from De Zerbi's Training Sessions

First published January 2024 by SoccerTutor.com
info@soccertutor.com | www.SoccerTutor.com

UK: 0208 1234 007 | **US:** (305) 767 4443 | **ROTW:** +44 208 1234 007
ISBN: 978-1-910491-66-9

Edited by
Alex Fitzgerald - SoccerTutor.com

Content contribution by
Allenatore.net

Diagrams
Diagram designs by SoccerTutor.com. All the diagrams in this book have been created using SoccerTutor.com Tactics Manager Software available from www.SoccerTutor.com

CONTENTS

Roberto De Zerbi's Build-up Play and Attacking Philosophy 47

Positional Possession Games 72

Positional Build-up Play 80

COACH PROFILE: ROBERTO DE ZERBI

COACHING ROLES

- **Brighton** (2022 - Present)
- **Shakhtar Donetsk** (2021-2022)
- **Sassuolo** (2018–2021)
- **Benevento** (2017–2018)
- **Palermo** (2016)
- **Foggia** (2014–2016)
- **Darfo Boario** (2013–2014)

- **Managing Brighton in the Premier League & Europa League:** In his first season, De Zerbi led Brighton to their highest ever Premier League finish (6th) and their first ever qualification for European competition. This season, they're continuing their strong performance, reaching the Europa League Last 16 by topping their group. As of this book's publication, Brighton's journey in Europe is still unfolding. De Zerbi's impressive impact has established him as one of the best young coaches in world football.
- **Managing Sassuolo in Serie A:** Took charge of Sassuolo in Serie A and over achieved by finishing in 8th position twice, playing attractive attacking football throughout his time there. He also helped develop and nurture the young players within the squad.
- **Coppa Italia Success:** Sassuolo reached the semi-finals of the Coppa Italia during the 2018-2019 season, a notable achievement for the club in a major domestic competition.
- **Ukrainian Super Cup:** Had a successful period at Shakhtar Donetsk before it was cut short due to the war in Ukraine. De Zerbi won the Ukrainian Super Cup in 2021 and left Shakhtar top of the Ukrainian Premier League before the season was cancelled.
- **Stint with Benevento:** Managed Benevento in the first ever season in Serie A, and his work with the team gained De Zerbi high praise and recognition for their possession-based attacking style of play, which led to him being appointed by Sassuolo for the next season.
- **Serie C Promotion with Foggia:** Gained recognition as a coach by guiding Foggia to promotion from Serie C to Serie B in the 2016-2017 season. This was a significant achievement for the club.

“Pay attention to what I’m going to say because I’m pretty convinced I’m right – Roberto De Zerbi is one of the most influential managers in the last 20 years.”

Pep Guardiola

DIAGRAM KEY

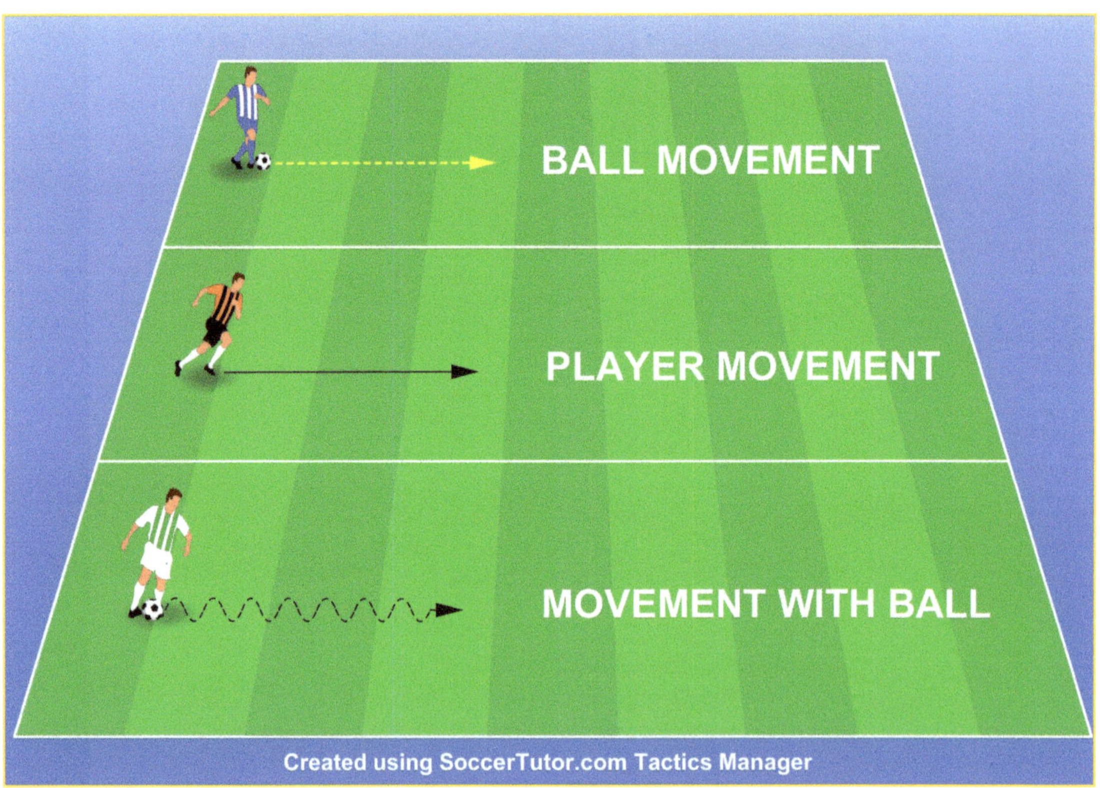

PRACTICE FORMAT

- The practices in this book are taken directly from Roberto De Zerbi's training sessions at Brighton, Shakhtar Donetsk, and Sassuolo between 2018 and 2023.
- Each practice includes the practice topic/name and clear diagrams with a detailed description.

Rondos

Direct from Roberto De Zerbi's Training Sessions

"To be a protagonist you have to keep the ball, to have the ball."

1. 5v2 Rondo to Maintain Possession with Short Passing and Pressing in Pairs to Win the Ball

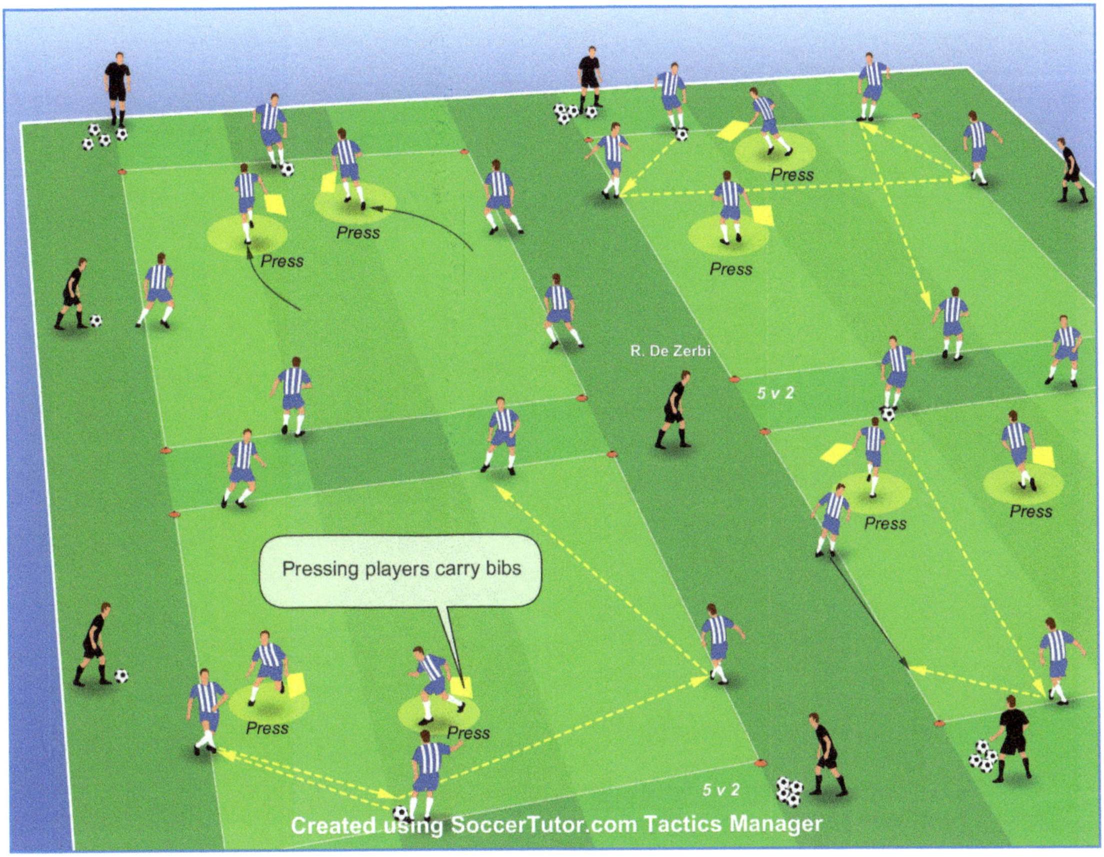

The 2 middle players carry bibs, which signify that they are the defenders.

Practice Description

- In this 5v2 Rondo, the players work in groups of 7 in an 8 yard square.
- The 5 outside players aim to keep possession of the ball and are only allowed to use **1 touch**. They are positioned on the outsides but must still play within the area.
- The 2 inside players (yellow bibs) work together to press, close the angles, and win the ball.
- If the 2 inside players win the ball within the first 10 passes, they BOTH switch roles with 2 outside players.

Source: Roberto De Zerbi's Brighton training session at the AMEX Elite Football Performance Centre - 2022

2. 4v2 +1 Middle Floating Player Rondo to Create Passing Angles and Pressing in Pairs to Win the Ball

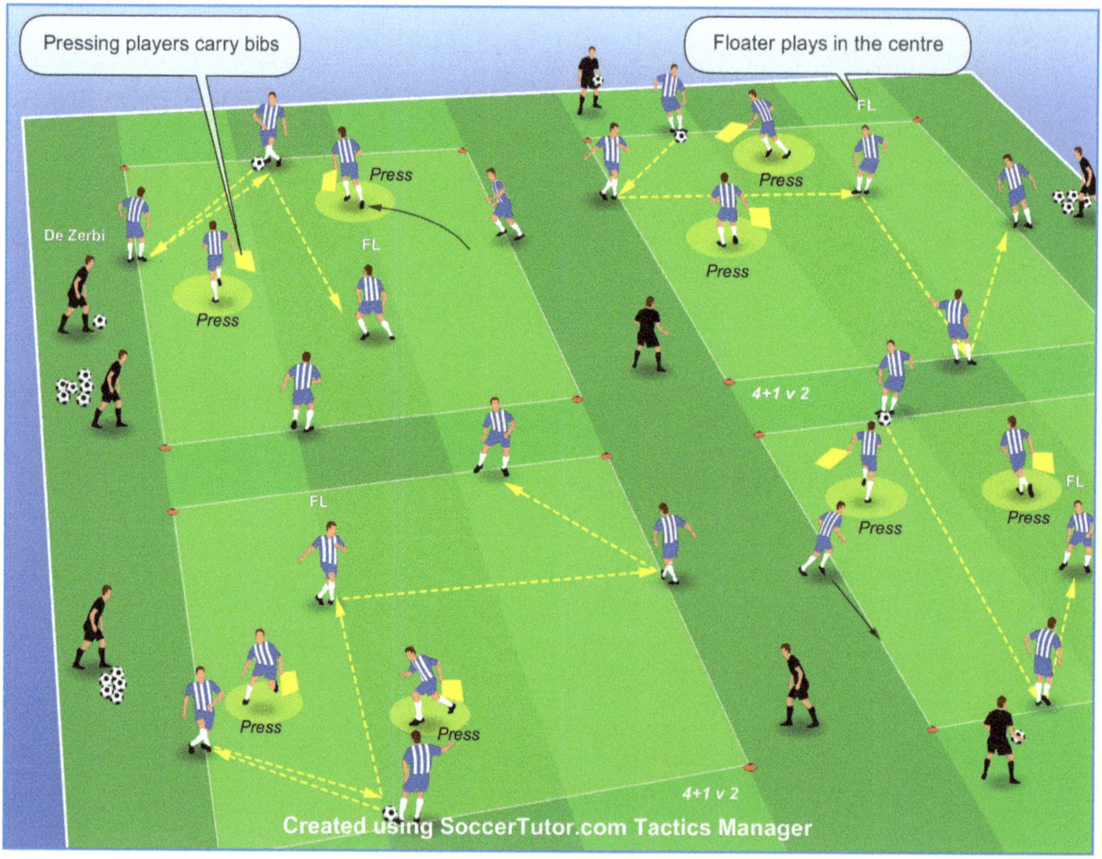

Pressing players carry bibs

Floater plays in the centre

The 2 middle players carry bibs, which signify that they are the defenders.

Practice Description

- In this variation of the traditional Rondo, there is an additional floating player (**FL**) in the middle who helps the 4 outside players keep possession.
- The players work in groups of 7 in an 8 yard square. The 4 outside players must play within the area using mainly 1 touch (2 touches allowed) and aim to keep possession of the ball with help from the floating player.
- The 2 defending players (yellow bibs) work together to press, close the angles for the potential passing lines and win the ball.
- The 2 players that touched the ball last when the ball is lost switch roles with the 2 defending players.

Source: Roberto De Zerbi's Brighton training session at the AMEX Elite Football Performance Centre - 2022

3. 6v2 +1 Middle Floating Player Rondo to Create Passing Angles and Pressing in Pairs to Win the Ball

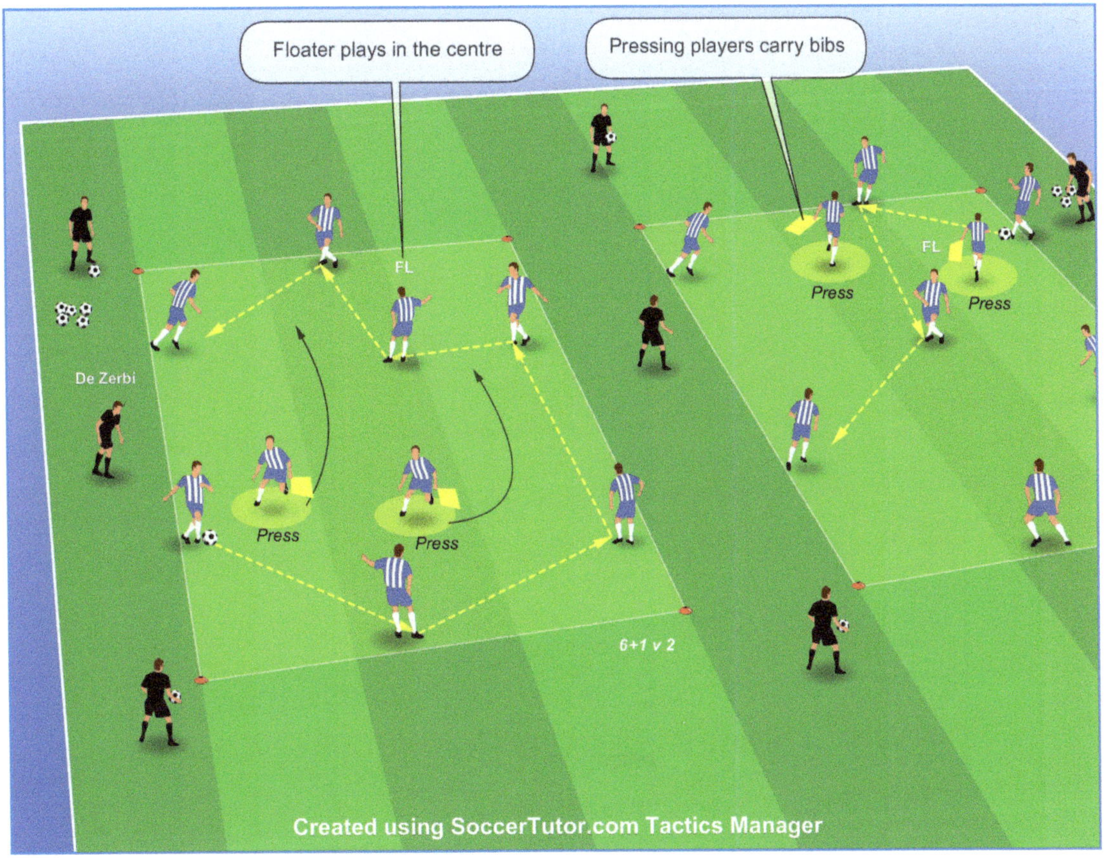

Floater plays in the centre

Pressing players carry bibs

FL

De Zerbi

Press

6+1 v 2

Created using SoccerTutor.com Tactics Manager

The 2 middle players carry bibs, which signify that they are the defenders.

Practice Description

- In this variation of the traditional Rondo, there is an additional floating player (**FL**) in the middle who helps the 6 outside players keep possession.
- The players work in groups of 9 in an 8x10 yard area. The 6 outside players must play within the area using mainly 1 touch (2 touches allowed) and aim to keep possession of the ball with help from the floating player.
- The 2 defending players (yellow bibs) work together to press, close the angles for the potential passing lines and win the ball.
- The 2 players that touched the ball last when the ball is lost switch roles with the 2 defending players.

Source: Roberto De Zerbi's Brighton training session at the AMEX Elite Football Performance Centre - 2022

SOCCER
TUTOR
.COM

4. 8v2 Rondo to Maintain Possession with Short Passing and Pressing in Pairs to Win the Ball

The players enjoyed the rondo and De Zerbi spontaneously joined in
De Zerbi
Press
Press
8 v 2
Pressing players carry bibs
Created using SoccerTutor.com Tactics Manager

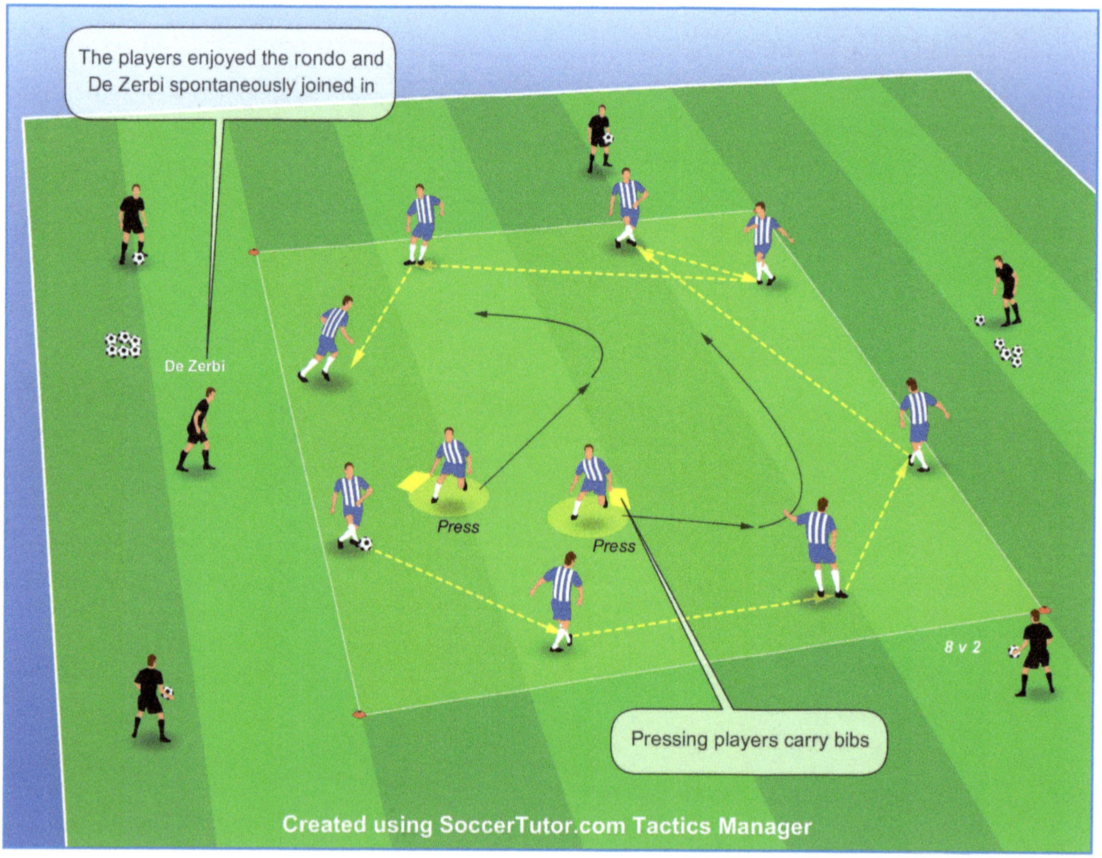

The 2 middle players carry bibs, which signify that they are the defenders.

Practice Description

- In this 8v2 Rondo, the players work in groups of 10 in a 10 yard square.
- The 8 outside players aim to keep possession of the ball and are only allowed to use **1 touch**. They are positioned on the outsides but must still play within the area.
- The 2 inside players (yellow bibs) work together to press, close the angles, and win the ball.
- If they win the ball within the first 10 passes, they BOTH switch roles with 2 outside players.

Source: Roberto De Zerbi's Brighton training session at the AMEX Elite Football Performance Centre - 2022

5. 8v2 +1 Middle Floating Player Rondo to Create Passing Angles and Pressing in Pairs to Win the Ball

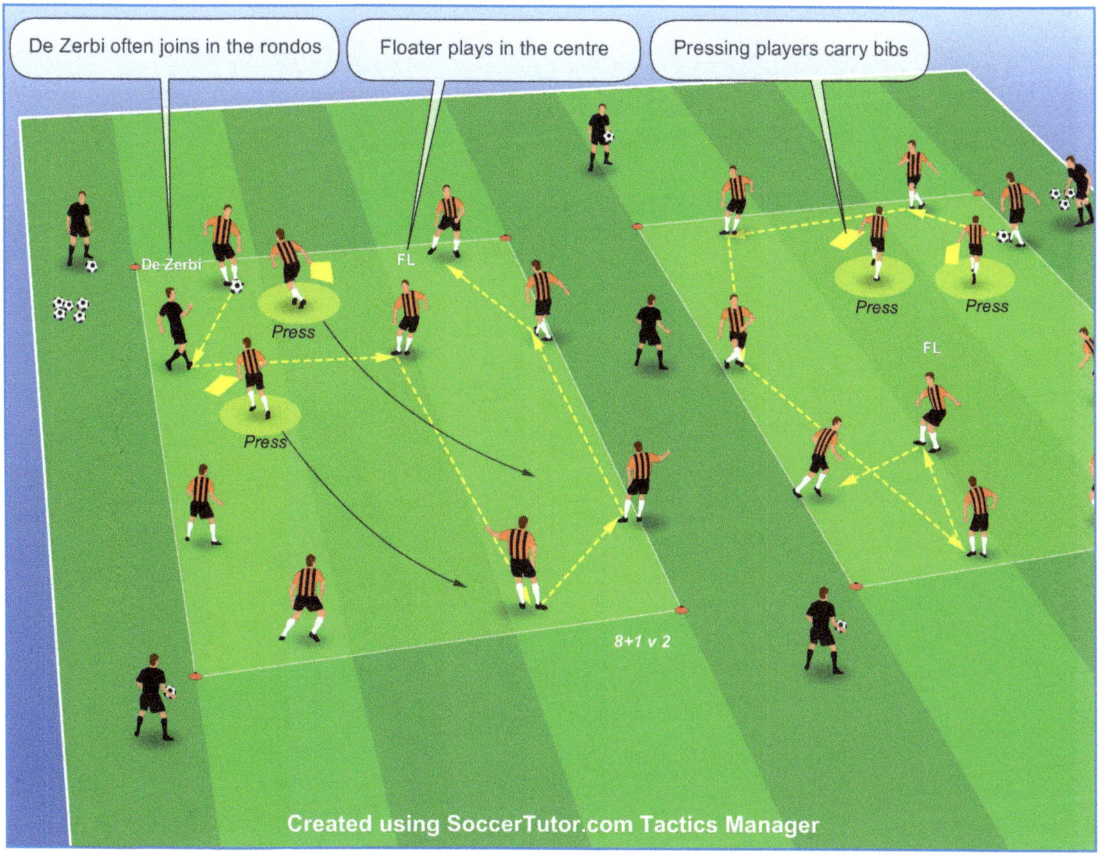

The 2 middle players carry bibs, which signify that they are the defenders.

Practice Description

- In this variation of the traditional Rondo, there is an additional floating player (**FL**) in the middle who helps the 8 outside players keep possession.
- The players work in groups of 11 in a 10x12 yard area. The 8 outside players must play within the area using mainly 1 touch (2 touches allowed) and aim to keep possession of the ball with help from the floating player.
- The 2 defending players (yellow bibs) work together to press, close the angles for the potential passing lines and win the ball.
- The 2 players that touched the ball last when the ball is lost switch roles with the 2 defending players.

Source: Roberto De Zerbi's Shakhtar Donetsk training session at Sviatoshyn Sports Complex -

Passing Combinations

Direct from Roberto De Zerbi's Training Sessions

"There is no permanence to technique. As a result, it suffers from a lack of practice. Therefore, it is important to challenge technique during training. We see this most often in small spaces."

1. 4-Player Combinations and Support Play with Rotations and Timing of Movement

Variation 1: One-Two, Forward Pass, and Move to Support

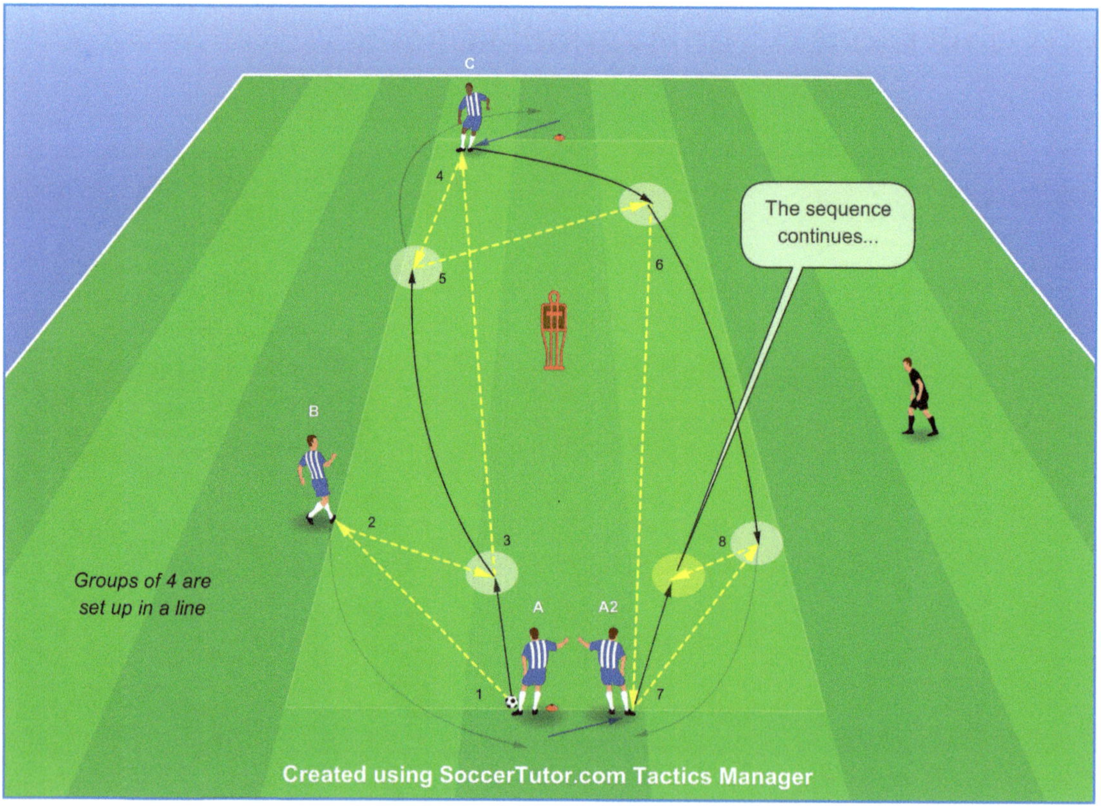

The sequence continues...

Groups of 4 are set up in a line

Created using SoccerTutor.com Tactics Manager

This passing combination normally involves 3 players, but 1 extra player is involved in this De Zerbi Brighton practice (groups of 4) to help the progression into Variation 2 shown on the following page.

Practice Description (Variation 1)

1-2. **A** plays a one-two with **B**, who moves to Position A.

3. **B** passes to **C** at the opposite end and moves forward.

4-5. **C** plays a one-two with **B**, who moves to Position C. **C** moves across to the other side to receive the return pass.

6. **C** passes to **A2** at the opposite end and moves forward.

7-8. **A2** plays a one-two with **C**, who moves to Position A2.

→ The same sequence continues with the players in their new positions (rotation).

Source: Roberto De Zerbi's Brighton training session at Elite Football Performance Centre - 21st July 2023

Variation 2: Short Combinations + Rotations (Progression)

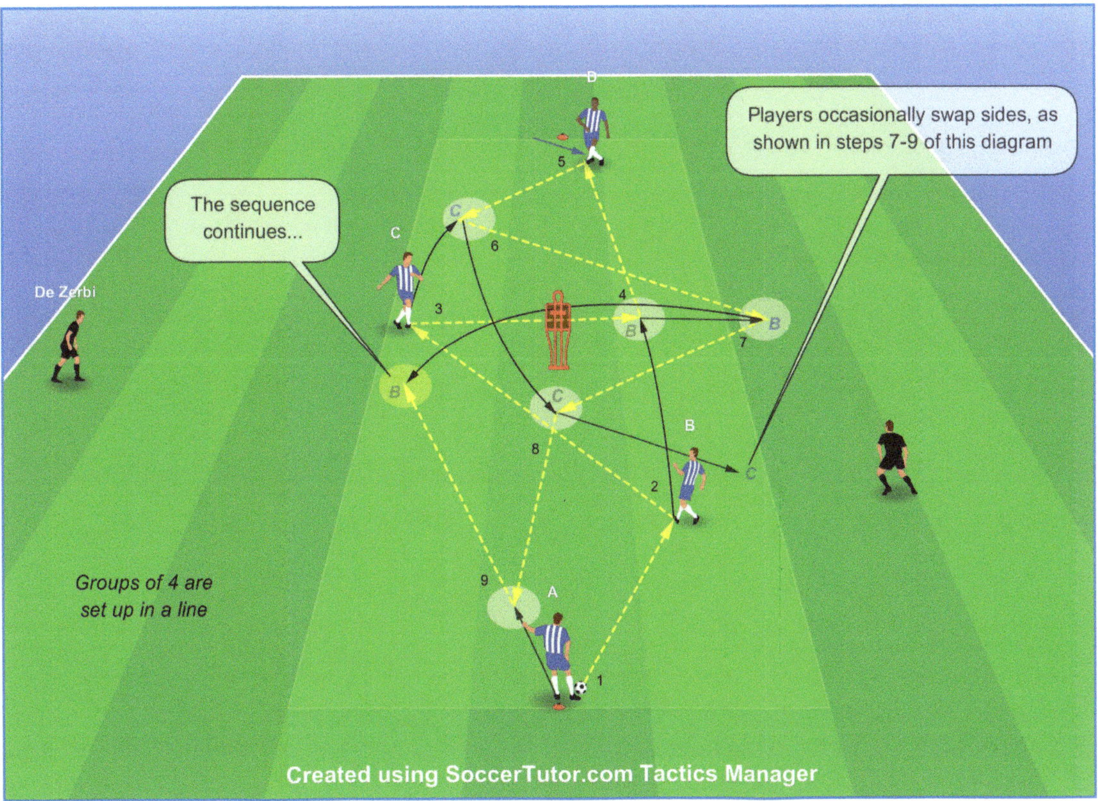

There are 2 players at the ends and 2 in the middle diagonally opposite to each other either side of the central mannequin.

Practice Description (Variation 2)

1. **A** passes to **B**.
2. **B** passes diagonally to **C**.
3. **C** passes inside well timed for the forward movement of **B** beyond the mannequin.
4. **B** passes forward to **D**, who checks off the cone.

5-6. **D** passes for the oncoming **C**, who then passes outside of the area for the outward movement of **B**.

7. **B** plays a return pass for the movement of **C** beyond the mannequin in the opposite direction.
8. **C** passes back to **A**, who moves forward off his cone to receive. **C** has also shifted across so the 2 middle players have swapped sides.
9. **A** passes to **B**, who shifts across from the other side behind the mannequin to receive.

→ The practice continues with the players using similar combinations and the middle players occasionally swapping, as shown in Steps 7-9.

Source: Roberto De Zerbi's Brighton training session at Elite Football Performance Centre - 21st July 2023

2. Creating Angles and Opening Up Pass and Receive at Speed Circuit

Variation 1: Diagonal Passing Inside to Outside

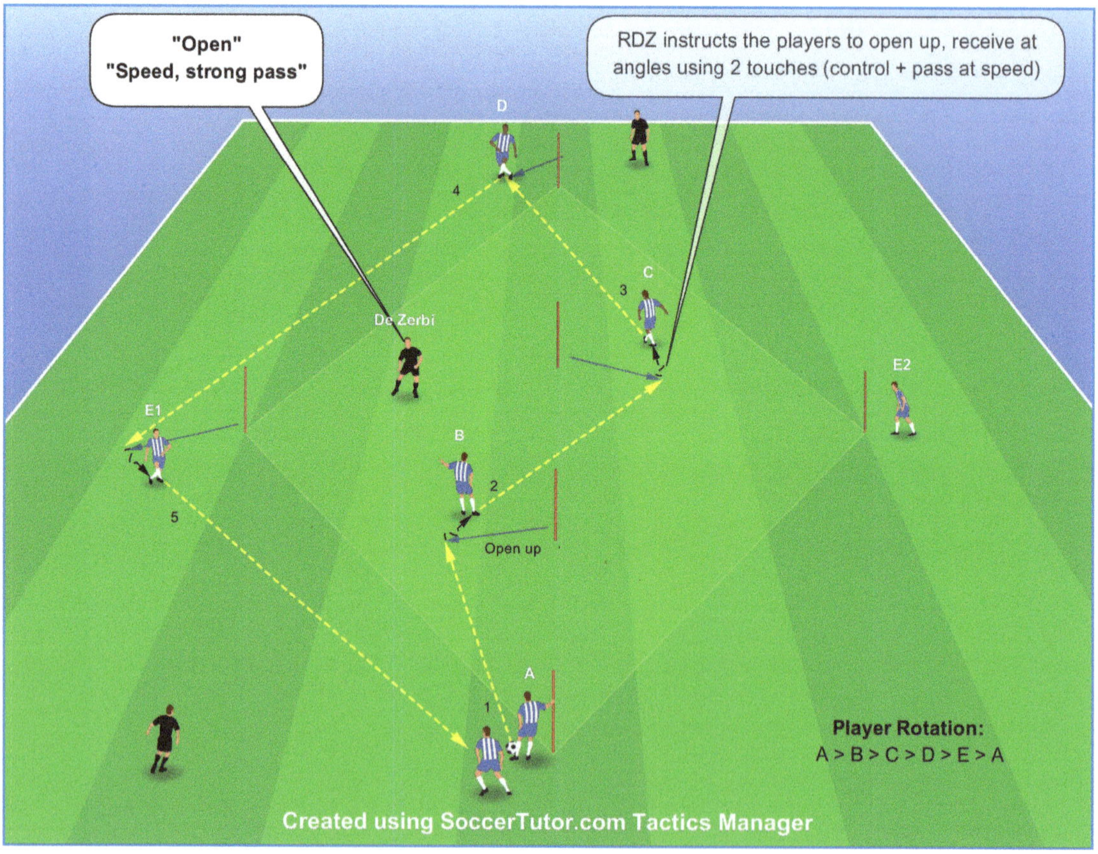

Practice Description (Variation 1)

1. **A** passes at a slight angle to **B**, who moves off the pole at an angle, and receives on the half-turn (opens up).
2. **B** passes diagonally to **C**, who also moves off the pole at an angle, and receives on the half-turn (opens up).
3. **C** passes to **D**, who moves across.
4. **D** passes to **E1**, who also moves off the pole at an angle, and receives on the half-turn (opens up).
5. **E1** passes to **Position A (Start)**.

→ The players rotate their positions around the circuit: **A** → **B** → **C** → **D** → **E**→ **A**. After the first set, repeat the sequence playing towards the right and using **E2**.

Source: Roberto De Zerbi's Brighton training session at Elite Football Performance Centre - 1st February 2023

Variation 2: Free Decision Making 1-Touch Play

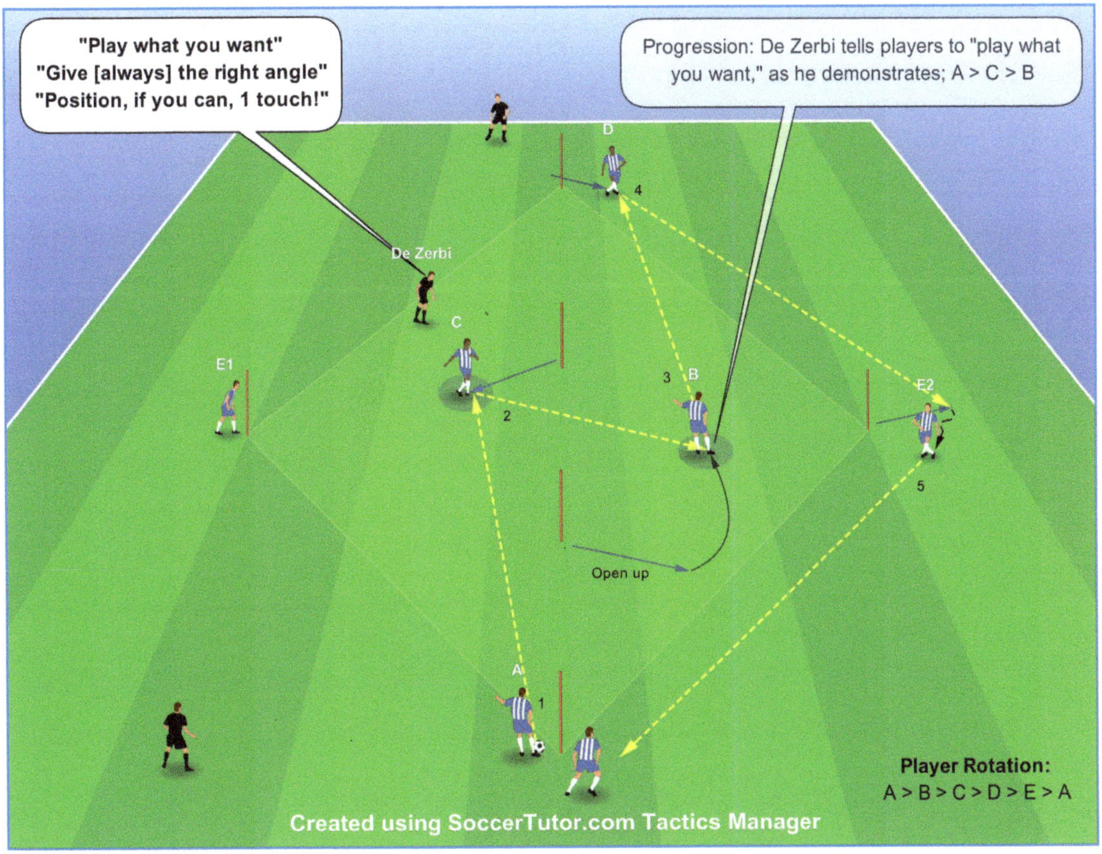

"Play what you want"
"Give [always] the right angle"
"Position, if you can, 1 touch!"

Progression: De Zerbi tells players to "play what you want," as he demonstrates; A > C > B

De Zerbi

Open up

Player Rotation:
A > B > C > D > E > A

Created using SoccerTutor.com Tactics Manager

Practice Description (Variation 2)

In this second variation, the players are encouraged to use 1 touch if possible. They also have free decision making - the diagram shows the example that De Zerbi demonstrated for the players.

1-2. **A** skips the first pole and plays a longer pass at a slight angle to **C**, who moves off the second pole at an angle, and sets the ball back for the oncoming **B** to receive.

3. **B** passes forward to **D**, who moves off the end pole to receive.

4. **D** passes diagonally to **E2**.

5. **E2** moves off the pole and opens up to receive, then passes to **Position A (Start)**.

→ The players rotate their positions around the circuit: **A** → **B** → **C** → **D** → **E**→ **A**. After the example shown, the players repeat using a different sequence.

Source: Roberto De Zerbi's Brighton training session at Elite Football Performance Centre - 1st February 2023

3a. Passing Diamond for High Speed of Play with 2 Balls and Fast Reactions to Switch Direction

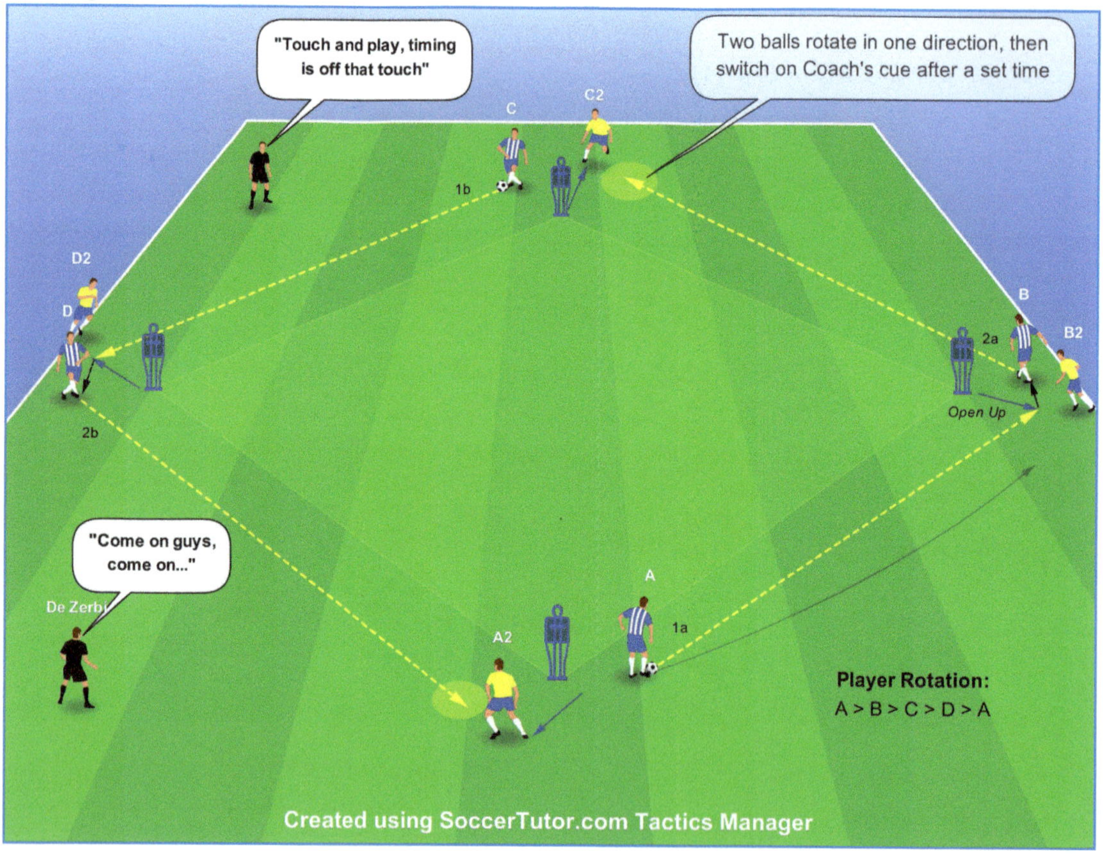

"Touch and play, timing is off that touch"

Two balls rotate in one direction, then switch on Coach's cue after a set time

C C2 1b D2 D B 2a B2 Open Up 2b

"Come on guys, come on..."

De Zerbi A A2 1a

Player Rotation:
A > B > C > D > A

Created using SoccerTutor.com Tactics Manager

Practice Description

There are 2 balls in play simultaneously starting from Positions A and C, as shown. The focus here is on speed of play using 2 touches (control out of your body + pass). In each position, the players drop off the mannequin at an angle, open up to receive with a good touch, and then play the next pass.

→ The players follow their pass: **A → B → C → D → A.**

Ball 1: A passes to **B**, **B** passes to **C2**, **C2** passes to **D2**, and **D2** passes to the start **Position A** *(D has rotated there to become new Player A).*

Ball 2: C passes to **D**, **D** passes to **A2**, and **A2** continues with a pass to **B2**.

→ On the Coach's cue, the direction of both balls in play is reversed e.g. from anti-clockwise to clockwise.

Source: Roberto De Zerbi's Brighton training session at Elite Football Performance Centre - 25th January 2023

3b. Diamond Passing Circuit with One-Two, Pass, Set, Switch, and Give & Go

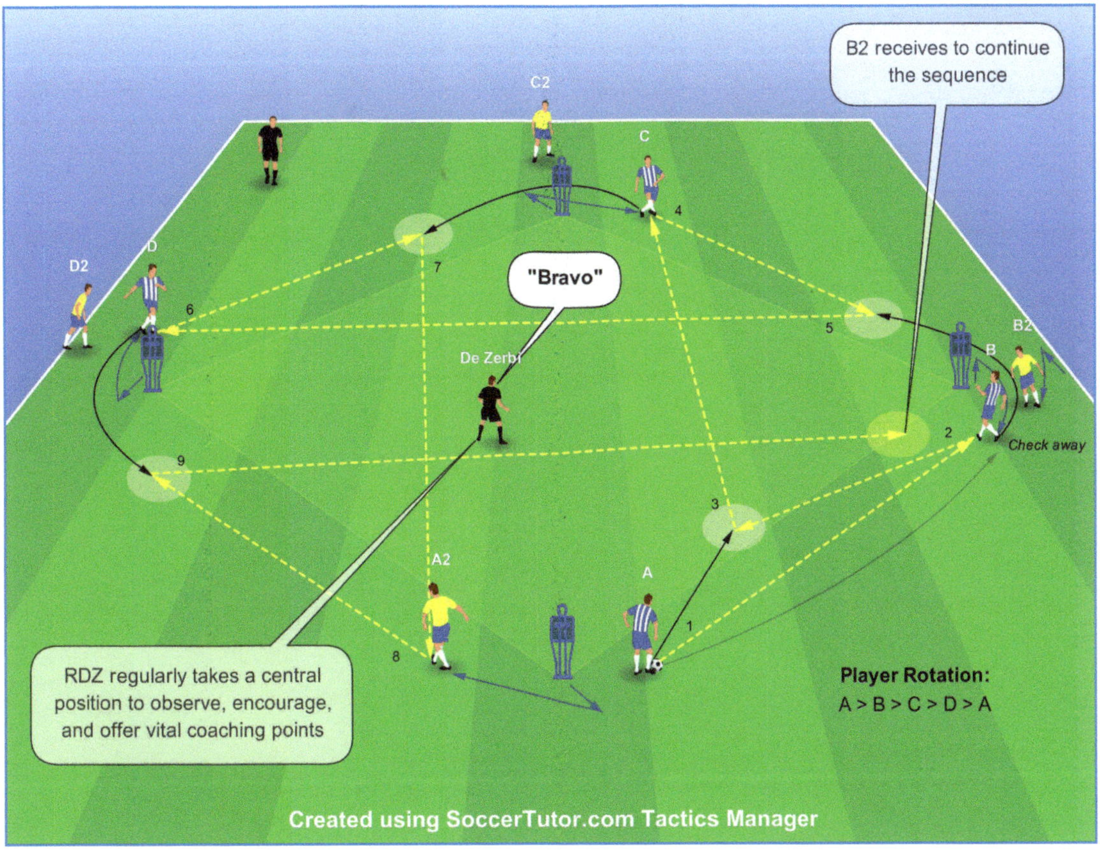

Practice Description

1-2. **A** plays a one-two with **B**, moving forward to receive the return. **B** checks away before moving to receive, and then makes a run around the mannequin.

3-4. **A** passes to **C**, who checks away and moves at an angle to receive, then sets the ball for the oncoming **B**.

5. **B** passes across the diamond to **D**, who also checks before moving to receive.

6. **D** sets the ball back for **C**, who moves around the mannequin to receive.

7-8. **C** passes to **A2**, who sets the ball for **D**, who also moves around the mannequin to receive.

9. **D** passes across the diamond to complete the circuit. As shown, **B2** receives to continue the sequence.

→ The players rotate their positions around the circuit: **A → B → C → D → A**.

Source: Roberto De Zerbi's Brighton training session at Elite Football Performance Centre - 25th January 2023

4. Diamond Passing Circuit with One-Two, Pass, Set, Switch, and Give & Go

RDZ

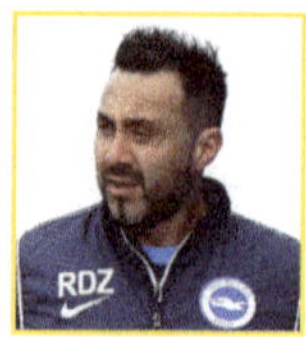

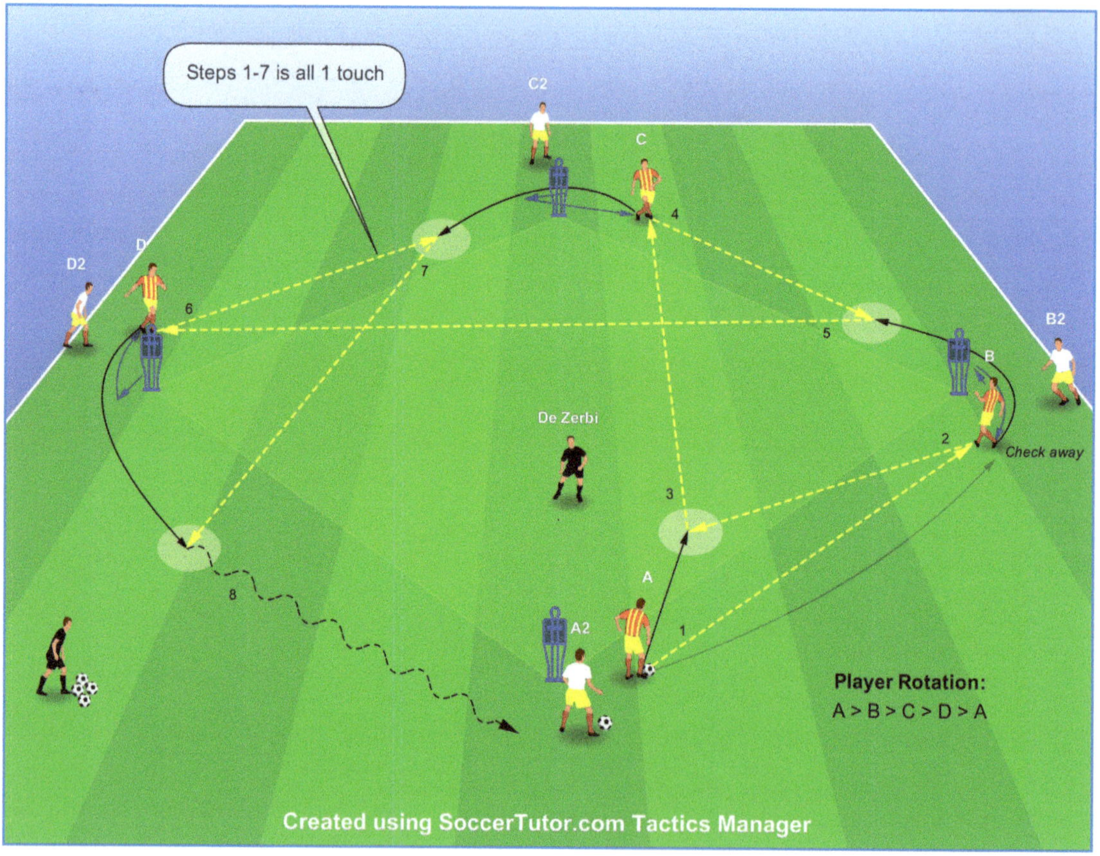

Steps 1-7 is all 1 touch
C2
C
D
D2
B2
B
Check away
De Zerbi
A
A2
Player Rotation:
A > B > C > D > A
Created using SoccerTutor.com Tactics Manager

Practice Description

1-2. **A** plays a one-two with **B**, moving forward to receive the return. **B** checks away before moving to receive, and then makes a run around the mannequin.

3-4. **A** passes to **C**, who checks away and moves at an angle to receive, then sets the ball for the oncoming **B**.

5. **B** passes across the diamond to **D**, who also checks before moving to receive.

6. **D** sets the ball back for **C**, who moves around the mannequin to receive.

7-8. **C** passes into space for **D**, who moves around the mannequin to receive. **D** dribbles to the start position as the circuit continues with **A2** (give & go).

→ The players rotate their positions around the circuit: **A** → **B** → **C** → **D** → **A2**.

Source: Roberto De Zerbi's Benevento Calcio training session in Benevento, Campania - 2017

5. Opposite Movements to Open Up Support Play Diamond Passing Circuit with Central Player

Variation 1: One-Two and Forward Pass

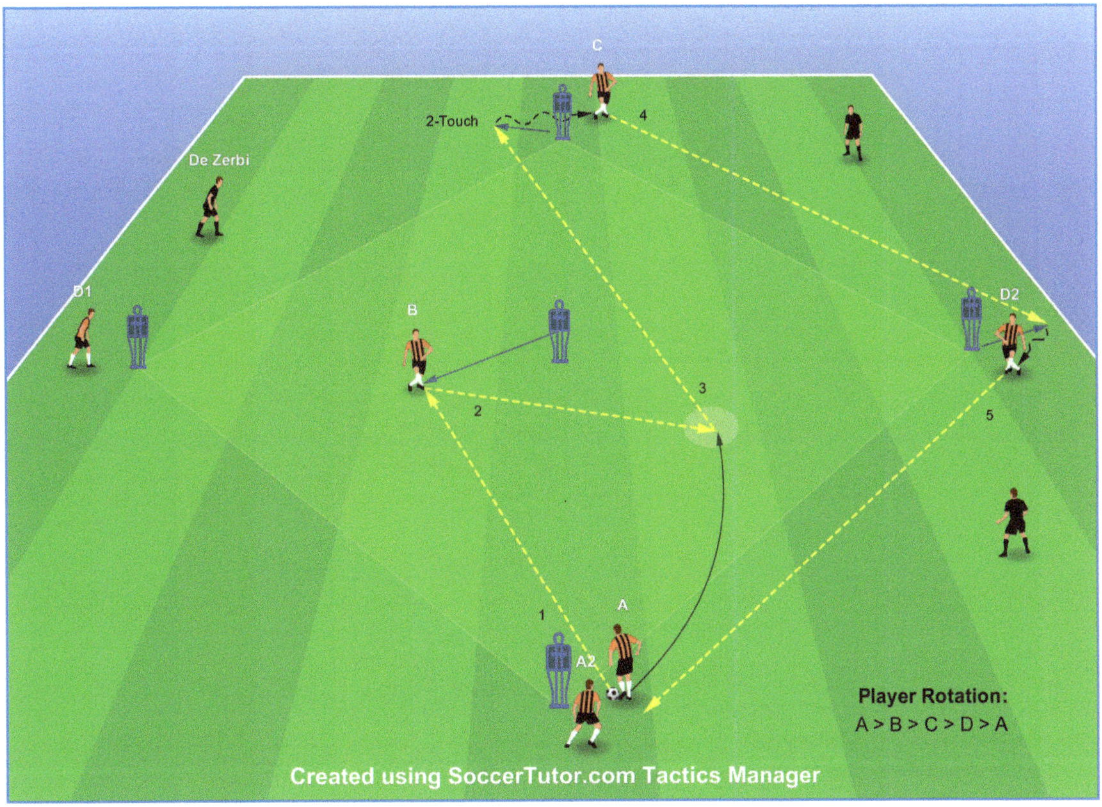

C
2-Touch
4
De Zerbi
D1
B
D2
3
2
5
1
A
A2
Player Rotation:
A > B > C > D > A
Created using SoccerTutor.com Tactics Manager

Practice Description (Variation 1)

1. **A** passes to one side of the central mannequin (left in diagram example) for **B** to drop off and receive.
2. **B** plays a return pass (one-two) for **A** to run forward onto.
3. **A** passes to the left of the end mannequin for **C**, who checks to receive and opens up to take a touch past the mannequin (behind), as shown.

4-5. **C** passes diagonally to **D2**, who checks to receive and opens up to take a touch past the mannequin. **D2** completes the sequence by passing to **A2**.

→ The players rotate their positions: **A → B → C → D → A2**.

→ The sequence is repeated with the passes going towards the right side of the mannequins and involving **D1** instead of **D2**.

Source: Roberto De Zerbi's Shakhtar Donetsk preseason training session in Austria - 23rd June 2021

Variation 2: One-Two, Pass, Lay-off, and Give & Go

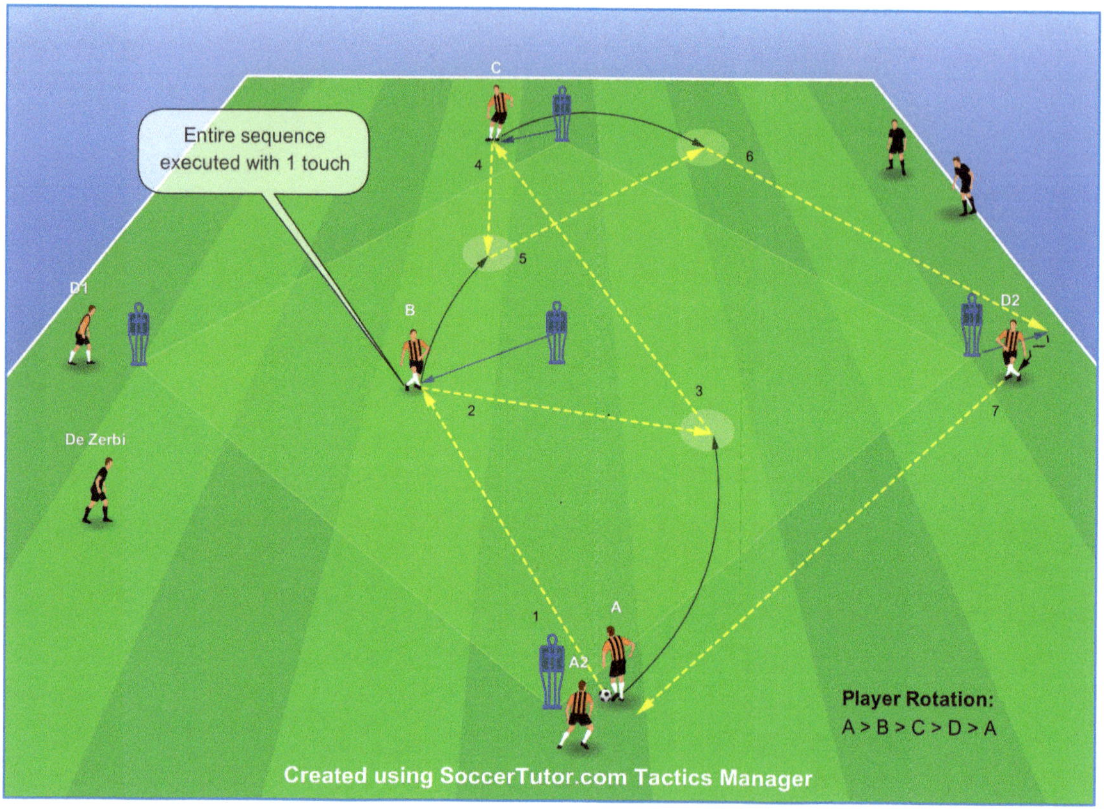

Entire sequence executed with 1 touch

Player Rotation:
A > B > C > D > A

Created using SoccerTutor.com Tactics Manager

Practice Description (Variation 2)

1. **A** passes to one side of the central mannequin (left in diagram example) for **B** to drop off and receive.
2. **B** plays a return pass (one-two) for **A** to run forward onto.

3-5. **A** passes to the left of the end mannequin for **C**, who sets the ball back for B's forward movement. This is the first part of a give & go as B plays the return well timed for C's movement around the mannequin, as shown.

6. **C** passes diagonally to **D2**, who also checks to receive and opens up to take a touch past the mannequin.
7. **D2** completes the sequence by passing to **A2**.

→ The players rotate their positions: **A → B → C → D → A2**.

→ The sequence is repeated with the passes going towards the right side of the mannequins and involving **D1** instead of **D2**.

Source: Roberto De Zerbi's Shakhtar Donetsk preseason training session in Austria - 23rd June 2021

6. Open Up to Receive Passing Hexagon Circuit with 2 Balls and Pass into Small Goals

Variation 1: Receive Angled Outside Pole and Finish

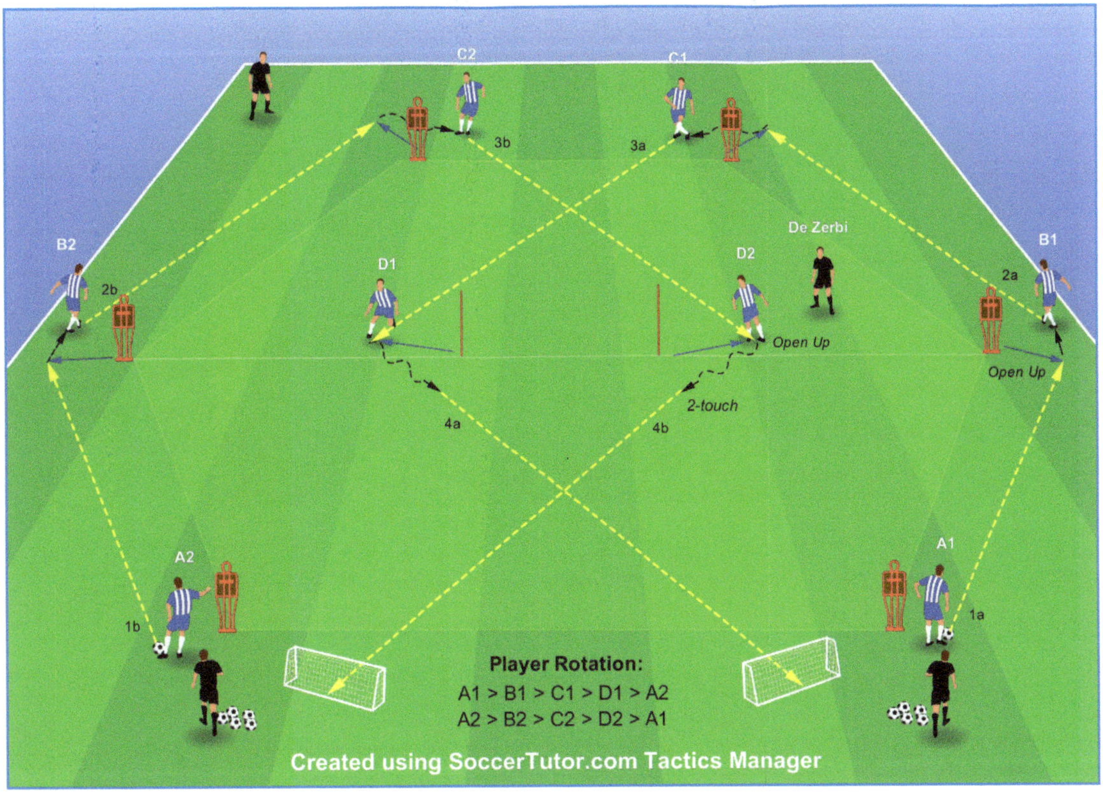

Player Rotation:
A1 > B1 > C1 > D1 > A2
A2 > B2 > C2 > D2 > A1

Created using SoccerTutor.com Tactics Manager

Practice Description (Variation 1)

There is the same set-up on both sides with 2 balls starting from A1 and A2 simultaneously. All players check off their pole/mannequin to open up and receive.

1-2. **A1/A2** pass to **B1/B2**, who open up outside the mannequin and pass to **C1/C2**, who do the same.

3. **C1/C2** pass diagonally to **D1/D2** in the centre.

4. **D1/D2** also open up to receive on the outside of the pole and pass into the small goal (diagonally). They then move to **Position A** of the opposite group.

→ The players rotate their positions:
A1 → B1 → C1 → D1 → A2
+ A2 → B2 → C2 → D2 → A1.

Source: Roberto De Zerbi's Brighton training session at Elite Football Performance Centre - 13th October 2022

Variation 2: Receive, Give & Go Around Pole, and Finish

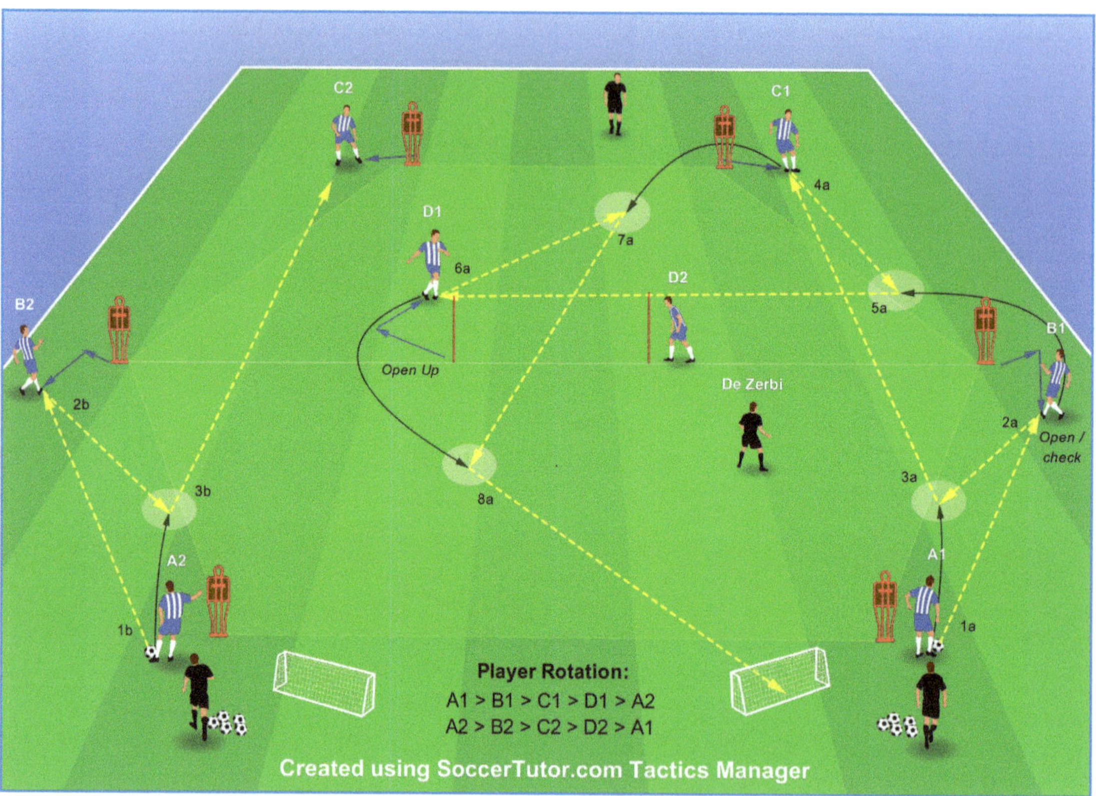

Practice Description (Variation 2)

In this variation of the example on the previous page, the full combination is shown on the right side, but not on the left. The left is an exact mirror image but is not shown on the diagram for simplicity.

1-2. **A1/A2** play a one-two with **B1/B2**, moving forward to receive the return.

3-4. **B1/B2** pass forward to **C1/C2**, who set the ball for the oncoming **B1/B2's** movement around the wide mannequin.

5-6. **B1/B2** pass inside to **D1/D2** in the centre, who set the ball for the oncoming **C1/C2's** movement around the mannequin.

7. **C1/C2** plays a through pass in between the 2 poles, timed for **D1/D2's** run around the pole.

8. **D1/D2** pass into the small goal (diagonally) and move to **Position A** of the opposite group.

→ The players rotate their positions: **A1 → B1 → C1 → D1 → A2** + **A2 → B2 → C2 → D2 → A1**.

Source: Roberto De Zerbi's Brighton training session at Elite Football Performance Centre - 13th October 2022

7. Open Up to Receive "Off the Pole" Hexagon Passing Circuit

Variation 1: Inside/Outside Pass and Receive (2-Touch)

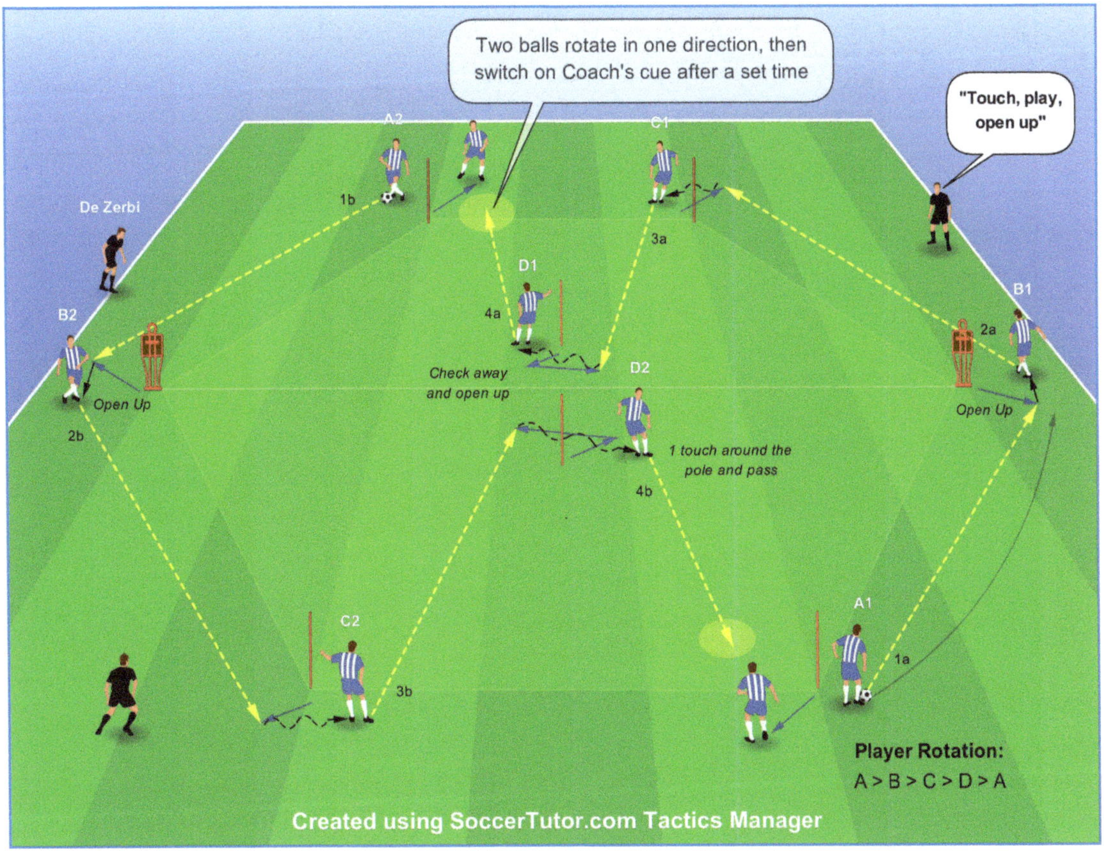

Practice Description (Variation 1)

There is the exact same set-up on both sides with 2 balls starting from A1 and A2 simultaneously. All the players check off the pole/mannequin to receive and rotate as one complete circuit (D1 → A2 / D2 → A1).

1-2. **A1/A2** pass to **B/B2**, who open up and pass to **C1/C2**.

3-4. **C1/C2** open up and receive behind the pole to move the ball forward at an angle, and then pass to **D1/D2** in the centre, who do the same, before passing to **Position A1/A2**.

→ The players rotate their positions around the circuit: **A → B → C → D → A**.

→ On the Coach's cue, the direction of both balls in play is reversed e.g. from anti-clockwise to clockwise.

Source: Roberto De Zerbi's Brighton training session at Elite Football Performance Centre - 2nd May 2023

Variation 2: Pass Inside to Out with One-Twos

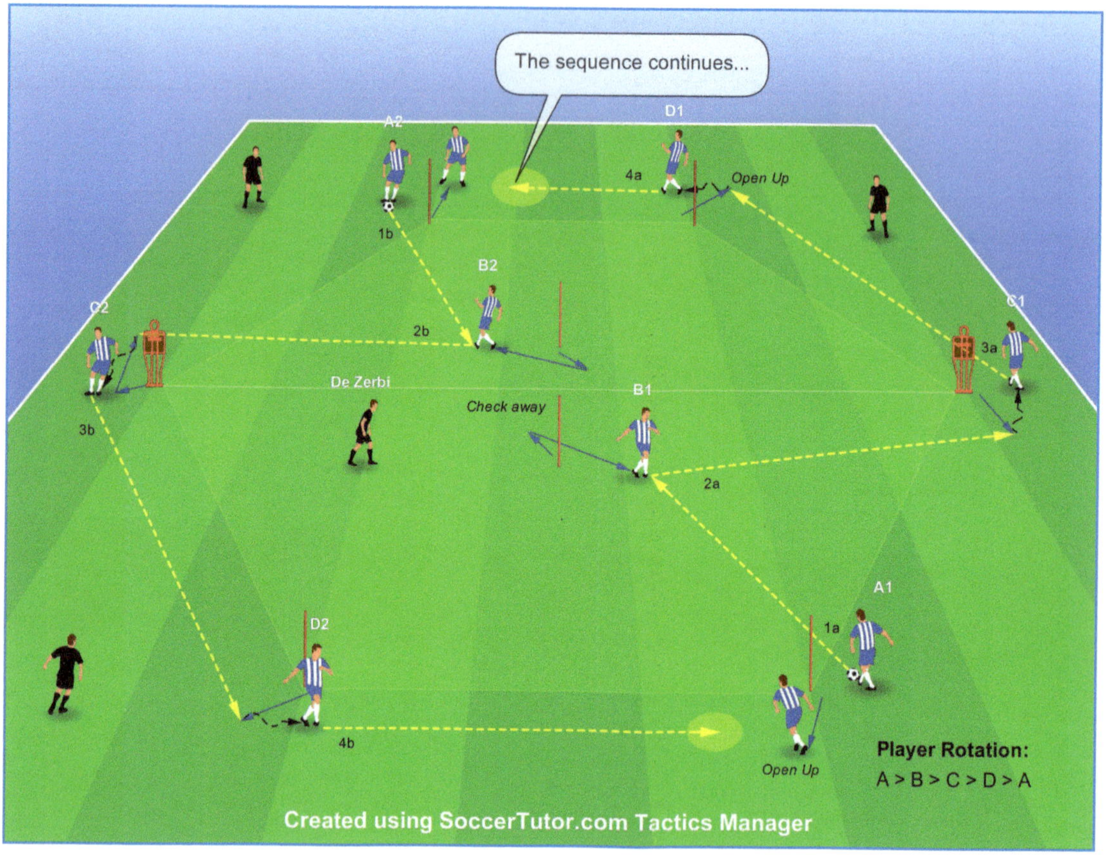

Practice Description (Variation 2)

There is the exact same set-up on both sides with 2 balls starting from A1 and A2 simultaneously. All the players check off the pole/mannequin to receive and rotate as one complete circuit (D1 → A2 / D2 → A1).

1-2. **A1/A2** pass to **B/B2**, who check off the pole, move to receive, and pass wide to **C1/C2**.

3-4. **C1/C2** drop, open up, receive behind the mannequin, move the ball forward at an angle, and then pass to **D1/D2** who take a directional touch behind the pole, and passes to **Position A1/A2**.

→ The players rotate their positions around the circuit: **A → B → C → D → A**.

→ On the Coach's cue, the direction of both balls in play is reversed e.g. from anti-clockwise to clockwise.

Source: Roberto De Zerbi's Brighton training session at Elite Football Performance Centre - 14th March 2023

Variation 3: Inside to Out with Give & Go

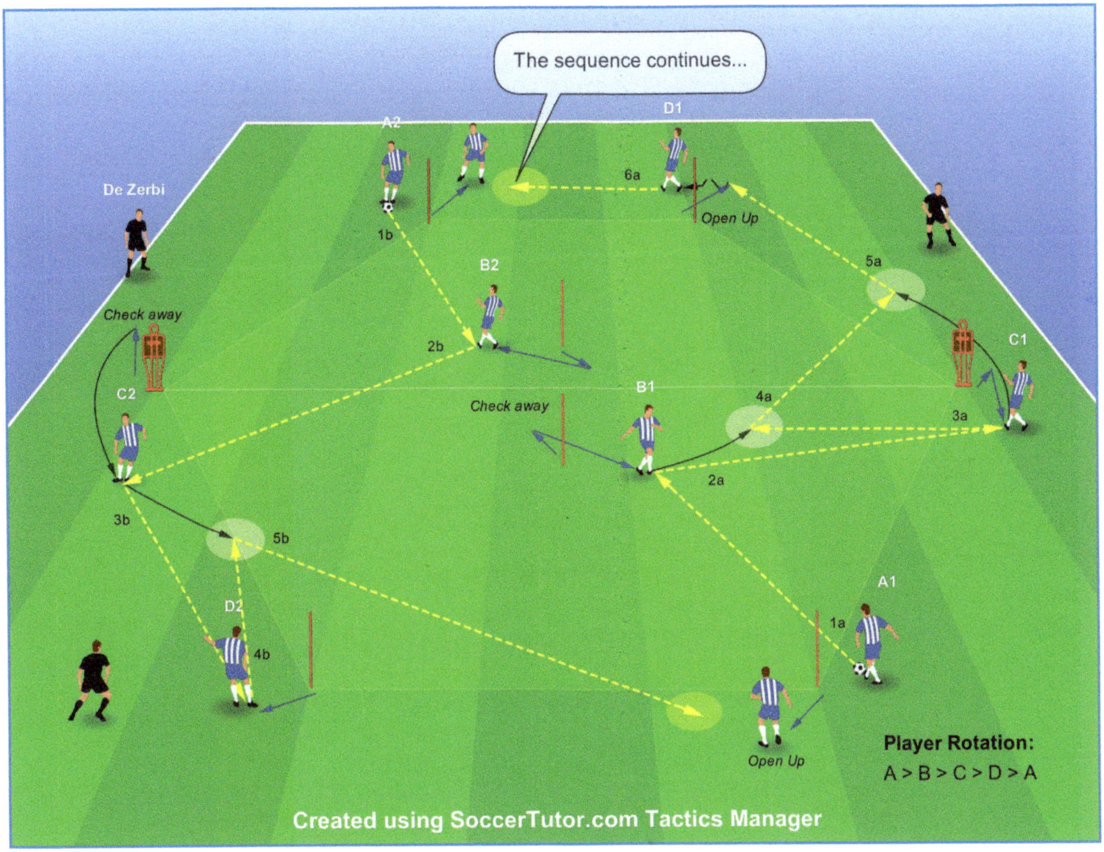

Practice Description (Variation 3)

All the players check off the pole or mannequin before moving to receive.

Ball 1 (on Right)

1-4a. **A1** passes to **B1**, who plays a one-two with **C1**, then plays another pass for **C1** to receive after running around the mannequin.

5-6a. **C1** passes to **D1**, who opens up and receives behind the pole at a sideways angle before passing to **Position A2**.

Ball 2 (on Left)

1-2b. **A2** passes to **B2**, who passes for **C2** on the other side of the mannequin.

3-5b. **C2** plays a one-two with **D2**, then passes to **Position A1**.

→ The players rotate their positions around the circuit: **A1 → B1 → C1 → D1 → A2 → B2 → C2 → D2 → A1**.

→ The same sequence is repeated in this continuous circuit. On the Coach's cue, the direction of both balls in play is reversed e.g. from anti-clockwise to clockwise.

Source: Roberto De Zerbi's Brighton training session at Elite Football Performance Centre - 2nd May 2023

Variation 4: Receive, One-Two, and Play Forward

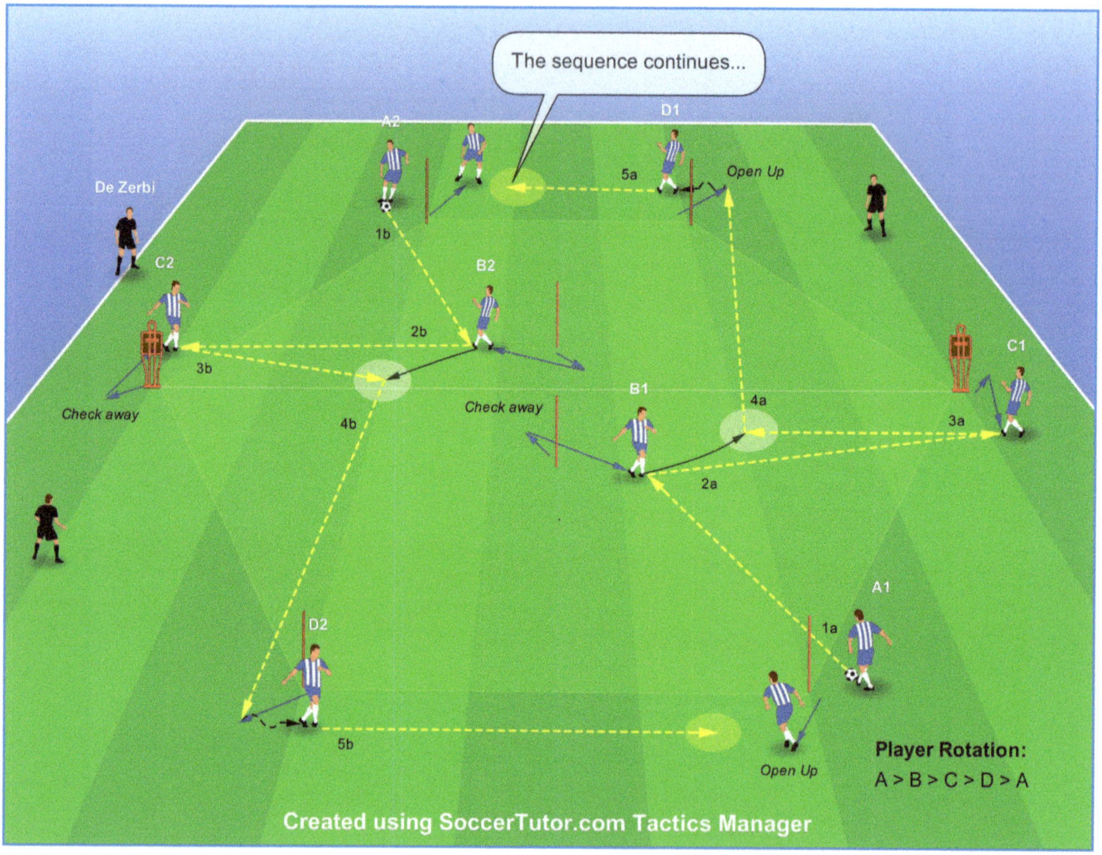

The sequence continues...

Player Rotation:
A > B > C > D > A

Created using SoccerTutor.com Tactics Manager

Practice Description (Variation 4)

There is the exact same set-up on both sides with 2 balls starting from A1 and A2 simultaneously. All the players check off the pole/mannequin to receive and rotate as one complete circuit (D1 → A2 / D2 → A1).

1. **A1/A2** pass to **B1/B2** in the centre.

2-3. **B1/B2** play a one-two with **C1/C2**, moving to meet the return.

4-5. **B1/B2** then pass forward to **D1/D2**, who open up and receive behind the pole, controlling the ball at a sideways angle before passing to **Position A1/A2**.

→ The players rotate their positions around the circuit: **A1** → **B1** → **C1** → **D1** → **A2** → **B2** → **C2** → **D2** → **A1**.

→ The same sequence is repeated in this continuous circuit.

→ On the Coach's cue, the direction of both balls in play is reversed e.g. from anti-clockwise to clockwise.

Source: Roberto De Zerbi's Brighton training session at Elite Football Performance Centre - 14th March 2023

Variation 5: Central Support with 2 & 3 Player Combinations

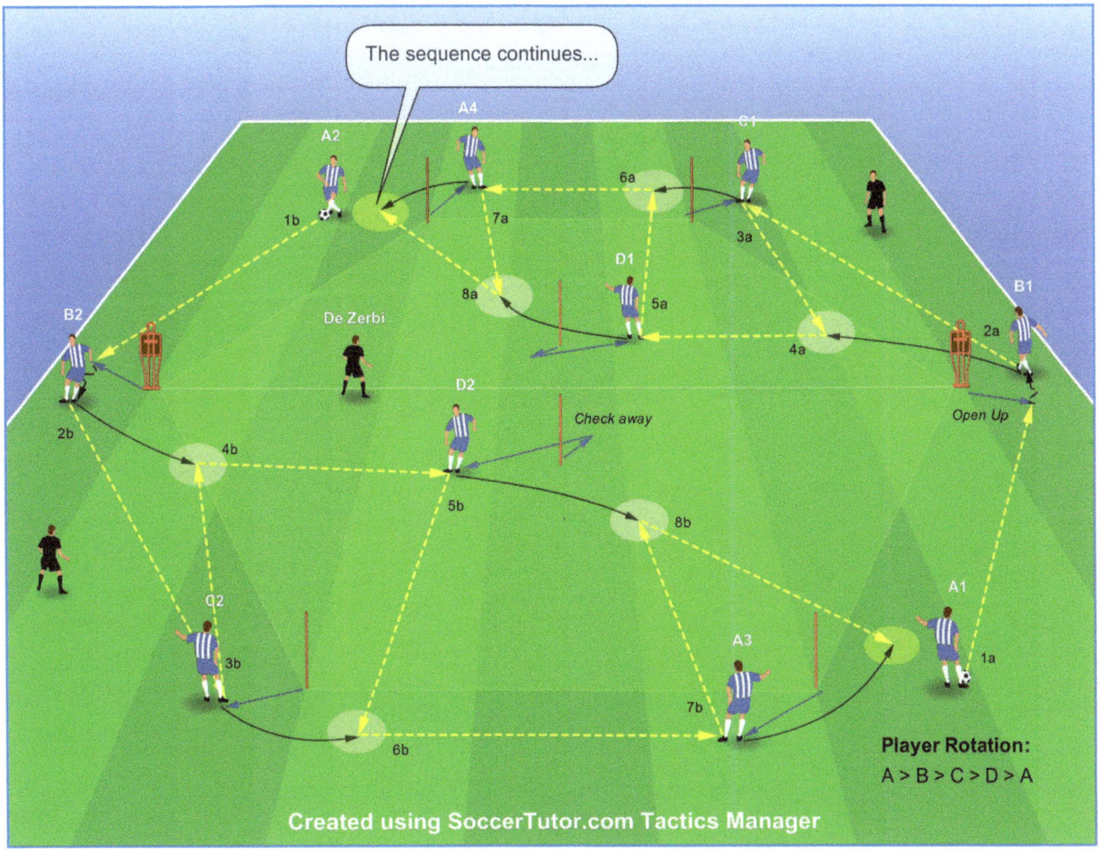

The sequence continues...

Player Rotation:
A > B > C > D > A

Created using SoccerTutor.com Tactics Manager

Practice Description (Variation 5)

There is the exact same set-up on both sides with 2 balls starting from A1 and A2 simultaneously. All the players check off the pole/mannequin to receive and rotate as one complete circuit (D1 → A2 / D2 → A1).

1-2. **A1/A2** pass to **B1/B2**, who open up and receive on the half-turn, and then pass to **C1/C2**.

3-4. **C1/C2** set the ball back for **B1/B2**, who move inside, and pass to **D1/D2** in the centre.

5-6. **D1/D2** pass for **C1/C2** on the other side of the pole, and they pass to **A2/A4**.

7-8. **A2/A4** pass for the movement across of **D1/D2**, who complete the sequence with a pass back to **A2/A4** to receive on the other side of the pole. The sequence resets from there and continues.

→ The players rotate their positions around the circuit: **A1 → B1 → C1 → D1 → A4 → A2 → B2 → C2 → D2 → A3 → A1**.

→ On the Coach's cue, the direction of both balls in play is reversed e.g. from anti-clockwise to clockwise.

Source: Roberto De Zerbi's Brighton training session at Elite Football Performance Centre - 4th October 2023

8. Inside and Outside Receiving Angles 2-Touch Continuous Passing Circuit

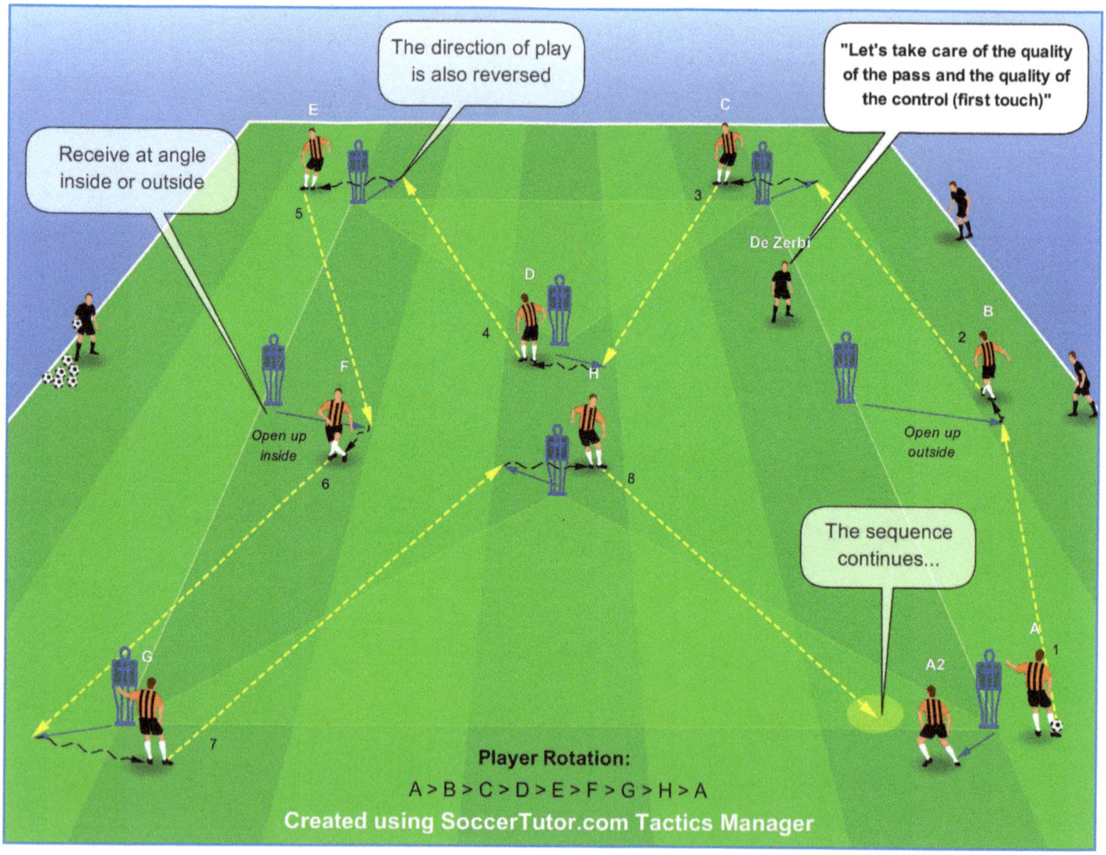

The direction of play is also reversed

"Let's take care of the quality of the pass and the quality of the control (first touch)"

Receive at angle inside or outside

Open up inside

Open up outside

The sequence continues...

Player Rotation:
A > B > C > D > E > F > G > H > A

Created using SoccerTutor.com Tactics Manager

Practice Description

The corner and middle players receive and open up (take a touch) behind the mannequins. The middle wide players can decide whether to receive at an angle with an inside or outside movement, as shown.

1-2. **A** passes to **B**, who opens up towards the outside and passes to the right of the mannequin for **C**.

[illegible] **C** [illegible]s to **D** in the centre, who passes [illegible]ft of the mannequin for **D**.

4-6. **D** passes to the right of the mannequin for **E**. **E** passes to **F**, who opens up towards the inside and passes to the right of the mannequin for **G**.

7-8. **G** passes to the left of the mannequin in the centre for **H**, who passes to **A2**. The same sequence continues.

→ The players rotate their positions: **A → B → C → D → E → F → G → H → A**.

→ On the Coach's cue, the direction of play is reversed to clockwise.

[illegible]berto De Zerbi's Shakhtar Donetsk training session at Sviatoshyn Sports Complex - 14th June 2021

9. Open Up with Correct Angles for Support Play Passing Circuit with Central Players

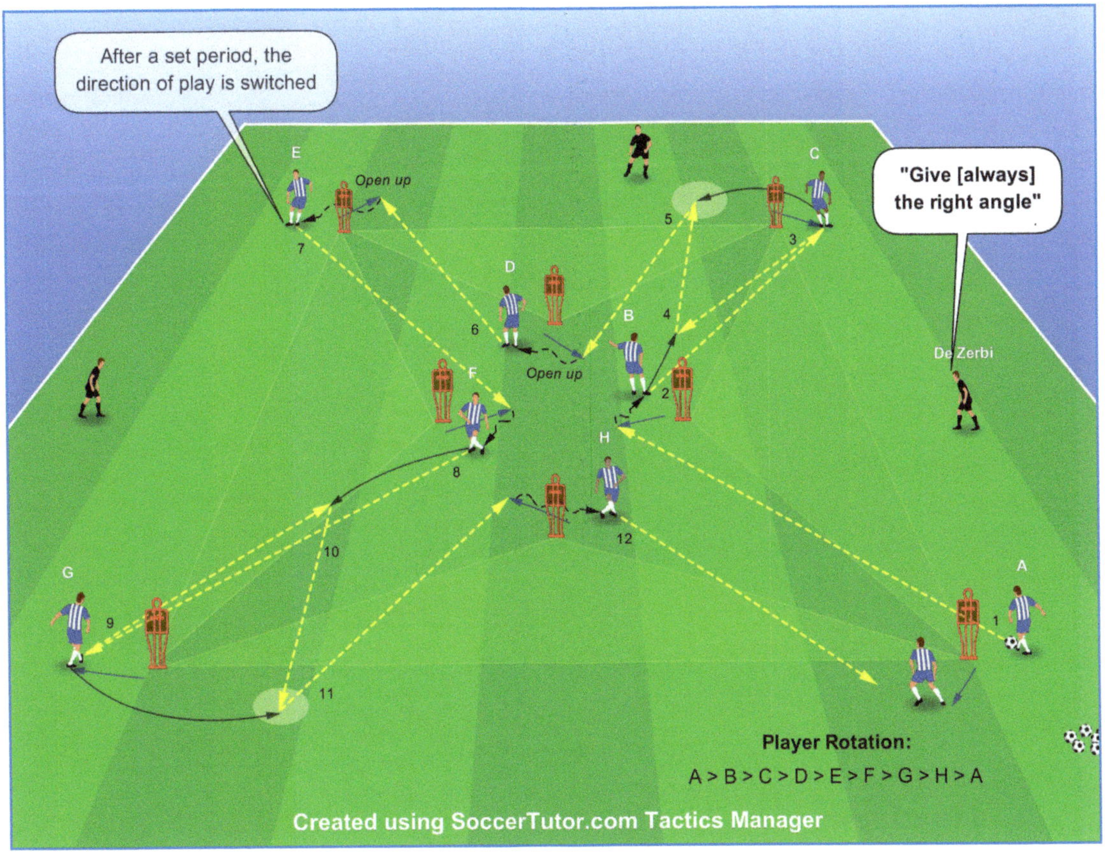

After a set period, the direction of play is switched

"Give [always] the right angle"

Player Rotation:
A > B > C > D > E > F > G > H > A

Created using SoccerTutor.com Tactics Manager

Middle players check away from mannequin, receive, opening up to play the next pass.

Practice Description

1. **A** passes to **B** in the centre.

2-4. **B** plays a one-two with **C**, and then passes (timed) for the movement of **C** around the mannequin.

5. **C** passes to **D** in the centre.

6. **D** passes to **E**, who receives and opens up around the mannequin.

7. **C** passes to **F** in the centre.

8-10. **F** plays a one-two with **G**, and then passes (timed) for the movement of **G** around the mannequin.

11-12. **G** passes to **H** in the centre, who passes to **Position A (Start)**.

→ Players rotate around the circuit: **A → B → C → D → E → F→ G → H → A.** After a set period of time, the direction of play is switched to clockwise.

Source: Roberto De Zerbi's Brighton training session at Elite Football Performance Centre - 26th September 2022

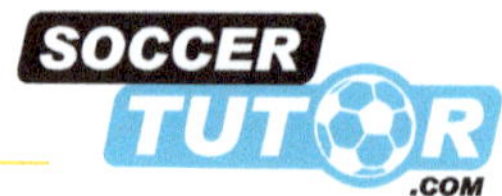

10. Open Up to Receive Passes at Diagonal Angles Passing Circuit with Inside/Outside Support Play

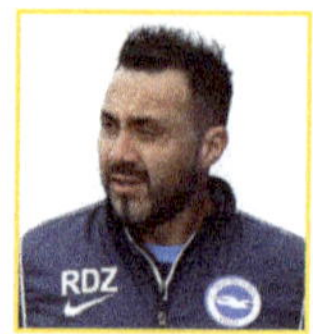

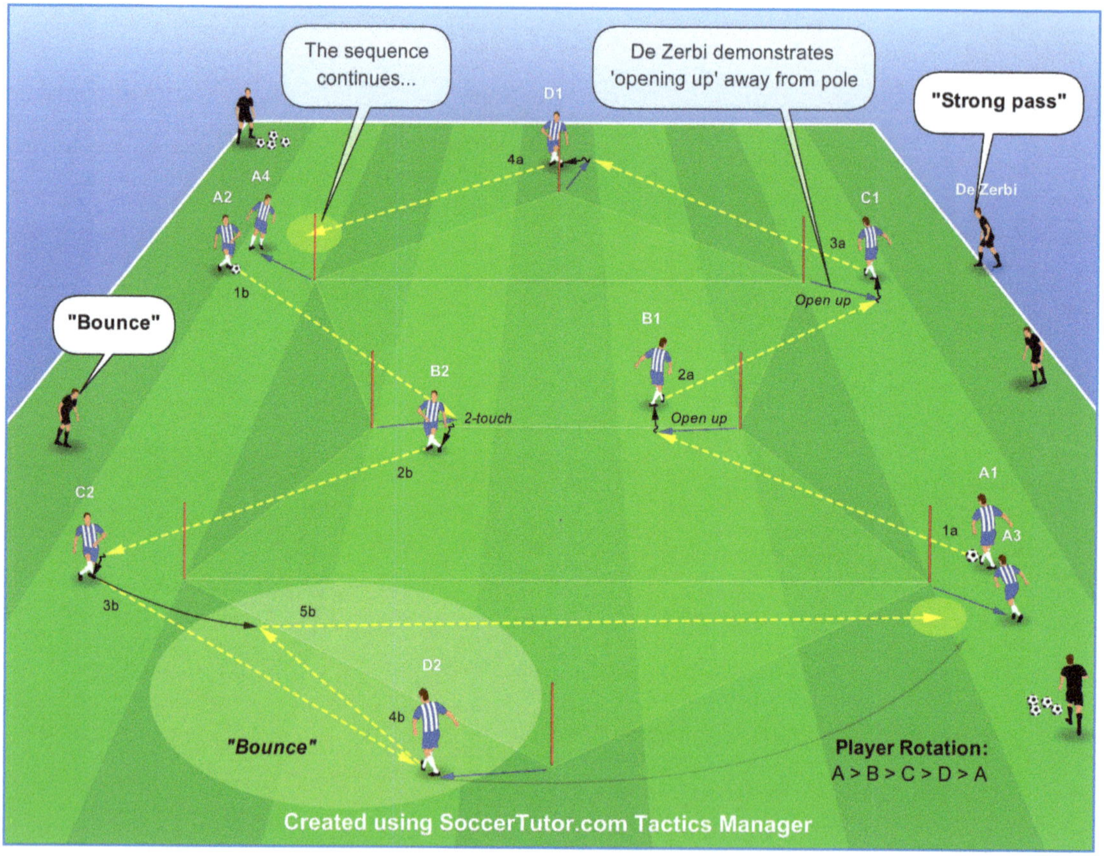

The sequence continues...
De Zerbi demonstrates 'opening up' away from pole
"Strong pass"
"Bounce"
De Zerbi
D1
4a
A4
A2
C1
3a
1b
Open up
B1
B2
2a
2-touch
Open up
2b
A1
C2
1a
A3
3b
5b
D2
4b
"Bounce"
Player Rotation:
A > B > C > D > A
Created using SoccerTutor.com Tactics Manager

*It is the same set-up on both sides with 2 balls starting from A1 & A2 simultaneously. There are extra players in these positions (A3 & A4). Players check off poles to open up, receive (control), and pass all at speed. When the **Coach calls "Bounce,"** that player sets the ball back to his teammate to pass to the next player, as shown with D2 (4b-5b).*

Practice Description (Ball 1)

1-2a. **A1** passes to **B1**, who passes to **C1**.

3-4a. **C1** passes to **D1**, who passes to **A4**.

Practice Description (Ball 2)

1-2b. **A2** passes to **B2**, who passes to **C2**.

3-5b. **C2** plays a one-two with to **D2**, moves inside to meet the return, and then passes to **A3**. This is because the Coach calls out **"Bounce"** which instructs D2 to set the ball for C2 to play the next pass.

→ The passing circuit is continuous and the players rotate their positions around the circuit: **A1 → B1 → C1 → D1 → A4 → A2 → B2 → C2 → D2 → A3 → A1.**

Source: Roberto De Zerbi's Brighton training session at Elite Football Performance Centre - 9th March 2023

11. Double Triangle and Forward Passing Circuit with One-Two Combinations (Match Day Warm-up)

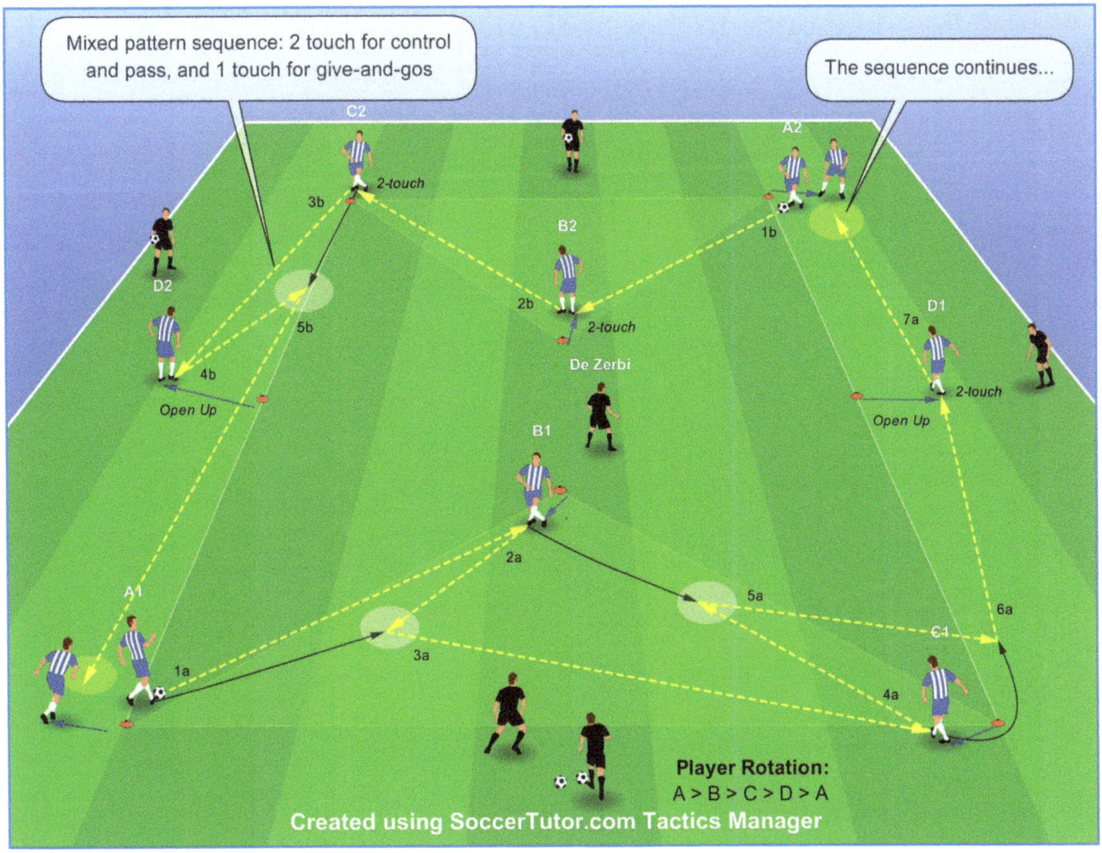

There is the same set-up at both ends with 2 balls starting from A1 and A2 simultaneously. All players move off their cone to receive. They use 2 touches for control and pass, and 1 touch for give & go.

Practice Description (Ball 1)

1-3a. **A1** plays a one-two with **B1** and then passes back at an angle to **C1**.

4-7a. **C1** plays a give & go with **B1** and then passes to **D1**, who opens up, receives, and passes forward to **Position A2**.

Practice Description (Ball 2)

1-2b. **A2** passes to **B2**, who passes to **C2**.

3-5b. **C2** plays a one-two with **D2**, moves to meet the return, and completes the sequence by passing to **Position A1**.

→ The players rotate their positions around the circuit: **A1 → B1 → C1 → D1 → A2 → B2 → C2 → D2 → A1**.

Source: Roberto De Zerbi's Brighton pre-match warm-up at Stanford Bridge (Chelsea) - 15th April 2023

12. Receiving Angles for Build-up Through Lines Support Play Passing Circuit

Variation 1: Combination with One-Two + Give & Go

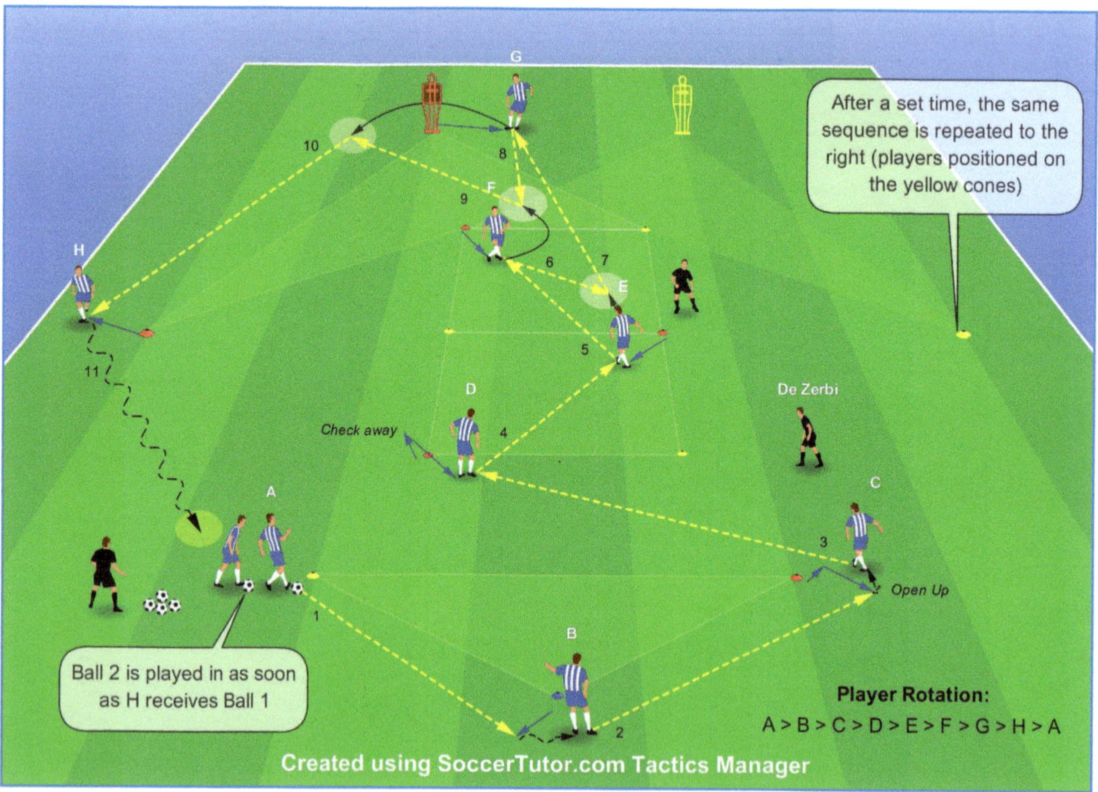

Practice Description (Variation 1)

This circuit is played with 2 simultaneous balls - the next pass from Position A is played after H receives.

1-2. **A** passes to **B**, then **B** to **C** with both opening up to receive around the triangle shape.

3-5. **C** passes diagonally to **D**, then **D** passes to **E**, and **E** to **F** with all players checking off their respective cones.

6-7. **F** sets the ball back for **E** to move forward and pass to **G**.

8-9. **G** plays a give & go with **F** to receive on the other side of the mannequin.

10-11. **G** passes to **H**, who receives and dribbles to the start position.

→ The players rotate their positions **A** → **B** → **C** → **D** → **E** → **F** > **G** → **H** → **A**, and the same sequence is repeated to the right with players positioned on yellow cones.

Source: Roberto De Zerbi's Brighton training session at AMEX Stadium - 11th April 2023

Variation 2: Combination with Lay-offs + Give & Go

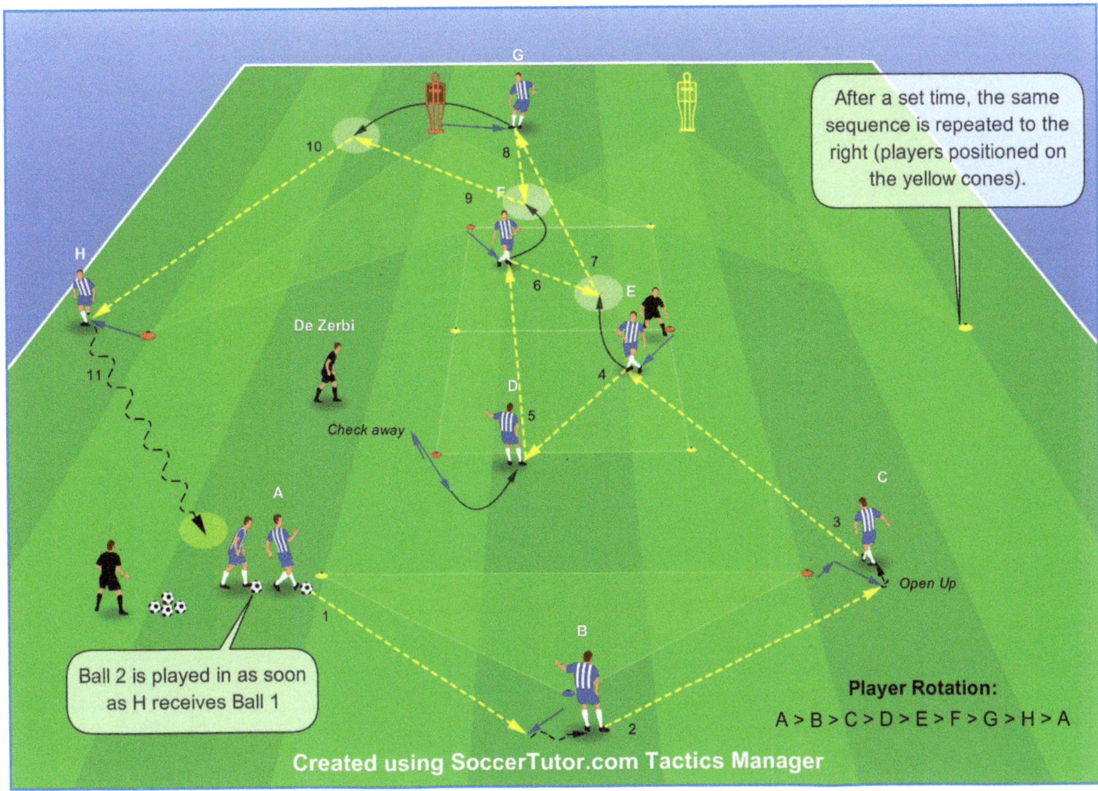

Practice Description (Variation 2)

This circuit is played with 2 simultaneous balls - the next pass from Position A is played after H receives. In this variation of the example on the previous page, the difference is that C now passes to E, who sets the ball back for D to pass to F (see full description below).

1-2. **A** passes to **B**, then **B** to **C** with both opening up to receive around the triangle shape.

3-5. **C** passes to **E**, who sets the ball back for **D**. **D** has checked away, dropped, and then made a curved forward movement to receive the lay-off before passing forward to **F**.

6-7. **F** sets the ball back for **E** to move forward and pass to **G**.

8-9. **G** plays a give & go with **F** to receive on the other side of the mannequin.

10-11. **G** passes to **H**, who receives and dribbles to the start position.

→ The players rotate their positions: **A → B → C → D → E → F > G → H → A**.

→ The same sequence is repeated to the right with players positioned on the yellow cones.

Source: Roberto De Zerbi's Brighton training session at AMEX Stadium - 11th April 2023

13. Positioning, Receiving, and Support Play Movements Passing Circuit

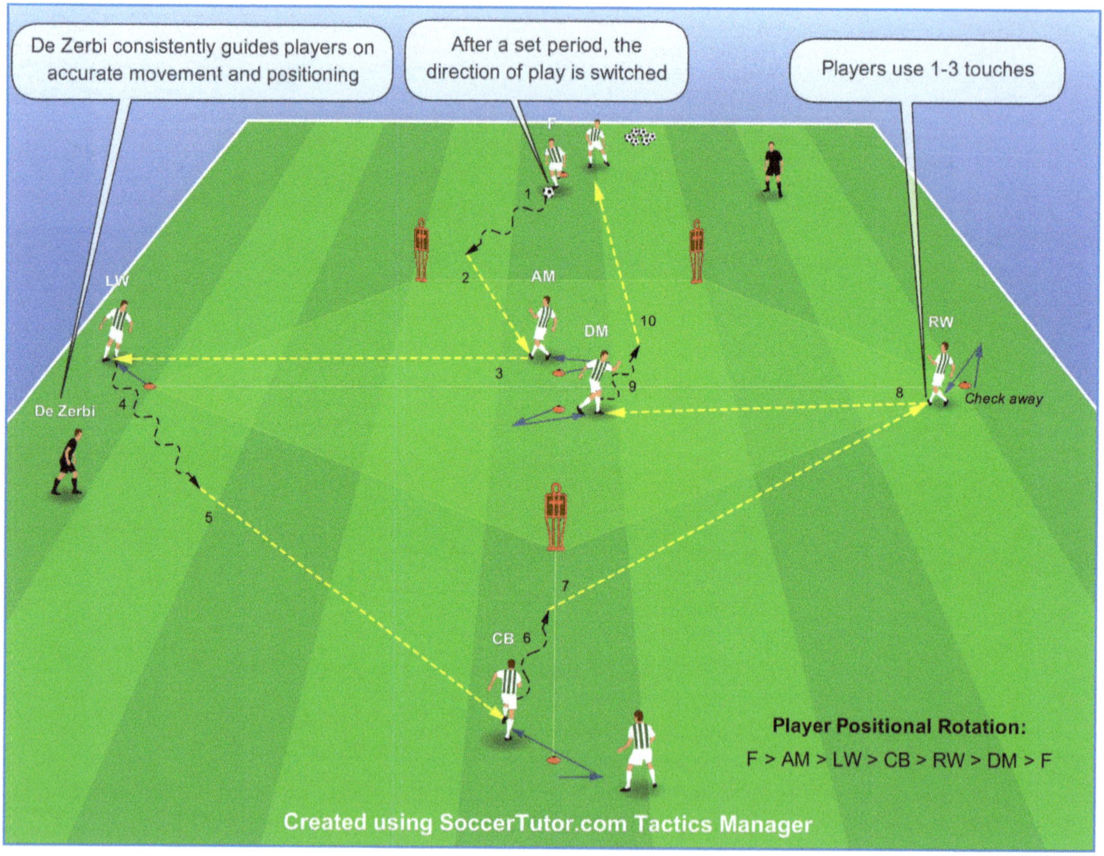

De Zerbi consistently guides players on accurate movement and positioning

After a set period, the direction of play is switched

Players use 1-3 touches

F
1
2
AM
LW
3
DM
10
9
RW
8
Check away
De Zerbi
4
5
7
CB 6

Player Positional Rotation:

F > AM > LW > CB > RW > DM > F

Created using SoccerTutor.com Tactics Manager

Practice Description

1-2. The **forward (F)** dribbles at an angle towards the mannequin and passes to the **attacking midfielder (AM)** in the centre.

3. **AM** checks off the cone, moves to receive, and passes wide to the **left winger (LW)**.

4-5. **LW** checks, receives, dribbles towards the **centre back (CB)**, and passes to him.

6-7. **CB** dribbles forward towards the mannequin and passes wide to the **right winger (RW)**, who checks before moving back to receive.

8-10. **RW** passes to the **defensive midfielder (DM)** in the centre, who checks, moves to receive, takes a touch forward, and plays the final pass to the **Start Position F** as the circuit continues.

→ After a set period of time, the direction of play is switched to clockwise.

Source: Roberto De Zerbi's Sassuolo Calcio preseason training session in Vipiteno, Italy - 18th July 2018

SOCCER
TUTOR
.COM

14. Positional Build-up Play Combinations and Movements

RDZ

Variation 1: 2-Touch (Control + Pass) Short Combinations

De Zerbi consistently guides players on accurate movement and positioning
Sequence restarts
All players take 2 touches (control and pass)
Double pass between RB and CB (steps 4-6)
Created using SoccerTutor.com Tactics Manager

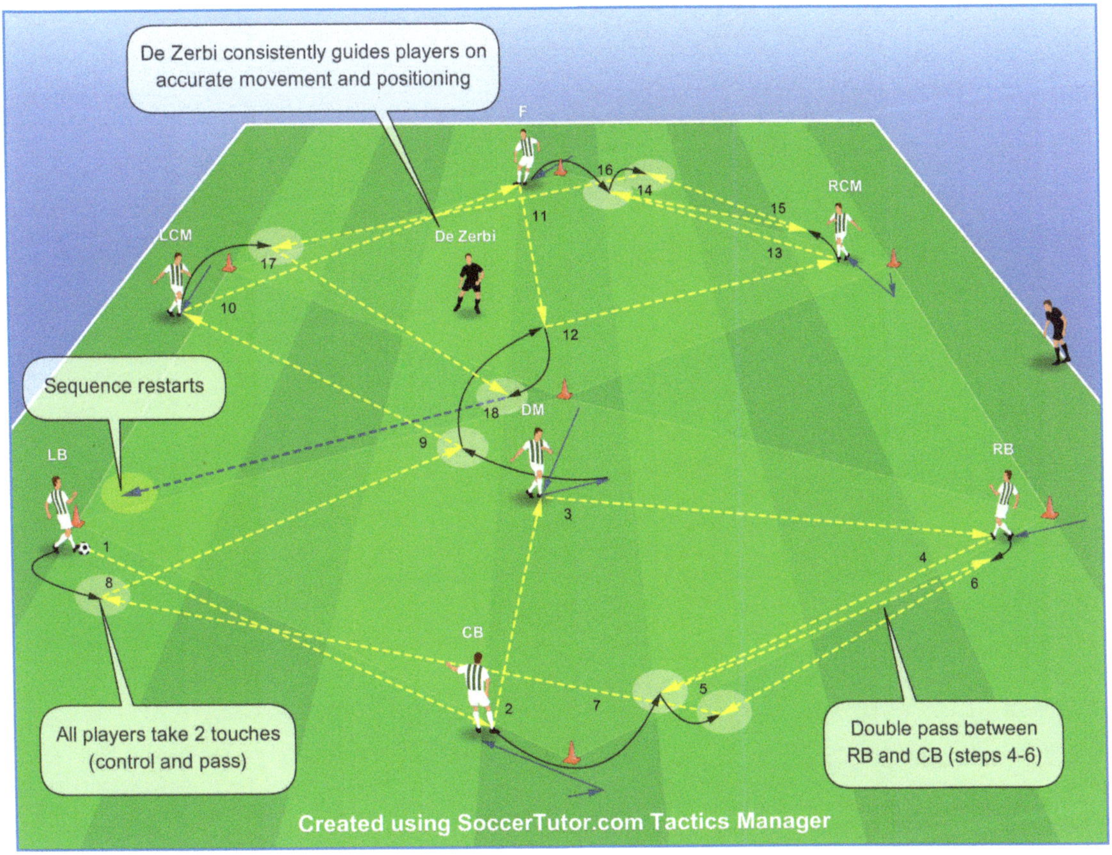

Practice Description (Variation 1)

1. **LB** passes back to **CB**.

2-3. **CB** passes forward to **DM**, who drops off the cone and passes across to **RB**.

4-6. **RB** plays a one-two with **CB**, and then returns the ball again back to **CB**.

7-9. **CB** passes to **LB**, who passes to **DM**. **DM** passes forward and wide to **LCM**.

10-11. **LCM** passes to the **forward (F)**, who sets the ball back for the oncoming **DM**.

12-13. **DM** passes right to **RCM**, who passes to **F** on the other side of the cone.

14-16. **F** plays a one-two with **RCM**, and then passes across to **LCM**.

17-18. **LCM** passes to **DM**, who passes to the start position (restarting sequence).

Source: Roberto De Zerbi's Sassuolo Calcio preseason training session in Vipiteno, Italy - 20th July 2018

Variation 2: De Zerbi's Coaching for Timing of Movement

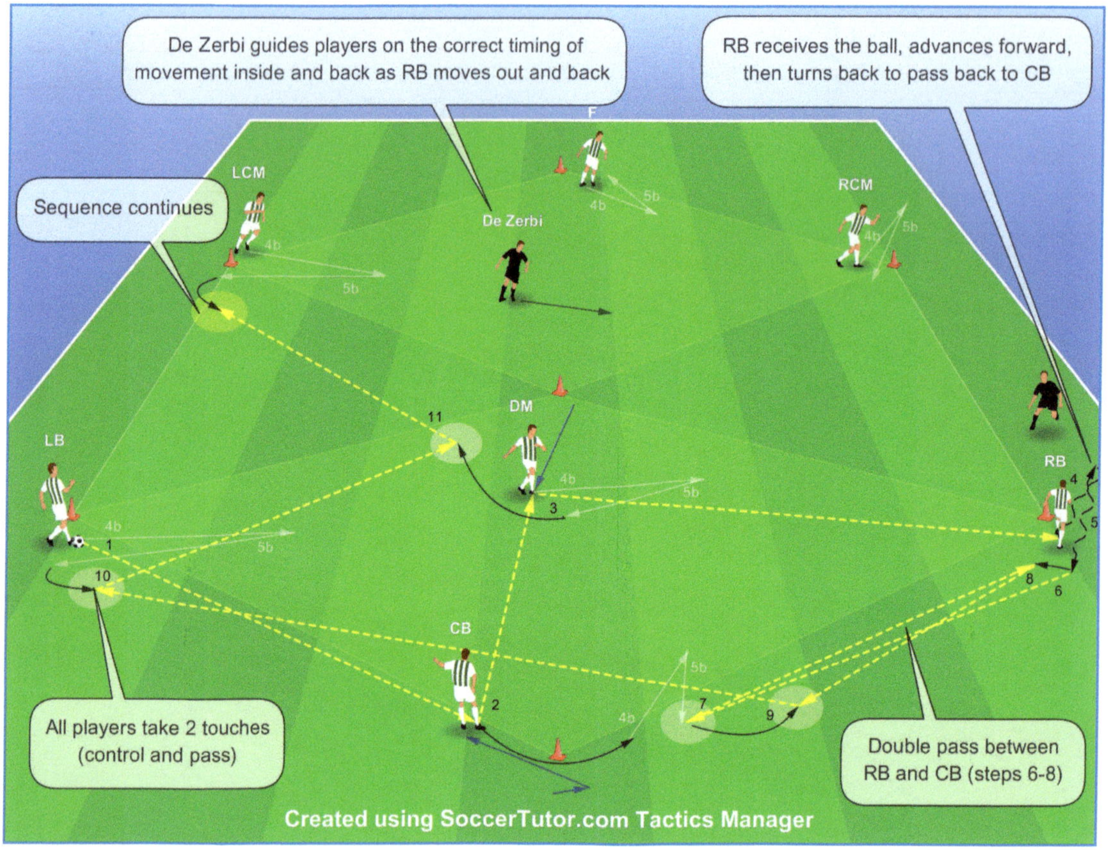

Practice Description (Variation 2)

1. **LB** passes back to **CB**.

2-3. **CB** passes forward to **DM**, who drops off the cone and passes across to **RB**.

4-5. **RB** receives, moves forward with the ball, turns, and moves back again.

... At this point, **De Zerbi** guides the players on the correct timing of their movement inside and then back as **RB** moves forward (outside) and back (inside).

6-8. **RB** plays a one-two with **CB**, and then returns the ball again back to **CB**.

9. **CB** passes across to **LB**.

10. **LB** passes forward to **DM**, who makes a curved movement to receive on the move.

11. **DM** plays a diagonal forward pass wide to **LCM**.

Sequence Continues → The same sequence as the previous example is repeated in the top rhombus (see steps 10-18 on the previous page).

Source: Roberto De Zerbi's Sassuolo Calcio preseason training session in Vipiteno, Italy - 20th July 2018

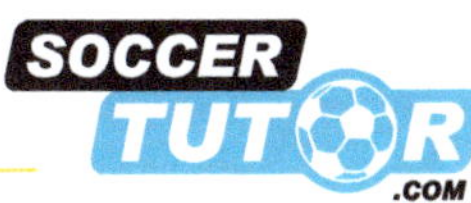

Variation 3: 1-Touch Faster Combinations with Switches

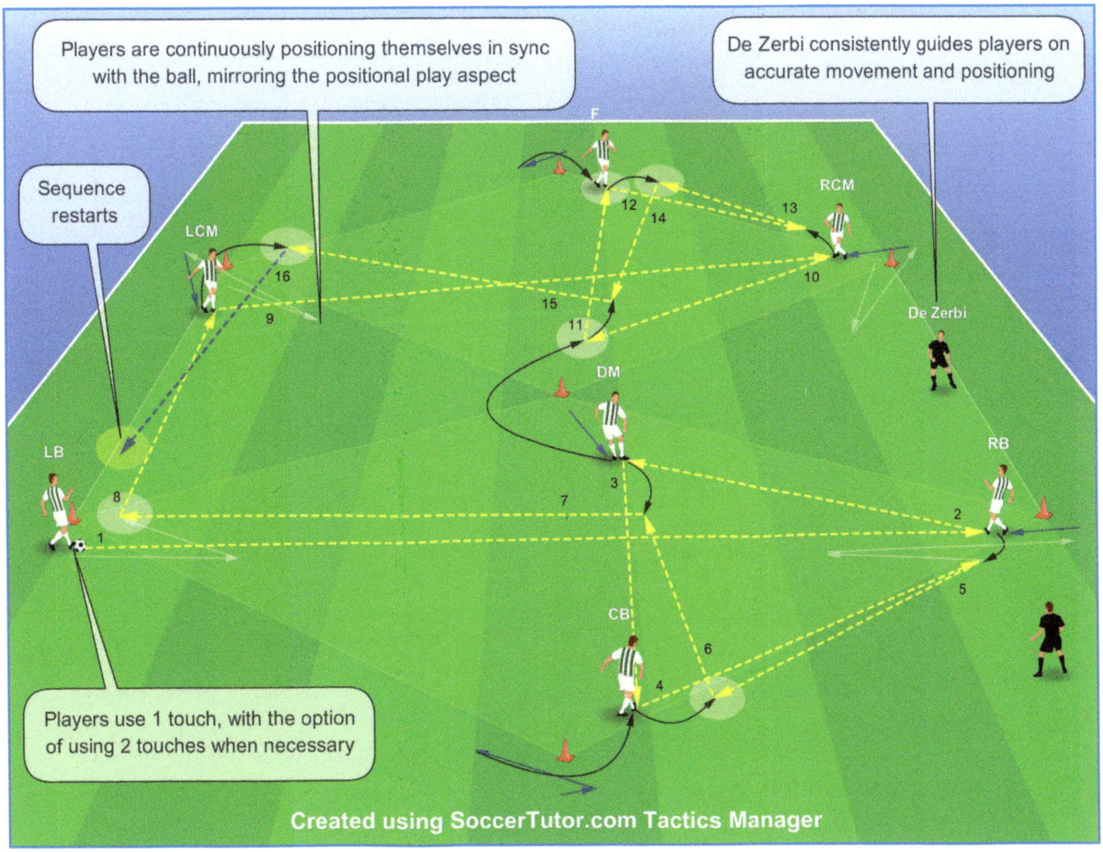

Players are continuously positioning themselves in sync with the ball, mirroring the positional play aspect
De Zerbi consistently guides players on accurate movement and positioning
Sequence restarts
Players use 1 touch, with the option of using 2 touches when necessary
F
RCM
LCM
De Zerbi
DM
LB
RB
CB
Created using SoccerTutor.com Tactics Manager

Practice Description (Variation 3)

1. **LB** passes across the rhombus to **RB**.

2-3. **RB** passes to **DM**, who drops off the cone and passes back to **CB**.

4-6. **CB** plays a one-two with **RB**, and then passes forward to **DM**.

7-8. **DM** has dropped back and passes wide to **LB**, who passes forward to **LCM**.

9. **LCM** passes the ball across to **RCM**.

10. **RCM** sets the ball back for the oncoming **DM**, who moves forward around the cone.

11-13. **DM** passes to the **forward (F)**, who plays a one-two with **RCM**.

14. **F** passes back to **DM.**

15. **DM** passes across to **LCM**, who moves around the cone to receive.

16. **LCM** passes to the start position to restart the same sequence.

Source: Roberto De Zerbi's Sassuolo Calcio preseason training session in Vipiteno, Italy - 20th July 2018

15. Positional Break the Lines 1-Touch Combination Play Double Passing Circuit with Central Box Midfield

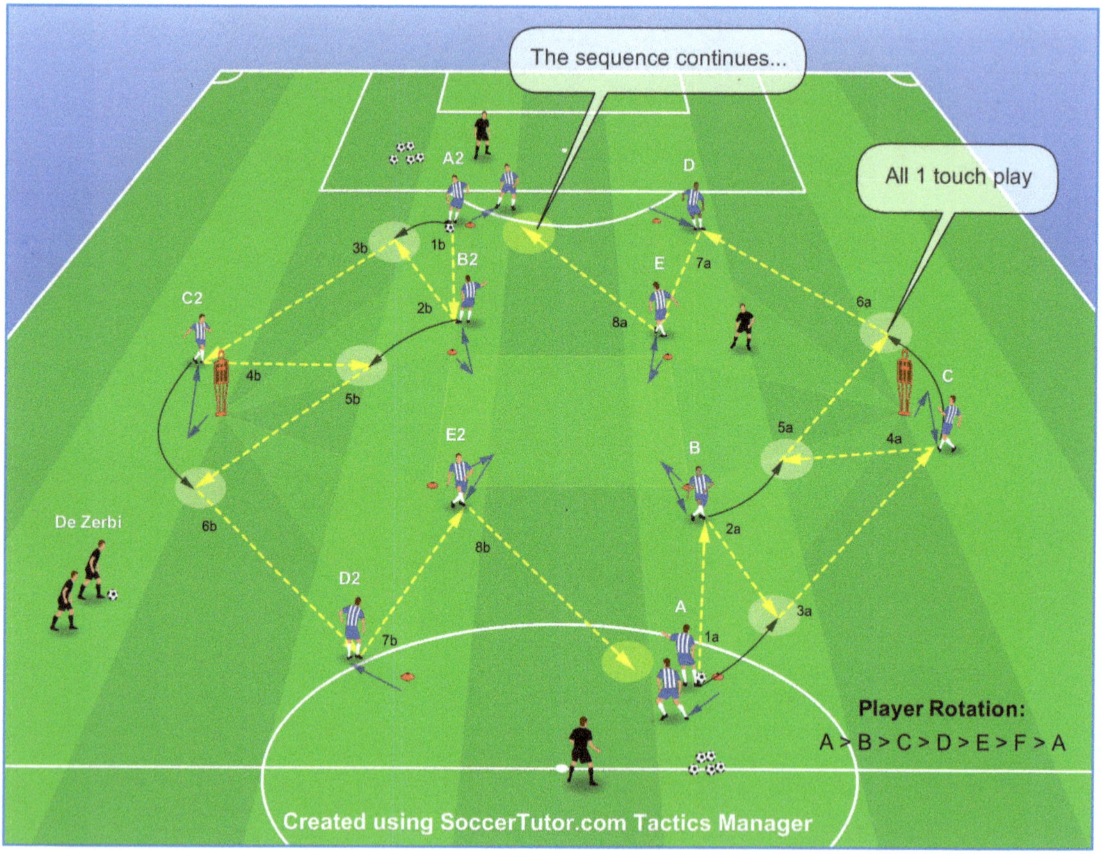

Practice Description

The same cones and number of players are set up on both sides with 2 balls starting from A and A2. All the players check before moving to receive and rotate as one complete circuit (E2 → A / E → A2).

1-3. **A/A2** play a one-two with **B/B2**, and then pass to **C/C2**.

4-5. **C/C2** play a give & go with **B/B2** and receive on the other side of the mannequin.

6. **C/C2** pass to **D/D2**.

7. **D/D2** pass to **E/E2**.

8. **E/E2** pass to **Start Position A/A2** with the next player waiting, and the passing circuit continues with the same sequence repeated.

→ The players rotate their positions around the circuit: **A → B → C → D → E → A**.

Source: Roberto De Zerbi's Brighton training session at Elite Football Performance Centre - 28th March 2023

Roberto De Zerbi's Build-up Play and Attacking Philosophy

Roberto De Zerbi's Key Game Principles for Build-up Play from the Back

1 Bait the Press (Draw Opponents Forward)

- Deliberately **invite pressure with players positioned deep during build-up**. The GK acts as the third centre back.
- **Draw in opponents** with short passes and maximise space further up the pitch to exploit.
- Put foot on ball with the sole of the boot so you can play any way and are not limited to only playing to one side when pressed.

2 Technical Execution

- Control of the ball with precise first touches, quality of pass, and the correct weight of pass.
- Prevent duels as much as possible by **limiting long passes (maintain control)**.
- Wait for the correct forward pass to a link player, who can play a wall pass to a teammate in space facing the opposition's goal.

3 Control the Opposition and the Game

- Control the game with good tactical knowledge, reading the game situation, and making the correct decisions.
- **Possession-based football** to control the game.
- Defensive midfielder/s deep to control the build-up play. Wingers push up high and pin back opposition's defensive line.
- Move the ball to the forward or attacking midfielder in the open space in the centre.

"If you receive the ball with the sole and from the front, you can play for the side you want. There you have total control of the ball."

Roberto De Zerbi's Tactical Shape for Build-up Play from Back in Open Play

1a. Build-up Shape with 2-4-4 Structure (Brighton 4-2-3-1)

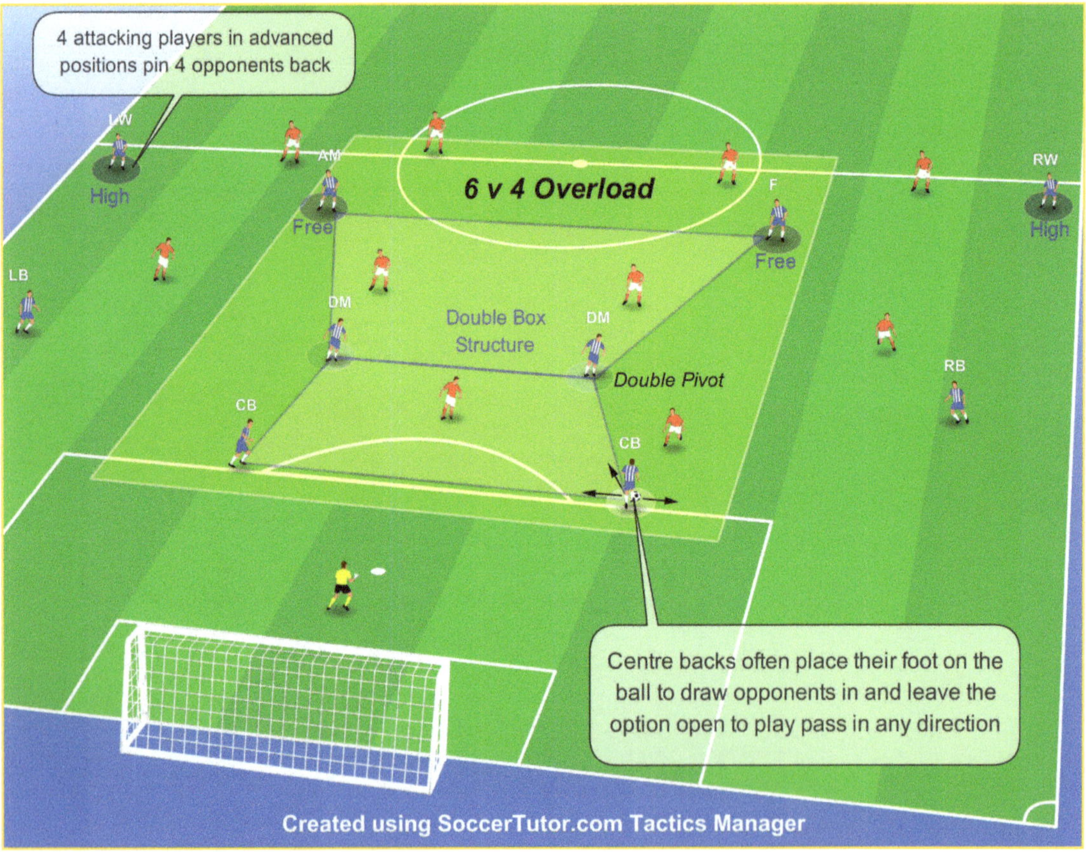

- Roberto De Zerbi's team invite the opposition's press and draw them deep into their half. The **centre backs (CB) often place their foot on the ball**, leaving the option open to play passes in any direction. The 2 full backs are wide and in line with the **2 defensive midfielders (double pivot)**. The 4 attacking players are in advanced positions to pin the 4 opposing defenders back and away from disrupting the build-up.
- As the opponents are forced to commit players forward, the Brighton **attacking midfielder (AM)** and **forward (F)** can occupy positions in free available space.
- With the **double box structure** shown, Brighton have a **6v4 Overload in the centre of the pitch (highlighted)**, which enables them to play through the opposition's organisation and move the ball forward to their attacking players.

1b. Square Pass (Bait to Press), Third Man Link Player to Move Ball to Free Player + Launch Attack

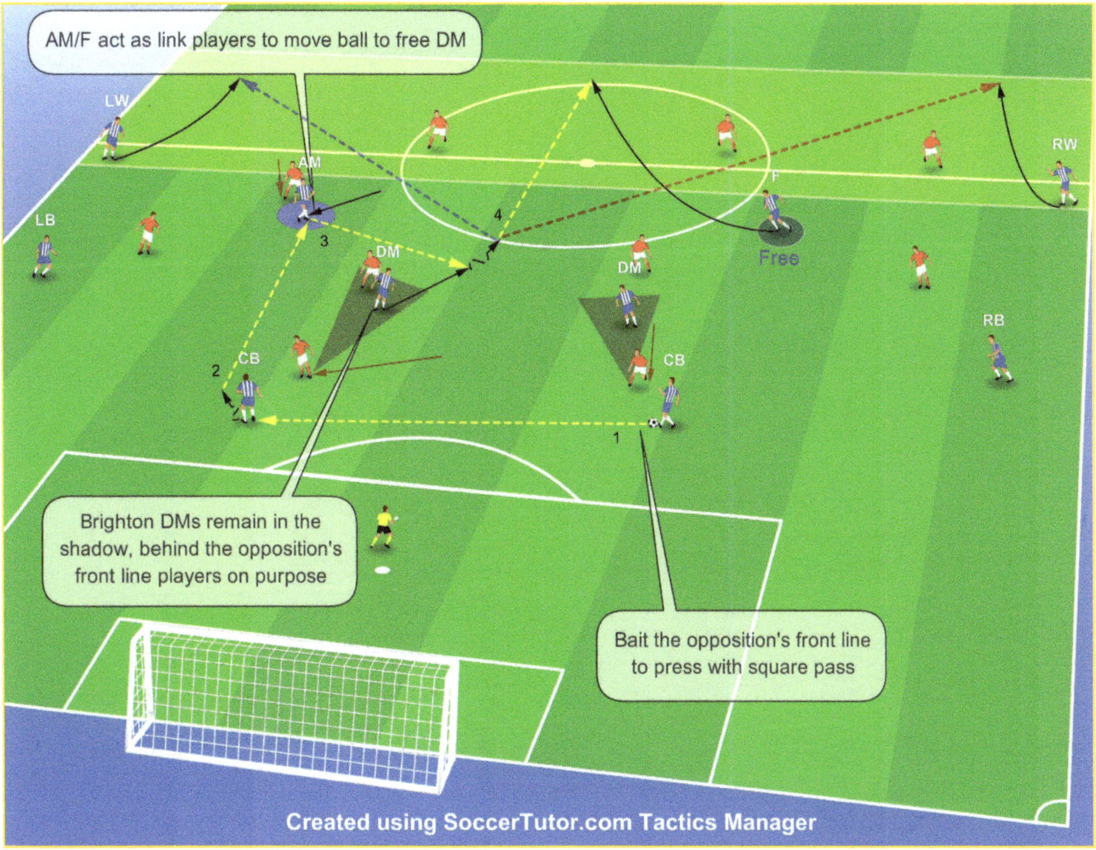

AM/F act as link players to move ball to free DM

Brighton DMs remain in the shadow, behind the opposition's front line players on purpose

Bait the opposition's front line to press with square pass

Created using SoccerTutor.com Tactics Manager

- De Zerbi's aims are to bait the opposition forward to press and draw them out of position and use a third man link player to move the ball to a free player behind the first line of pressure. Square passes like the one in the diagram example are used to bait the press.
- The **defensive midfielders (DM)** stay behind the 2 red forwards (in shadow) with the aim of receiving via a link player. They do not move at angles to receive directly from the **centre backs (CB)**.
- Once their opponents commit, Brighton play out from the back successfully by following this set tactical structure and principles. Once a link player is used to "bounce" the ball to a free **DM**, Brighton can move the ball into the free available space (highlighted yellow). This space to play is there because the opposition's back 4 were pinned back by the wingers.
- In the diagram example, the **attacking midfielder (AM)** is the link player and the **DM's** pass breaks the midfield line to play through to the **forward (F)**. A good attacking opportunity has been created very quickly with 6 or 7 opponents taken out of the game.

2a. Adjusting Build-up Shape to 2-3-5 Structure (4-2-3-1)

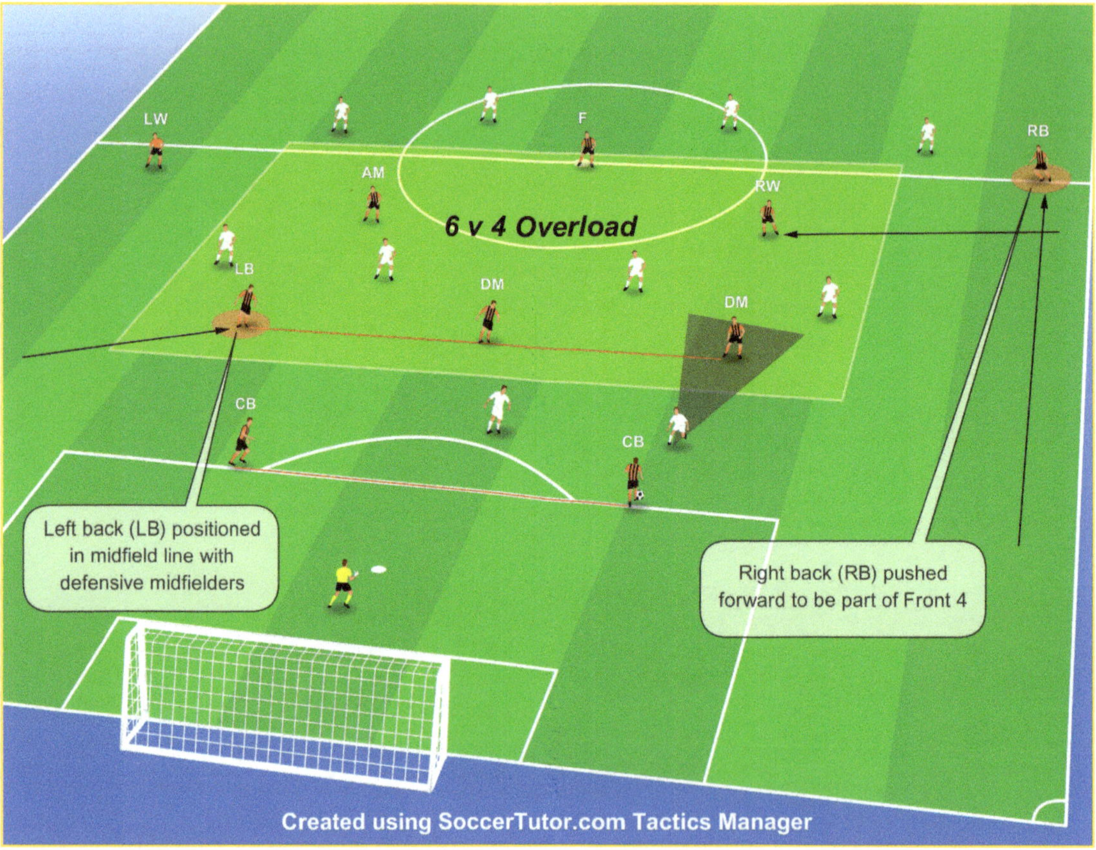

6 v 4 Overload

Left back (LB) positioned in midfield line with defensive midfielders

Right back (RB) pushed forward to be part of Front 4

Created using SoccerTutor.com Tactics Manager

- **This analysis is taken from De Zerbi's Shakhtar Donetsk team (4-2-3-1).**
- On occasion, De Zerbi switches the build-up shape of his team depending on the game situation or the different number of opponents involved in the first and second lines of pressure.
- The diagram shows an adjustment from the 2-4-4 structure shown on the previous 2 pages to a 2-3-5 shape.
- In this structure, one full back (**LB** in diagram example) joins the 2 defensive midfielders in the second line. The other one (**RB**) moves into a winger position to join the front 5.
- The **attacking midfielder (AM)** and **right winger (RW)** occupy central positions in the free available space (highlighted yellow). This is one variation of how the players move positions, but there are a few that De Zerbi uses.
- There is a 6v4 overload in the centre of the pitch (highlighted) as shown, but for the **initial build-up the central area is condensed and difficult to play through**.
- Therefore, the **aim is to play out from the back towards the wide areas**, and an example is shown on the following page...

2b. Square Passes Between Centre Backs (Bait to Press) + Move the Ball Wide and Away from Condensed Centre

LW
AM
F
RW
RB
5 v 4 Overload
LB
DM
DM
CB
Condensed
CB
With a condensed centre of the pitch, look to play wide into space
Bait the opposition's front line to press with square pass
Created using SoccerTutor.com Tactics Manager

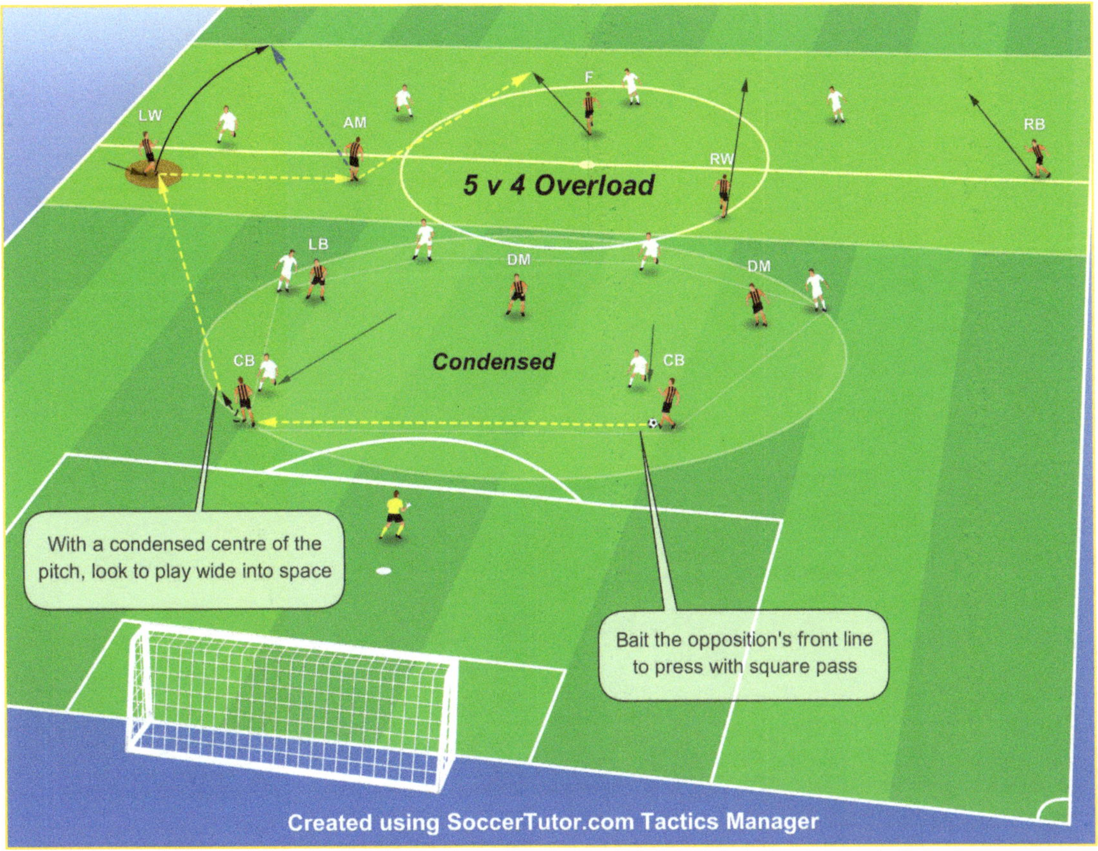

- With De Zerbi's **2-3 build-up shape** in his own half, the opposition need to be compact in the centre, as shown with the 2 white wingers in narrow positions.
- An irregular hexagon shape is formed which includes Shakhtar Donetsk's back 5 + **6 opponents, who are advanced to stop Shakhtar from building up play too easily** with equal or greater numbers.
- The aim for De Zerbi's team when in this shape is to **play quickly to the wide players**, so that they can take 6 opponents out of the game for a very promising attack.
- They again use short passes and specifically sideways passes between the centre backs (as shown) to **bait the press and create space**.
- In this example, the 2 white players in the front line of the press are baited forward, and the **centre back (CB)** is able to play wide to the **left winger (LW)** in the available space (highlighted yellow).
- From there, Shakhtar potentially have a **5v4 numerical advantage (overload) to try and score** with their attack.

3a. Build-up Shape with 4-3-3 Structure (Sassuolo)

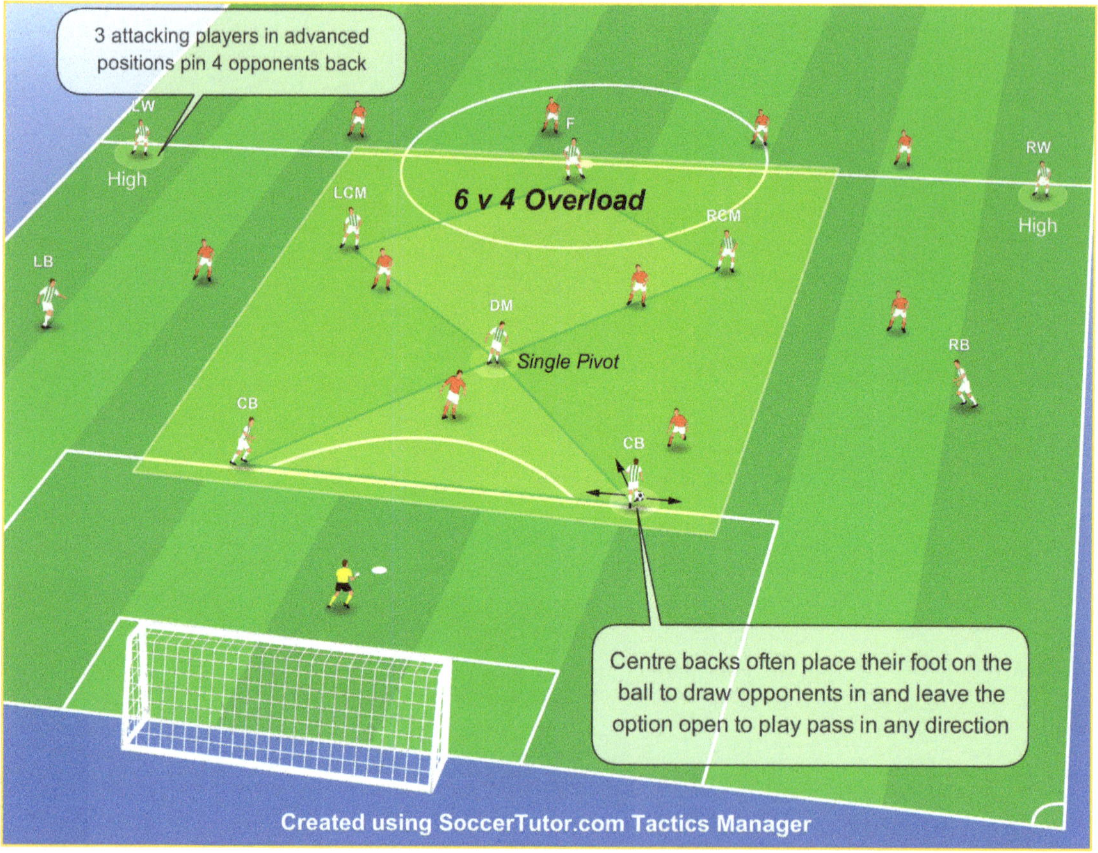

3 attacking players in advanced positions pin 4 opponents back

LW High F RW High LCM 6 v 4 Overload RCM LB DM Single Pivot RB CB CB

Centre backs often place their foot on the ball to draw opponents in and leave the option open to play pass in any direction

Created using SoccerTutor.com Tactics Manager

- **This analysis is taken from De Zerbi's Sassuolo team (4-3-3).**
- 5 players (or 6 including the GK) are involved in playing out from the back, and 3 attacking players (2 wingers + forward) are in advanced positions to pin the 4 opposing defenders back.
- In contrast to Brighton and Shakhtar Donetsk's 2 defensive midfielders (DM), **Sassuolo have 1 DM (single pivot)**.
- As the opponents are forced to commit players forward, the Sassuolo **central midfielders (LCM & RCM) can occupy positions in free available space** just behind the opposition's midfield line.
- NOTE: ***The structure of the Positional Build-up Play and Attacking Positional Patterns of Play practices included later in the book is based on De Zerbi's Sassuolo training sessions when using the 4-3-3 formation and the 2-3-2-3 attacking phase shape. You can adapt them for 4-2-3-1 by including a double pivot (2 defensive midfielders).***
- However, the current Brighton team do use either 2-3 / 3-2 build-up shapes in parts of games or against specific opponents. You still have a **6 v 4 Overload in the centre of the pitch (highlighted)**, which enables the team to play through the opposition's organisation.

3b. Adjusting Build-up Shape to 2-3-2-3 Structure with Inverted Full Backs (4-3-3)

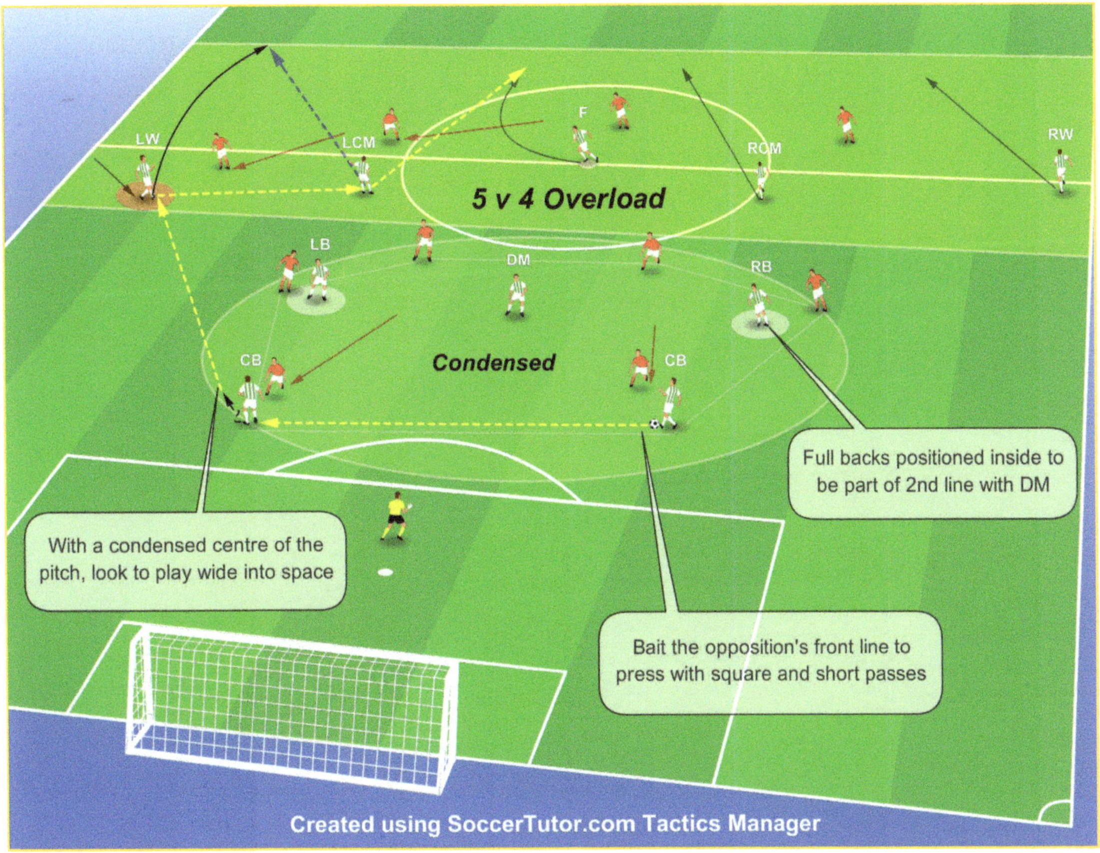

5 v 4 Overload

Condensed

Full backs positioned inside to be part of 2nd line with DM

With a condensed centre of the pitch, look to play wide into space

Bait the opposition's front line to press with square and short passes

Created using SoccerTutor.com Tactics Manager

- With De Zerbi's **2-3 build-up shape** (2 full backs in second line), the opposition need to be compact in the centre, as shown with the 2 red wingers in narrow positions. With this adjusted shape, the **2 full backs (LB & RB) join the second line with the defensive midfielder (DM)**.
- De Zerbi's team invite the opponent's press, drawing them in deep in their own half using square and short passes.
- The **centre is condensed, so the aim is to play wide**. Sassuolo can take 6 opponents out of the game and attack with a numerical advantage.
- In this example, the 2 red players in the front line of the press are baited forward, and the **centre back (CB)** is able to play wide to the **left winger (LW)**, who drops back to receive.
- The red right back follows **LW's** movement, so he passes to the **left central midfielder (LCM)**, who has plenty of space to receive and turn, then play in behind the defensive line.
- From there, Sassuolo potentially have a **4v3 or 5v4 overload** to try and score with their attack.

Roberto De Zerbi's Brighton Build-up Play from Goal Kicks

1a. Build-up Shape from Goal Kicks (4-2-4)

LW
RW
AM
F
DM
DM
LB
RB
CB
CB

Full backs deep and narrow - Brighton play out from GK with 6 or 7 players

Created using SoccerTutor.com Tactics Manager

- This **analysis is taken from De Zerbi's Brighton team (4-2-3-1)**. 7 players including the GK are involved in playing out from the back, and 4 attacking players are in advanced positions to pin the 4 opposing defenders back.
- The 2 **full backs (LB & RB)** are deep and narrow. The 2 **defensive midfielders (DM)** position themselves behind the 2 most advanced opponents.
- This creates an **advantage of 4 (+GK) v 2 to play through the first line of pressure.**
- The **attacking midfielder (AM) and forward (F) are ready to help create a 4v2 overload in the centre of the pitch once the ball has been progressed** (see highlighted area). The red centre backs cannot move forward to mark them because they would leave space for the Brighton wingers to run into.

SOCCER
TUTOR
.COM

1b. Build-up with Third Man Link Player + Central Overload

Opposing centre backs stay back to protect space behind them
Opposing centre backs stay to protect space behind them
LW
AM
F
RW
4 v 2 Overload
DM
DM
LB
RB
CB
CB
Link player enables Brighton to break first line of pressure
Created using SoccerTutor.com Tactics Manager

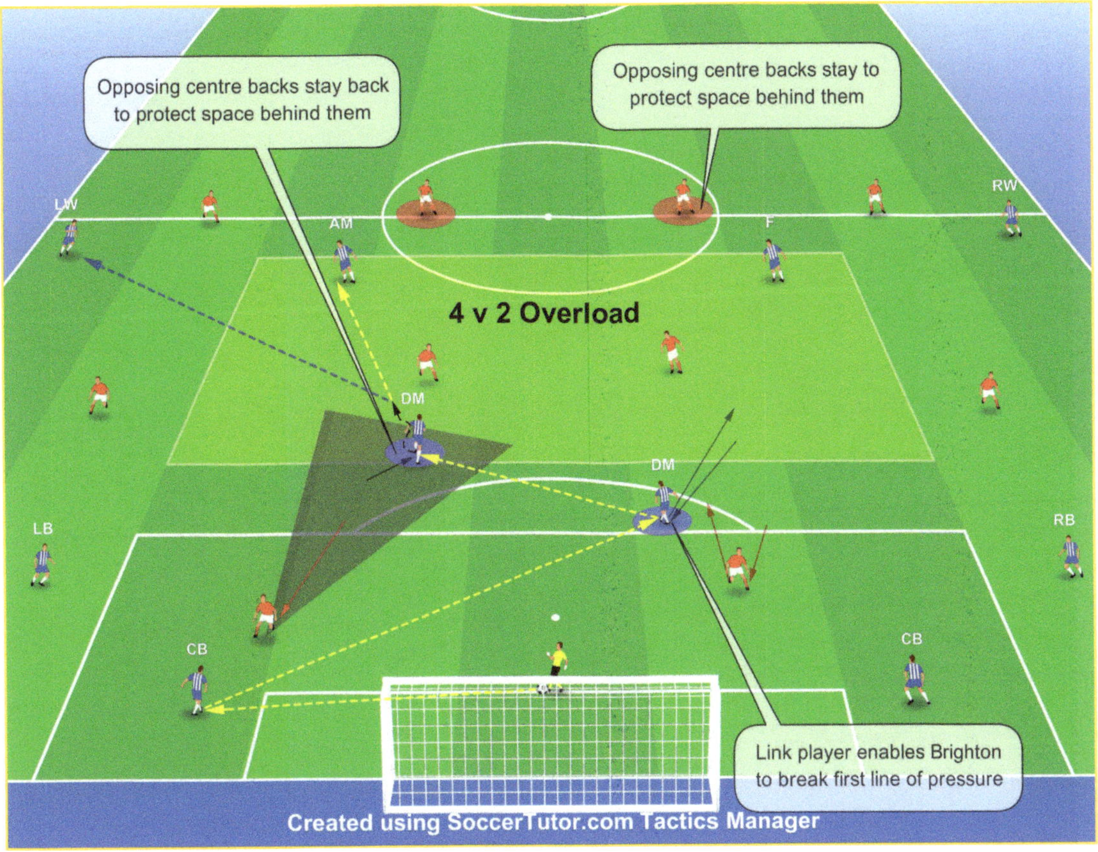

- Brighton's aim is to **use a link player to play a "bounce" pass to a free player in the centre**, to then progress the attack.
- The GK plays the ball short to one of the centre backs to **bait the press of the 2 red attackers** and make it easier to play out from the back.
- One of the **defensive midfielders (DM)** is positioned behind the red player who moves to press the ball (in shadow). The other **DM** drops back a little to create a passing angle for the **centre back (CB)**. **CB** passes diagonally to **DM**, who is able to easily play forward to the other **DM**. Brighton have broken the first line of pressure.
- As mentioned on the previous page, the opposing centre backs have stayed back to protect the space behind them, so a **4v2 overload is created in the centre with 2 x DMs, the attacking midfielder (AM), and the forward (F) vs 2 red central midfielders**.
- Brighton are now in a great position to easily beat the opposition's second line of pressure and attack the back 4 with a numerical advantage.
- **NOTE:** ***This is just one pattern Brighton used to build-up play from goal kicks and 3 more are shown on the next 3 pages...***

2. Build-up when Opposing Centre Backs Push Forward

When opposition CBs move to mark AM/F, they leave a large space behind to attack
4 v 2 Overload
Space
Created using SoccerTutor.com Tactics Manager

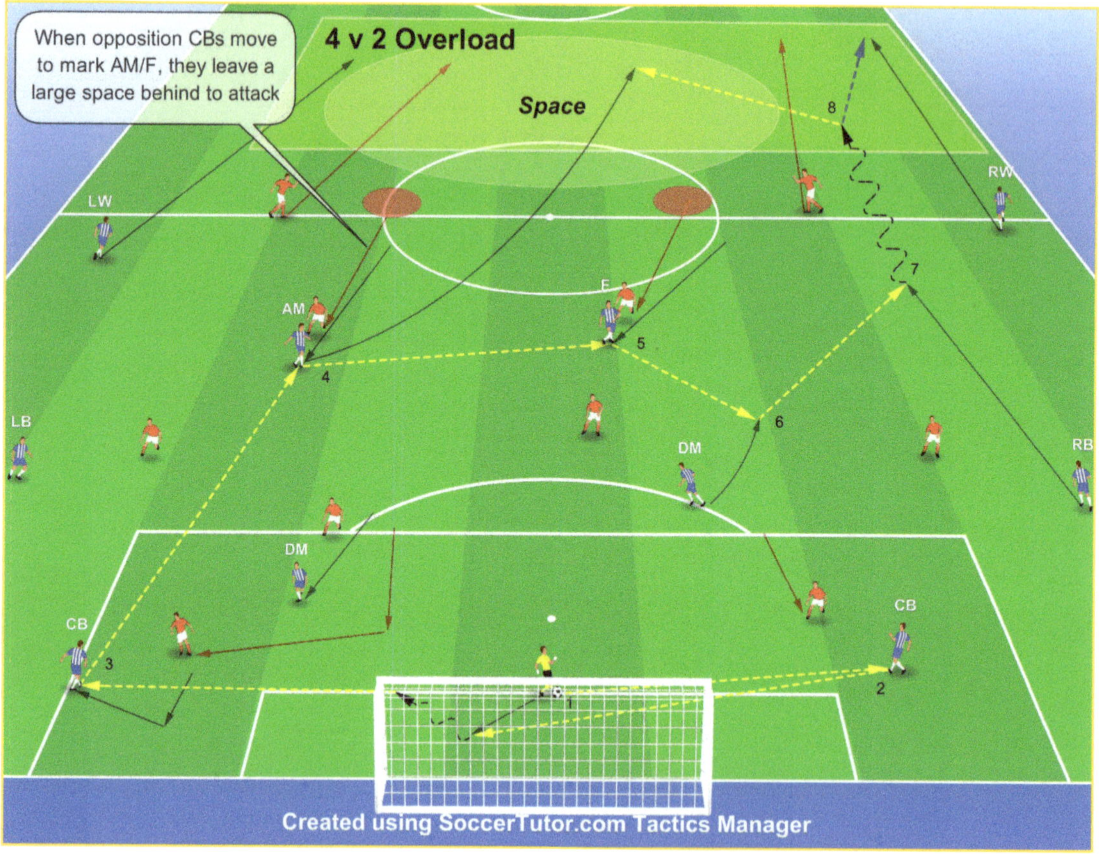

- This example is a variation of the example on the previous page and shows you what can happen if the opposing centre backs move forward to mark Brighton's **attacking midfielder (AM)** and **forward (F)**, trying to avoid a 4v2 overload being created in the centre of the pitch.
- They leave their half open to be attacked with ease if Brighton are able to play out from the back successfully.
- In this example, the GK passes to the right **centre back (CB)**, who is pressed and returns the ball to the GK. The GK then plays to the other **CB**.
- Brighton always aim to break through pressure with forward passes (as long as it's not too risky). In this situation, **CB** is able to break the midfield line with a through pass to the **attacking midfielder (AM)**. As he is put under pressure from behind, **AM** passes across to the **forward (F)**, who is also closed down. Now both red centre backs are out of position leaving a large hole in their defence.
- **F** lays the ball off for the **defensive midfielder (DM)**, who is able to play for the **right back (RB)** to run forward onto. From here, De Zerbi's Brighton have a potential 4 or 5 v 2 overload to finish their attack and score.

3. Invite Press on One Side and Switch Play into Space

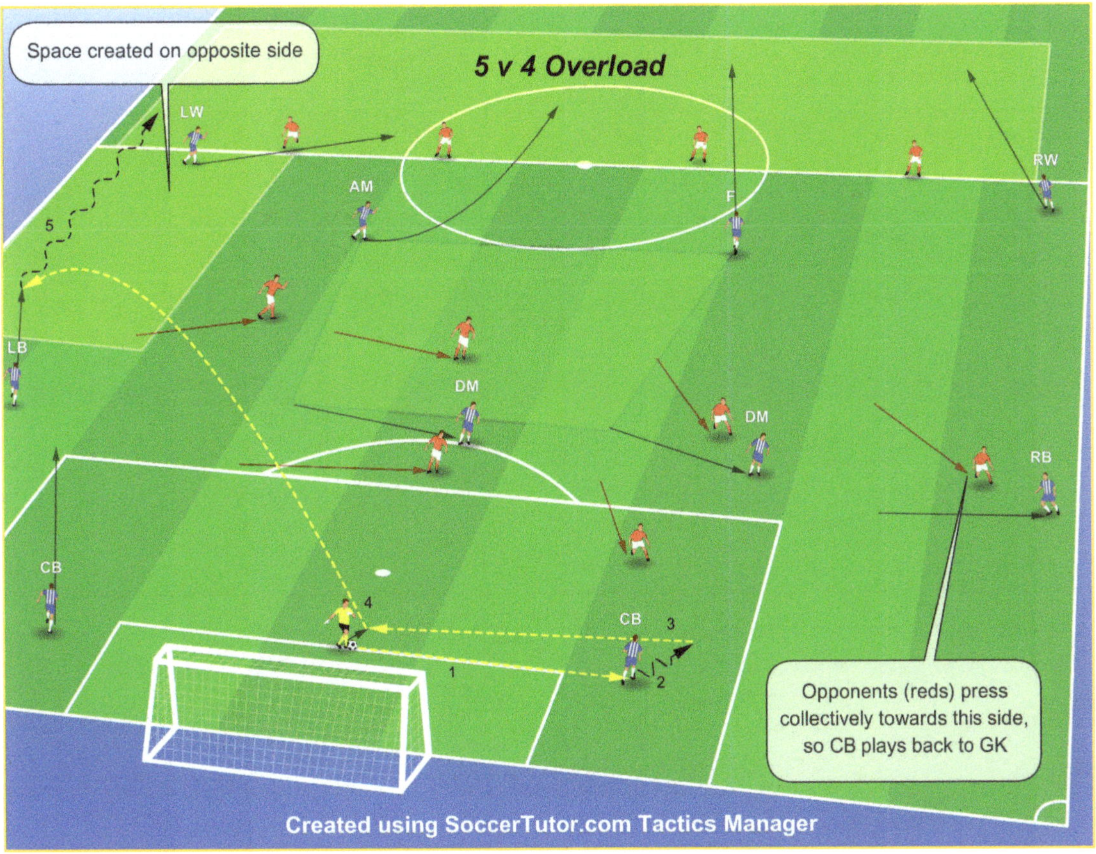

Space created on opposite side
5 v 4 Overload
LW
AM
F
RW
LB
DM
DM
RB
CB
CB
1
2
3
4
5
Opponents (reds) press collectively towards this side, so CB plays back to GK
Created using SoccerTutor.com Tactics Manager

- In this example, Brighton aim to attract the opposition to press towards one side of the pitch, and then switch play into the space out wide on the opposite side.
- In this example, the GK passes to the **centre back (CB)**, who takes a forward touch. The **right back (RB)** moves wide.
- **CB** is closed down by the red forward and all the other red players in the first and second line of pressure shift across to that side.
- **CB** passes back across to the **GK**, so that he can play a long aerial pass for the forward run of the **left back (LB)**.
- The **left winger (LW)** makes a run inside, which creates space for **LB** to dribble forward quickly.
- The **attacking midfielder (AM)**, **forward (F)**, and **right winger (RW)** all make forward runs and Brighton have a potential 5v4 numerical advantage (overload) to finish their attack.
- **NOTE:** ***The central blue box shows the starting positions of both DMs, AM, & F, as displayed on Page 56.***

4. Third Man Link Player, Lay-off, and Through Pass

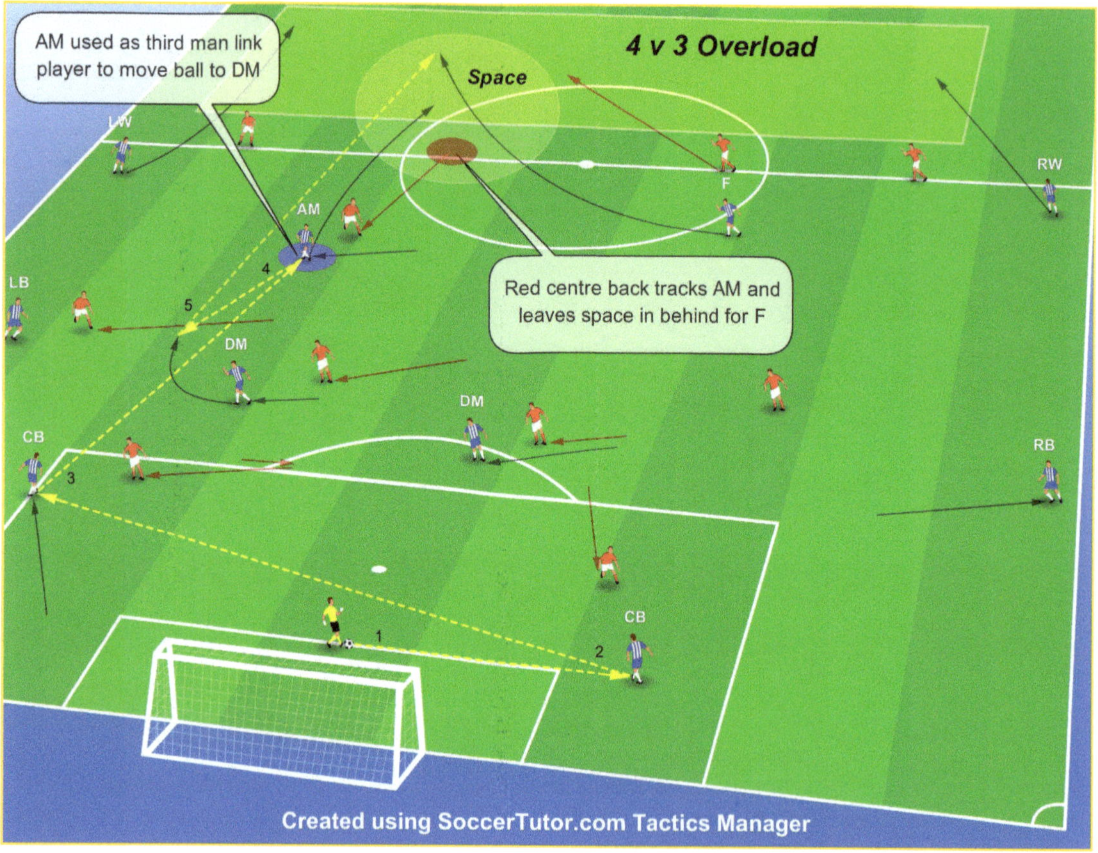

- In this example, Brighton use a third man link player to move the ball to a **defensive midfielder (DM)** free in the centre, and then launch their attack from there.
- The **DMs** stay behind the 2 red forwards with the aim of receiving via a link player. They do not move at angles to receive directly from the **centre backs (CBs)**.
- Once their opponents commit, Brighton look to pass to an attacking player beyond the opposition's midfield line.
- In this example, the GK passes to one of the **centre backs (CB)**, who passes across to the other one.
- **CB** sees an open passing lane towards the **attacking midfielder (AM)**.
- **AM** plays a "bounce" pass back to the free **DM**, who moves to meet the pass.
- The red centre back has tracked Brighton's **AM**, so there is **space created in behind (highlighted)**.
- **DM** plays a through pass for the curved run of the **forward (F)** into the space, and Brighton have a 3v3 situation to finish their attack. In addition, **AM** makes a run forward which can help create a **4v3 overload** if the red centre back is unable to track back at the same speed.

Roberto De Zerbi's Possession Based Style of Play

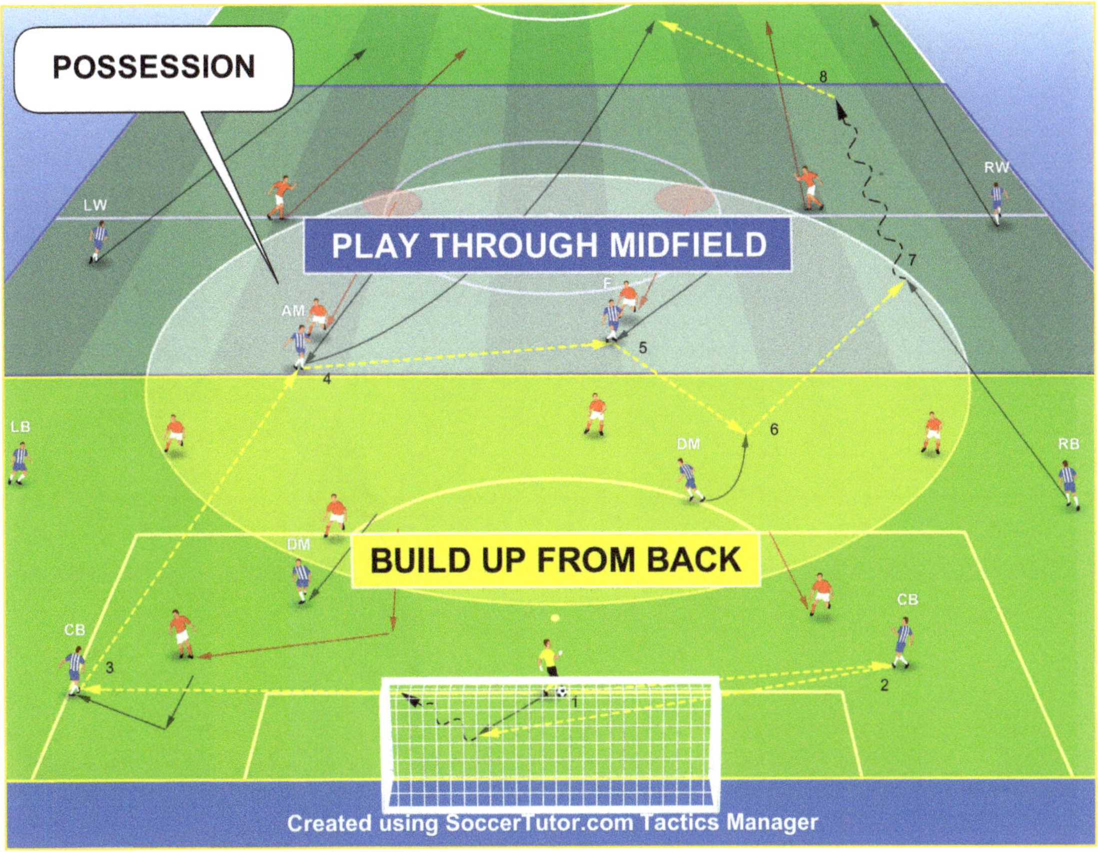

POSSESSION

PLAY THROUGH MIDFIELD

BUILD UP FROM BACK

Created using SoccerTutor.com Tactics Manager

BUILD UP FROM BACK

De Zerbi encourages his teams to build up play from the back, starting with the goalkeeper distributing the ball to the centre backs, who then play out from the defensive third.

POSSESSION (CONTROL)

De Zerbi's teams aim to control possession of the ball. This involves playing out from the back, maintaining a high passing accuracy, and circulating the ball.

PLAY THROUGH MIDFIELD

De Zerbi's possession-based style involves playing through midfield. The 2 defensive midfielders (double pivot) play a crucial role in controlling the tempo of the game, circulating the ball, linking up with the defensive unit to progress the play, and linking up with the attacking unit to create scoring opportunities.

"[Centre backs] have the pleasure of holding the ball, of building the game, knowing that everything starts from them."

Roberto De Zerbi's Attacking Tactics and Game Principles

1. Build-up Play from the Back (Brighton 4-2-4 Shape)

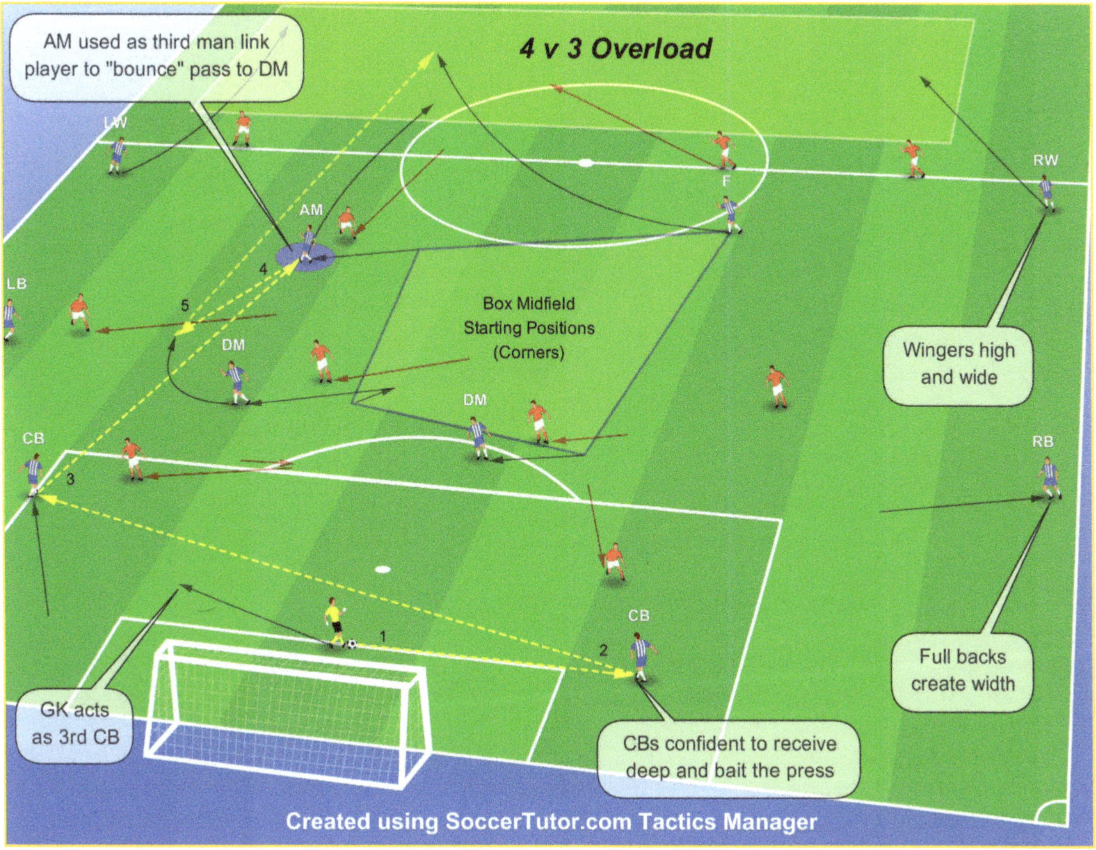

This example is a repetition of the match example on Page 60, where you will find the full description of this build-up play sequence. The central blue box shows the starting positions of both **DMs**, **AM**, & **F**, as displayed on Page 56.

It is repeated here to outline the key points and best illustrate Roberto De Zerbi's game principles in relation to build up play from the back:

1. Players encouraged to **play short**, **bait the press**, and use **quick ball circulation**.
2. **Open up** to receive at angles (support).
3. Maintain **good ball control** at all times.
4. Midfielders must **dictate the tempo of the game** (key players for De Zerbi's tactics).
5. Third man link player **bounce passes**!

2a. Keep Possession + Break the Lines at Right Moment (Play Out from the Back)

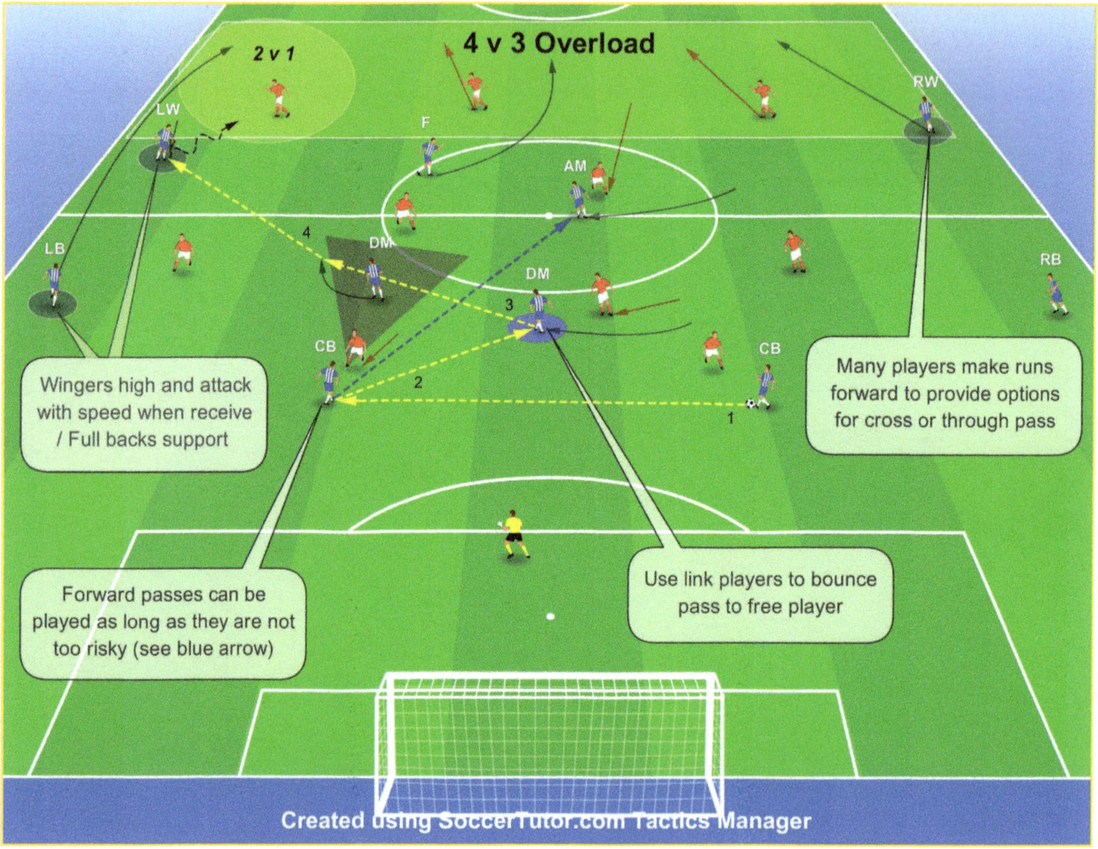

Roverto De Zerbi wants his teams to move the ball to a free player facing the opponent's goal.

To achieve this (after attracting the opposition's first line press), here are the principles he implements:

- **Play the forward pass** as long as it is not too risky (good decision making - see blue arrow in diagram) to play through the midfield line.
- **Utilise link players** (even if marked) to play first time bounce passes to move the ball to a free player, who can then advance the attack.
- **Wingers stay in advanced wide positions** and attack at speed if they receive, exploiting the numerical situation due to many opponents being too far away to track back successfully.
- The **central midfielders can then exploit the available space in the centre** with supporting runs, as the opposing defensive line moves backwards to defend their goal.
- Many players **make runs into the box to provide plenty of goal scoring options** for potential crosses or through passes.

SOCCER
TUTOR
.COM

2b. Keep Possession + Break the Lines at Right Moment (Possession in Attacking Half)

Disrupts the opposition's defensive structure to draw players out of position to create space and score chances
Play incisive through passess + Aim to play ball in between the lines
10
9
LW
RW
F
AM
Space
LB
DM
DM
RB
CB
CB
Midefielders dictate tempo as "Key Players" + Open up to receive at angles (support play)
Created using SoccerTutor.com Tactics Manager

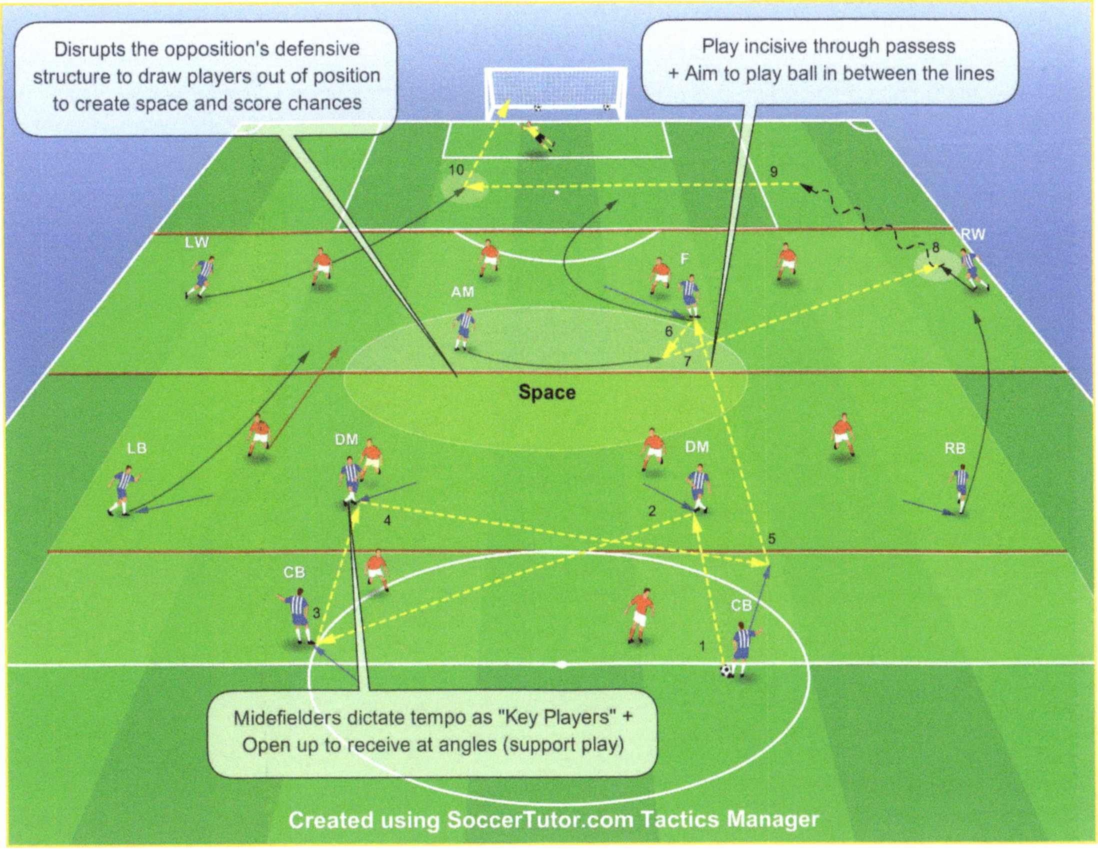

Now we show the tactics for Roberto De Zerbi's Brighton team when building their attack in their opponent's half. Here are the principles he implements:

- **Midfielders must dictate the tempo of the game as they are "key players"** for Brighton and De Zerbi's tactics. Together with the centre backs, they can play short passes to keep possession, waiting for the right time to break the lines.
- Play forward as long as it is not too risky (good decision making) to **play through the midfield line**. Play **incisive passes to receive in between the lines**.
- **Utilise link players** (even if marked like the forward in the diagram example) to play **first time bounce passes** to move the ball to a free player, who can then advance the attack.
- **Disrupt the opposition's defensive structure and draw players out of position** to create space and scoring chances.
- **Wingers stay in advanced wide positions** and attack at speed if they receive.
- Many players **make runs into the box to provide plenty of goal scoring options** for potential crosses or through passes.

3. Wide Play (Control, Switching Play, Overloads on Flank)

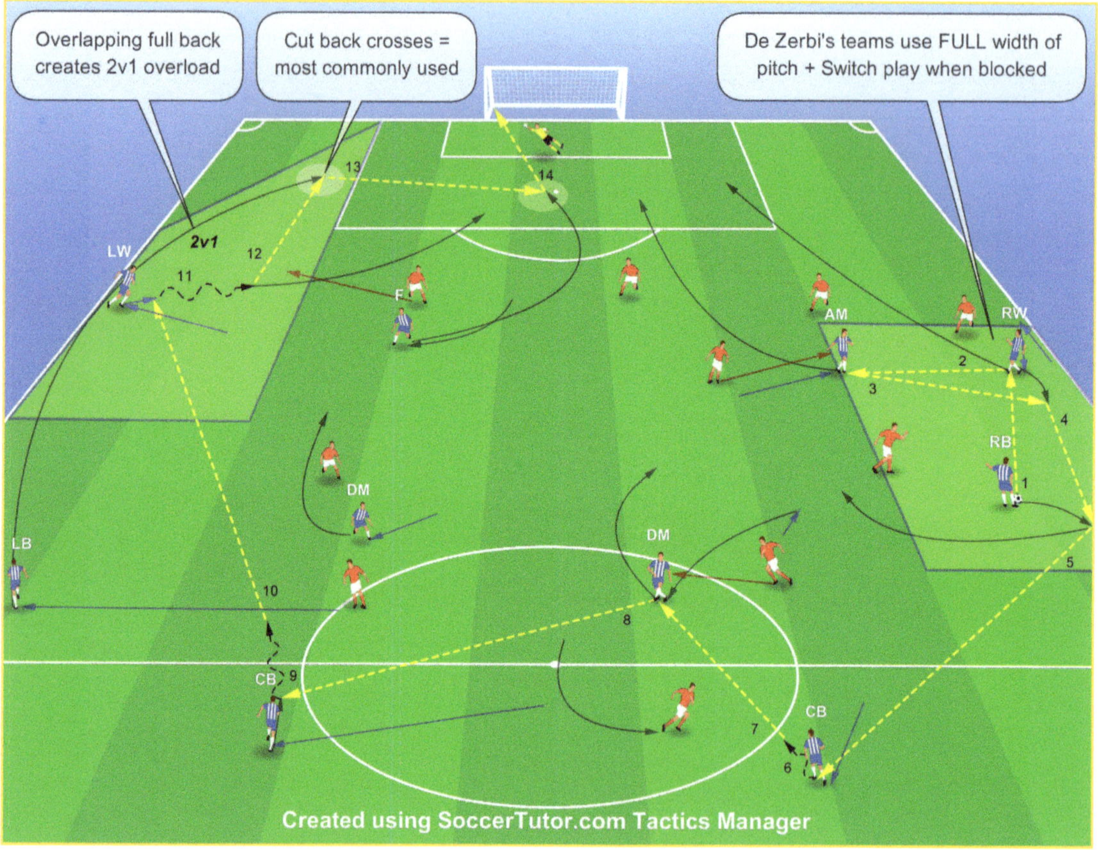

Overlapping full back creates 2v1 overload

Cut back crosses = most commonly used

De Zerbi's teams use FULL width of pitch + Switch play when blocked

Created using SoccerTutor.com Tactics Manager

In this example of Roberto De Zerbi's Brighton team breaking down the opposition's defensive structure, we want to best illustrate the game principles in relation to wide play:

- Roberto De Zerbi's teams make sure to use the **FULL width of the pitch**.
- They still make sure to **keep possession with short passes (control)** when there is not a good vertical or through passing option.
- When blocked from progression on one flank, De Zerbi's teams look to **switch play into the space on the opposite side**.
- In this example, the **centre back (CB) is used to reset the play and recycle the ball** to the left side of the pitch.
- The **defensive midfielder (DM) is also key**, making sure to provide a passing angle and keep the ball moving to switch the play.
- With wide positioning, the **winger (LW) is able to receive in space**. From there, Brighton can create a **2v1 overload** with the **full back pushing forward**.
- **Wide players are encouraged to overlap and deliver crosses into the box**.
- **Cut back crosses** are most commonly used.

4. Quick and Incisive Attacking Play

De Zerbi's optimal attacking zone

Timing runs to exploit the space in behind the defensive line

Thurd man runs to receive "Bounce" passes + Quick and incisive passes in behind

Created using SoccerTutor.com Tactics Manager

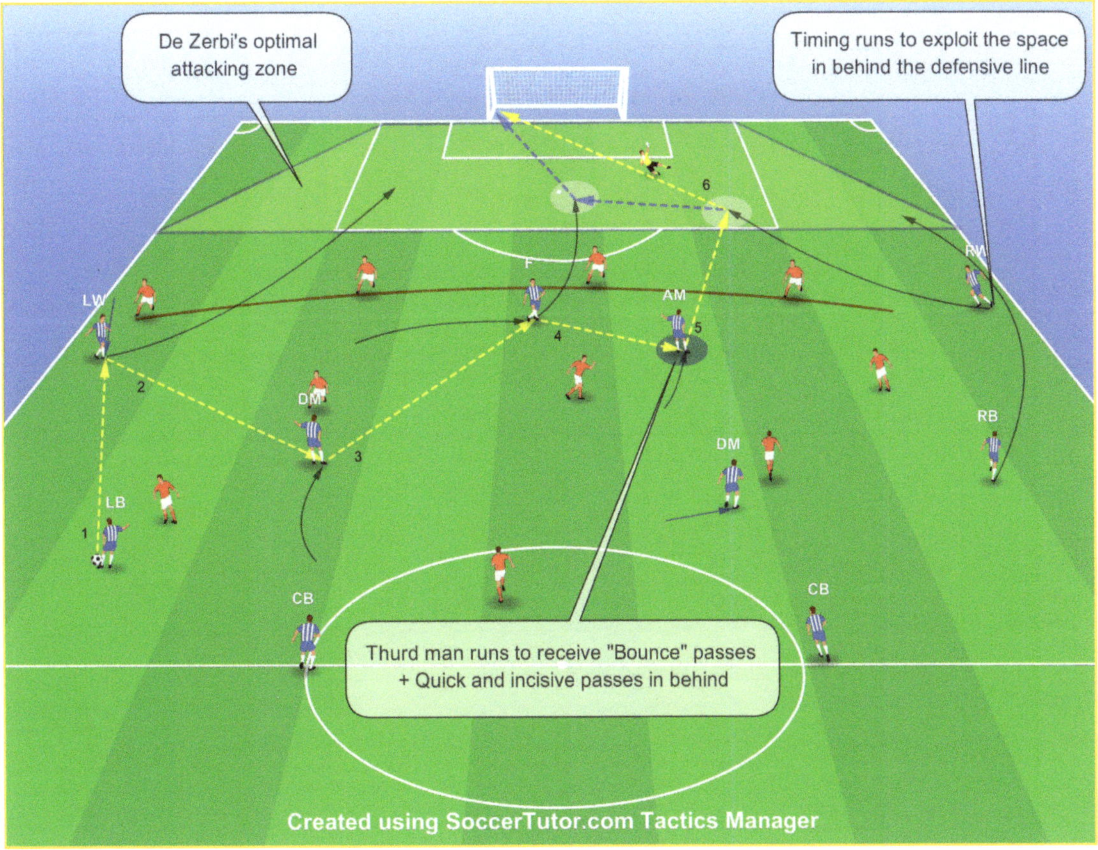

This diagram illustrates the game principles in relation to quick and incisive attacking play in the opposition's half for De Zerbi's Brighton team:

- Play forward as long as it is not too risky (good decision making) to **play through the lines**.
- Dynamic **patterns of play** that can penetrate opposing teams' defences.
- **Receive between the lines** and use third man runs to receive **"bounce passes"** free in space!
- **Intelligent off-the-ball runs** to create space and scoring opportunities.
- Create difficulties for opposing defences in tracking players and maintaining defensive shape.
- Quick and **incisive through passes** in behind.
- **Timing runs** to exploit the space in behind the defensive line.
- De Zerbi's **optimal attacking zone** is highlighted, wanting his players to avoid going too far into the corner or towards the by-line to deliver crosses.

"There is no team playing in the way they play – it is unique. I had the feeling when he arrived in the Premier League that the impact would be great, but I couldn't expect he would do this in this short a time."

Pep Guardiola

Positional Roles in Roberto De Zerbi's Build-up Play and Attacking Philosophy

1. Play Out from the GK with Ball Playing Centre Backs and Full Backs Supporting the Attack

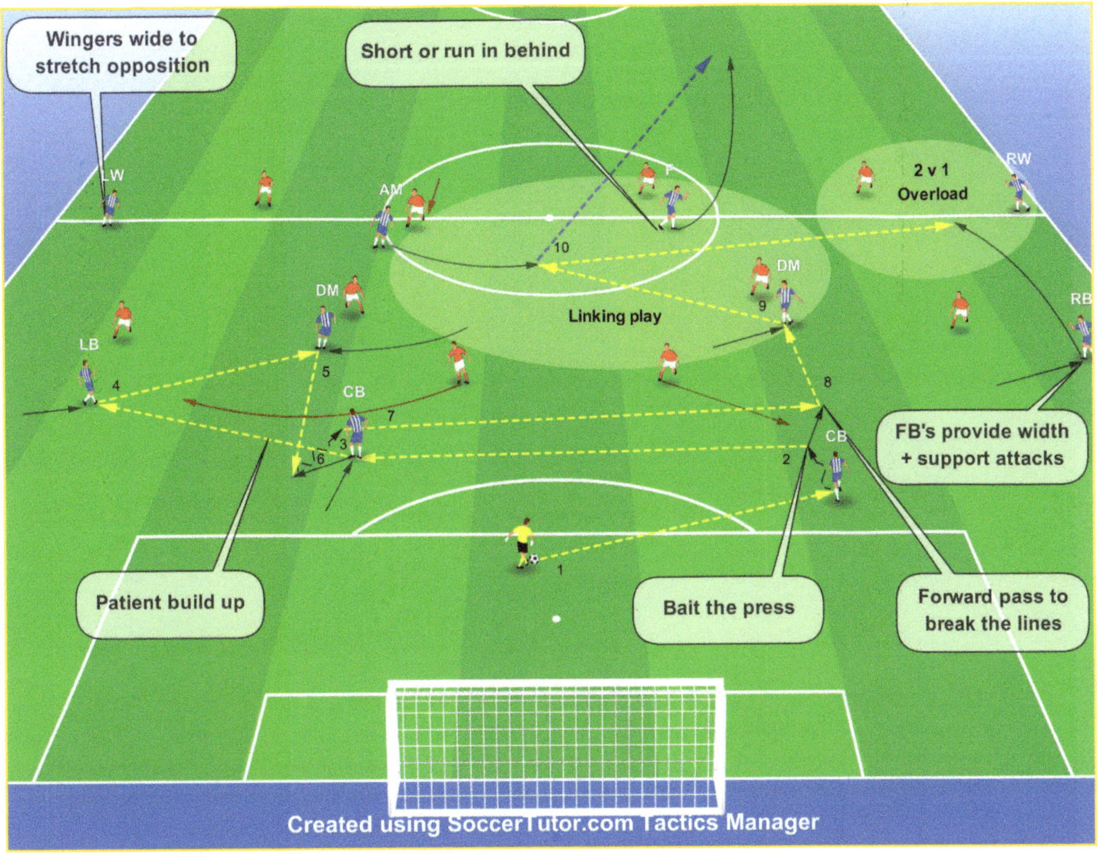

- **Play out from the goalkeeper** and the centre backs. Establish possession deep in the defensive third and build up play patiently from there, **baiting the press**.
- **Ball playing centre backs** actively participate in the build up play. They play short passes to maintain possession, stop with the ball, carry the ball, etc. They also play forward passes to break the lines.
- **Full backs play a crucial role in providing width** during the build-up phase. They are positioned to receive wide and **push forward to support the attack**.
- With the **wingers high and wide**, De Zerbi likes to **create overloads on the flanks** and stretch the opposition's defensive line.

2. Midfield Structure for Ball Progression, Forward Link Play, and Overloads on the Flank (Create and Score Goals)

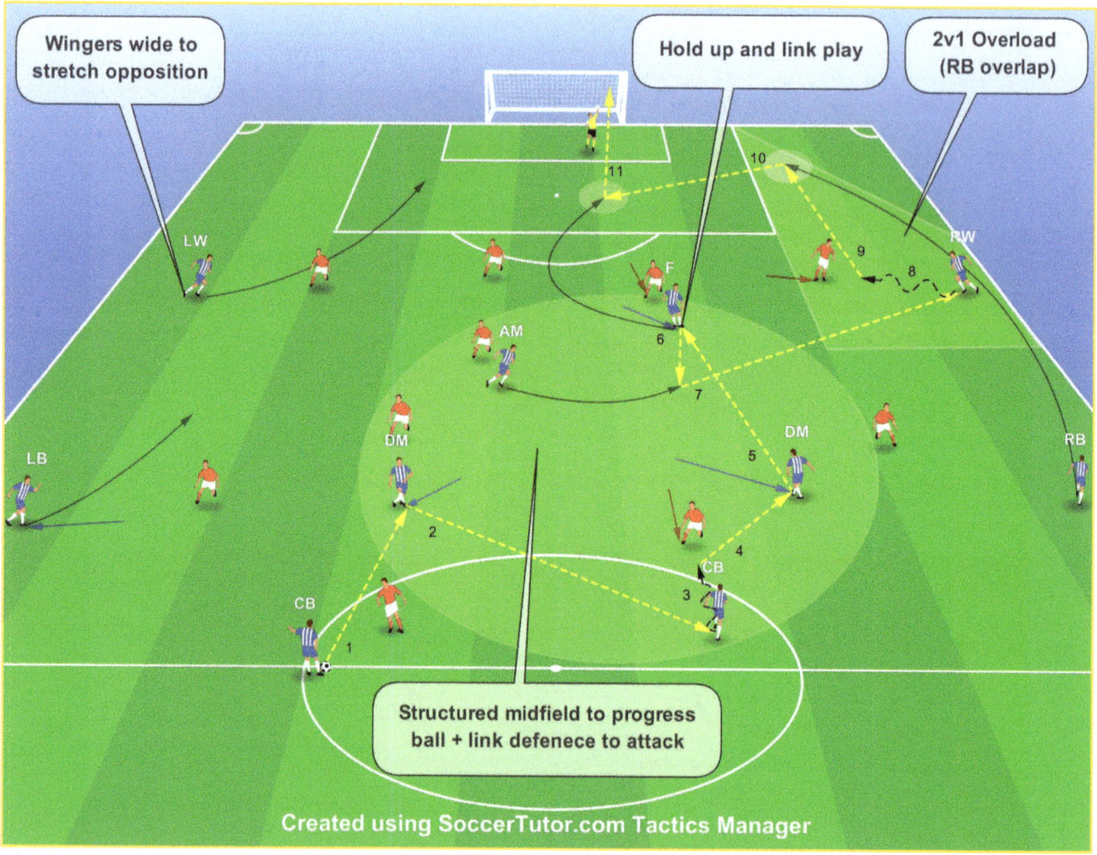

Wingers wide to stretch opposition

Hold up and link play

2v1 Overload (RB overlap)

Structured midfield to progress ball + link defenece to attack

Created using SoccerTutor.com Tactics Manager

- **Well structured midfield** that facilitates ball circulation and **ball progression**.
- Midfielders play a key role in linking the defenders and attacking players, ensuring a smooth transition through the centre of the pitch.
- **Wingers** occupy the wide positions in the front 3 and **stretch the opposition**. They also deliver crosses or cut inside to create goal scoring chances.
- The full backs make deep overlapping runs to help **create 2v1 overloads high up the flank**, as shown in the diagram example.
- The **forward (F)** is the centre point of the attack with responsibilities for hold up play, linking the midfielders with the wingers, making runs in behind, and attacking the box to score goals!

Roberto De Zerbi's High Pressing and Regaining Possession Tactics

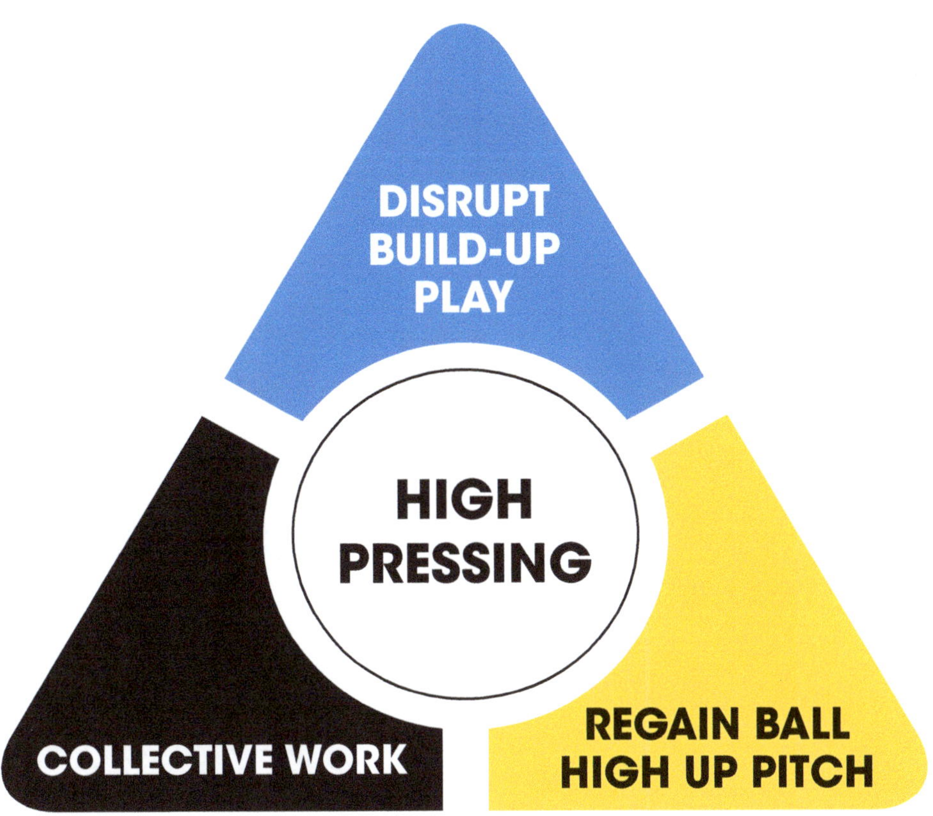

DISRUPT BUILD-UP PLAY

Roberto De Zerbi's teams employ a high pressing strategy to prevent the opposition from being able to play out, which creates pressure and forces mistakes.

COLLECTIVE WORK

Players work collectively to press the opposition high up the pitch, disrupting their build-up play and committing many players forward and around the ball area.

REGAIN BALL HIGH UP PITCH

While focused on possession, De Zerbi's teams also tend to engage in high pressing to win the ball back quickly when out of possession. This style helps disrupt the opponent's build-up and win the ball in advanced areas, where they can then attack the opposition's goal very quickly while their defence is unorganised.

Positional Possession Games

Direct from Roberto De Zerbi's Training Sessions

"I love to try to win the game with the ball. I love when my team keep the ball, try to lead the game and my players show their quality."

1. 3v3 (+4) Positional Possession Game with Outside Support Players

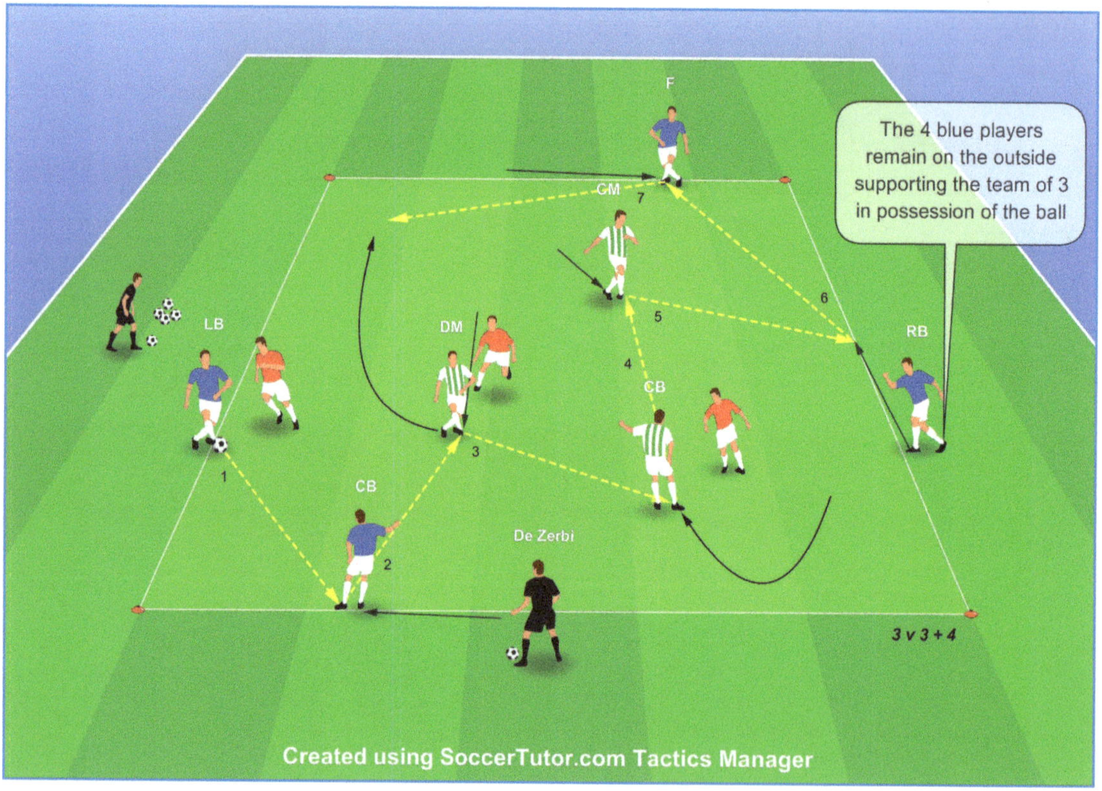

Practice Description

- In a 10 yard square, there are 3 white players vs 3 reds, and 4 blue outside who play with the team in possession.
- All 4 blue players are positioned on the sides and represent the centre back (**CB**), left back (**LB**), right back (**RB**), and forward (**F**) depending on the direction of play at the time.
- The white team have 3 players inside ... a defensive midfielder ... back (**CB**), and a central ...M).
- The focus for the team in possession is quick combinations, and intelligent support play.
- The red defending team are also all positioned inside and work together (pressing) to close off the angles and try to win the ball.
- If the reds are able to win the ball, they switch roles with the white team and the game continues with the reds keeping possession and the whites defending.

...to De Zerbi's Sassuolo Calcio preseason training session in Vipiteno, Italy - 16th July 2019

2. 5v5 (+4) Positional Possession Game with Middle and End Support Players

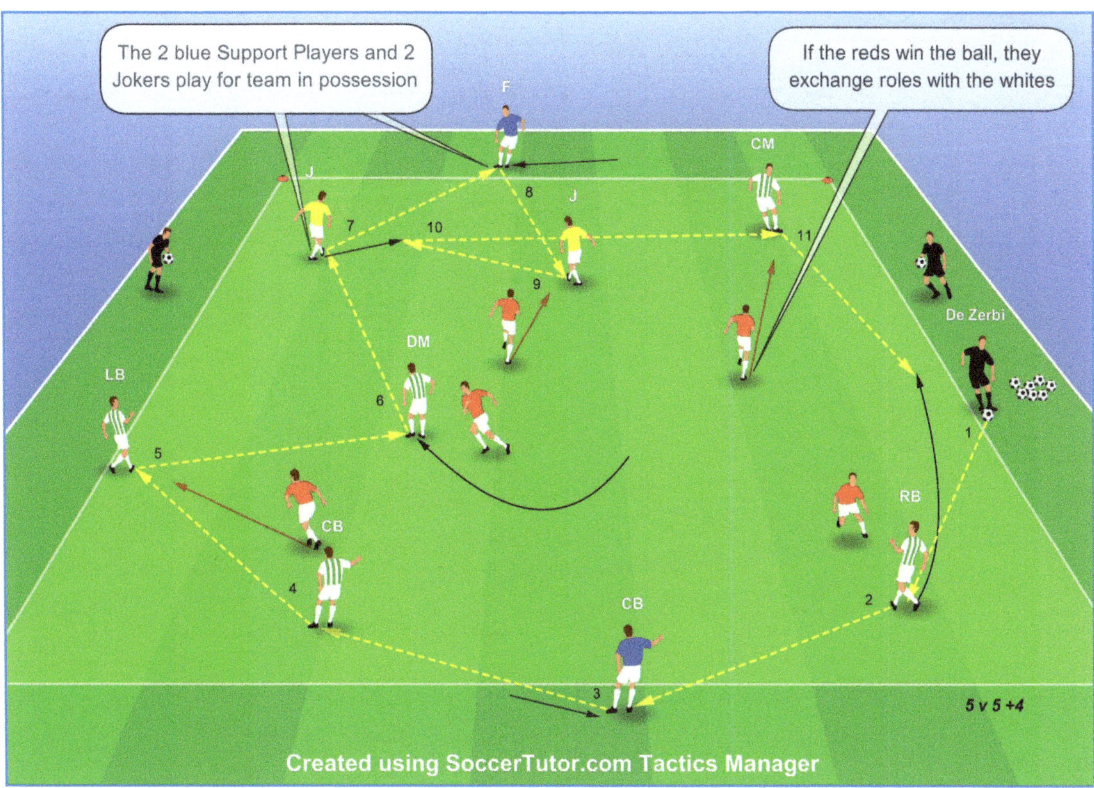

Practice Description

- In a 15 yard square, there are 5 white players vs 5 reds + 2 inside yellow jokers and 2 blue outside end players, who play with the team in possession.
- The white team have 5 players inside representing a centre back (**CB**), a left back (**LB**), a right back (**RB**), a defensive midfielder (**DM**), and a central midfielder (**CM**). The blue players represent the other centre back (**CB**) and forward (**F**).
- The aim is to keep possession and move the ball from end to end, and back again.
- The red defending team are all positioned inside and work together (pressing) to close off the angles and try to win the ball.
- If the reds are able to win the ball, they switch roles with the white team and the game continues with the reds keeping possession and the whites defending.

Source: Roberto De Zerbi's Sassuolo Calcio preseason training session in Vipiteno, Italy - 20th July 2018

3. 4v4 (+3) Positional Possession Game in Central Area of the Pitch

RDZ

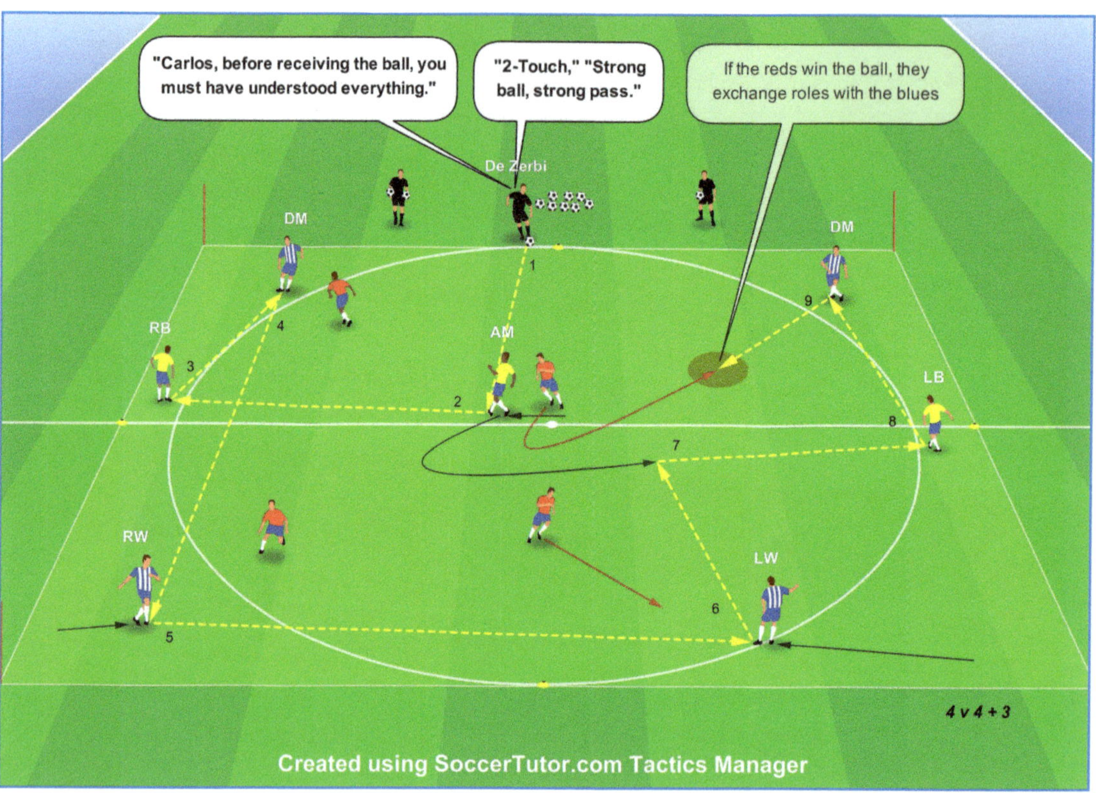
"Carlos, before receiving the ball, you must have understood everything."
"2-Touch," "Strong ball, strong pass."
If the reds win the ball, they exchange roles with the blues
De Zerbi
DM
DM
RB
AM
LB
RW
LW
1
2
3
4
5
6
7
8
9
4 v 4 + 3
Created using SoccerTutor.com Tactics Manager

Practice Description

- In the area shown, we have 4 blue players with 2 defensive midfielders (**DM**) and 2 wingers (**LW** & **RW**) vs 4 red players.
- The team in possession (blues) are supported by the 3 yellow neutral players, who play with the team in possession: The right back (**RB**), left back (**LB**), and attacking midfielder (**AM**).
- The game starts with De Zerbi's pass in and the blue team (with help from yellows) aim to maintain possession against the red players' pressing.
- All 7 players in possession make movements to support as shown but must retain their positional roles.
- The red defending team all work together (pressing) to close off the passing angles and try to win the ball.
- If the reds are able to win the ball, they switch roles with the blue team and the game continues with the reds keeping possession supported by the yellows, and the blue players defending.

Source: Roberto De Zerbi's Brighton training session at Elite Football Performance Centre - 2022

4. 4v4 (+4) Positional Possession Game in Centre of the Pitch

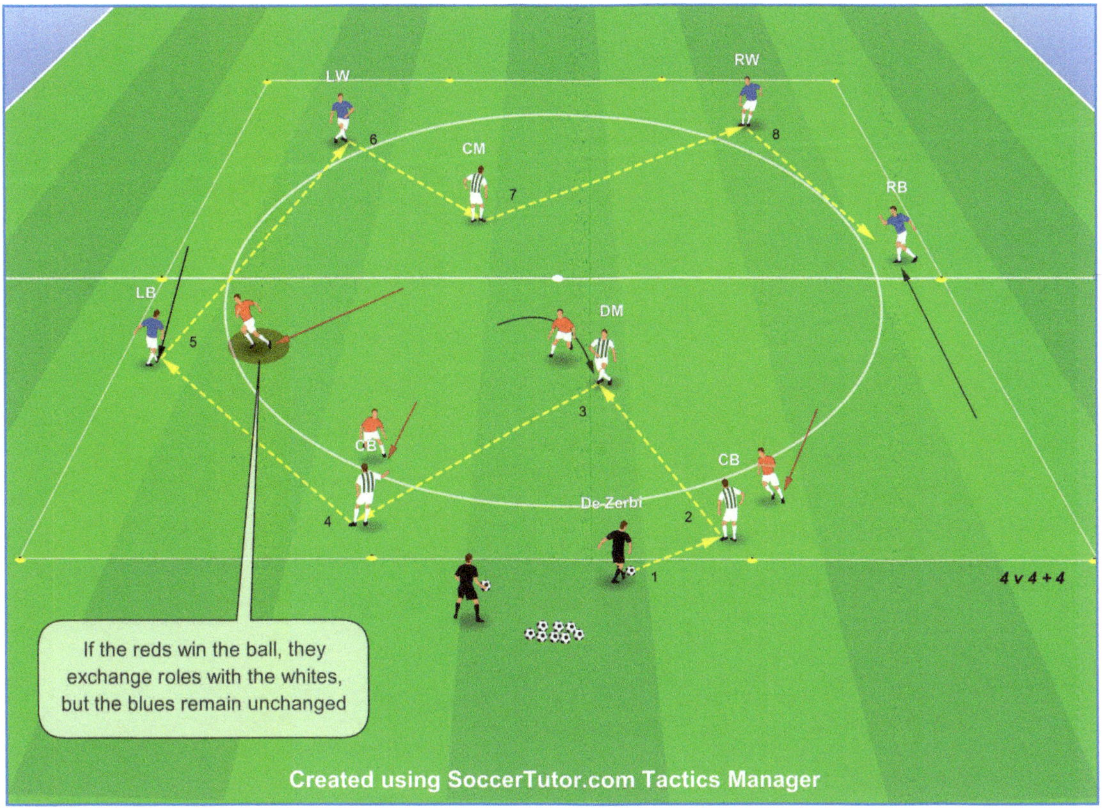

If the reds win the ball, they exchange roles with the whites, but the blues remain unchanged

Created using SoccerTutor.com Tactics Manager

Practice Description

- In the area shown, we have 3 sets of 4 players (whites, reds, and blues).
- The whites have 2 centre backs (**CB**), a defensive midfielder (**DM**), and a central midfielder (**CM**).
- The blues have the left back (**LB**), right back (**RB**), left winger (**LW**), and right winger (**RW**).
- The game starts with De Zerbi's pass and the whites and blues keep possession against the red players' pressing.
- All 8 players in possession make movements to support, especially the full backs as shown.
- The red defending team are all work together (pressing) to close off the passing angles and try to win the ball.
- If the reds are able to win the ball, they switch roles with the white team and the game continues with the reds and blues keeping possession, and the white players defending.

Source: Roberto De Zerbi's Sassuolo Calcio preseason training session in Vipiteno, Italy - 16th July 2019

5. 6v6 (+4) Positional Build-up Play Possession Game in Centre of the Pitch

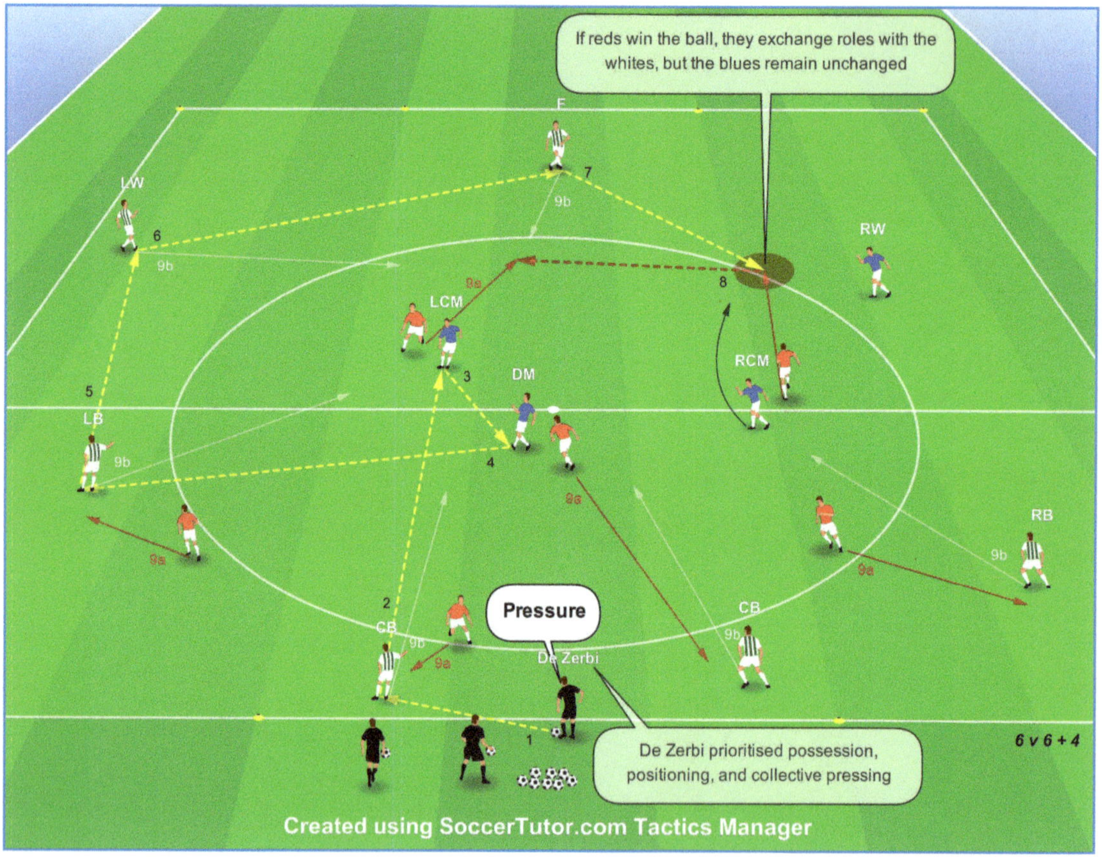

If reds win the ball, they exchange roles with the whites, but the blues remain unchanged

Pressure

De Zerbi prioritised possession, positioning, and collective pressing

6 v 6 + 4

Created using SoccerTutor.com Tactics Manager

Practice Description

- The whites have 6 players with 2 centre backs (**CB**), the left back (**LB**), the right back (**RB**), and the left winger (**LW**).
- The blues have 4 players with the defensive midfielder (**DM**), 2 central midfielders (**LCM** & **RCM**), and the right winger (**RW**).
- The whites and blues keep possession against the 6 red players' pressing.
- **De Zerbi** coaches the players and prioritises possession, support play, positioning, and collective pressing.
- The red defending team all work together (pressing) to close off the passing angles and try to win the ball.
- If the reds are able to win the ball, they switch roles with the white team and the game continues with the reds keeping possession with support from the blues, and the white players defending.

Source: Roberto De Zerbi's Sassuolo Calcio preseason training session in Vipiteno, Italy - 16th July 2019

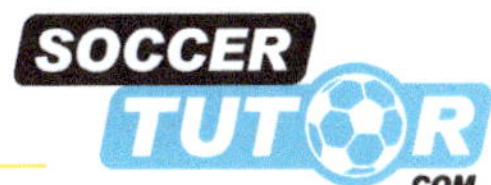

6. 7v7 (+2) Positional Build-up Play Possession Game in Centre of Pitch + GK End Players

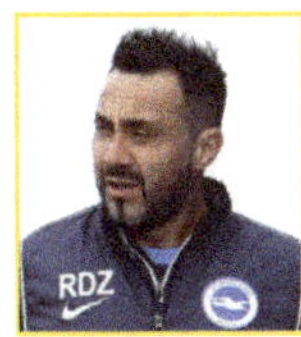

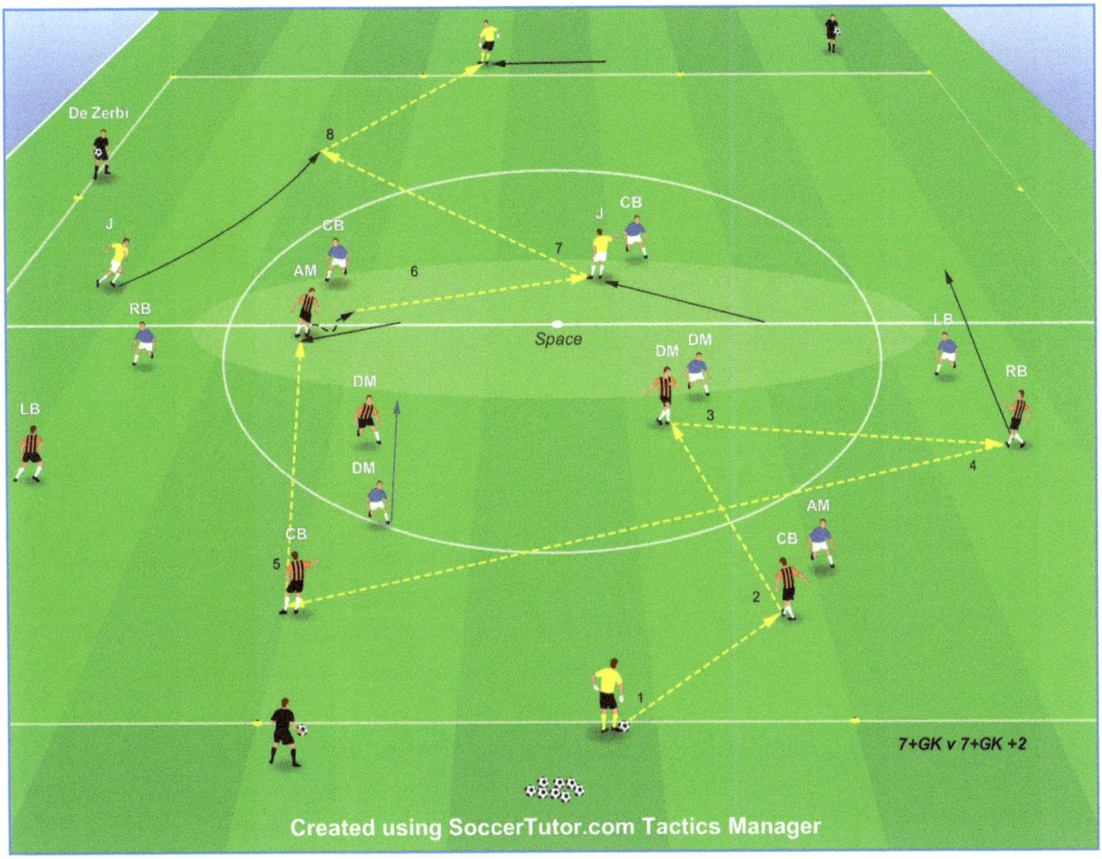

De Zerbi
J
CB
AM
RB
LB
DM
DM
CB
8
7
6
J
CB
Space
DM
DM
LB
RB
3
4
AM
CB
5
2
1
7+GK v 7+GK +2
Created using SoccerTutor.com Tactics Manager

Practice Description

- In the marked out area shown, we have 2 teams of 7 players and 2 yellow Jokers inside the playing area + 2 GKs acting as end players.
- Both the orange and blue teams have their back 4, 2 defensive midfielders, and 1 attacking midfielder (from 4-2-3-1). The 2 Jokers take the positions of winger and forward for the team in possession (orange team in diagram example).
- The GK starts and the aim is to keep possession and play through the defending team for the GK at the opposite end to receive. He then passes to a blue defender, and the blues have the same aim in the opposite direction. The 2 Jokers move to become the winger and forward for the blues.
- If a team wins the ball from their opponents, they play to the GK to reset and start with the build-up.

Source: Roberto De Zerbi's Shakhtar Donetsk training session at Sviatoshyn Sports Complex - 2021

Positional Build-up Play

Direct from Roberto De Zerbi's Training Sessions

"To show quality, they have to be put in the right situations to play. And so starts the build-up, because we have to reach the No7, No9, No10, No11 with the ball in a good situation."

1. Centre Backs Build-up Through the Centre with Vertical Movements + Final Diagonal Through Pass (5+GK v1)

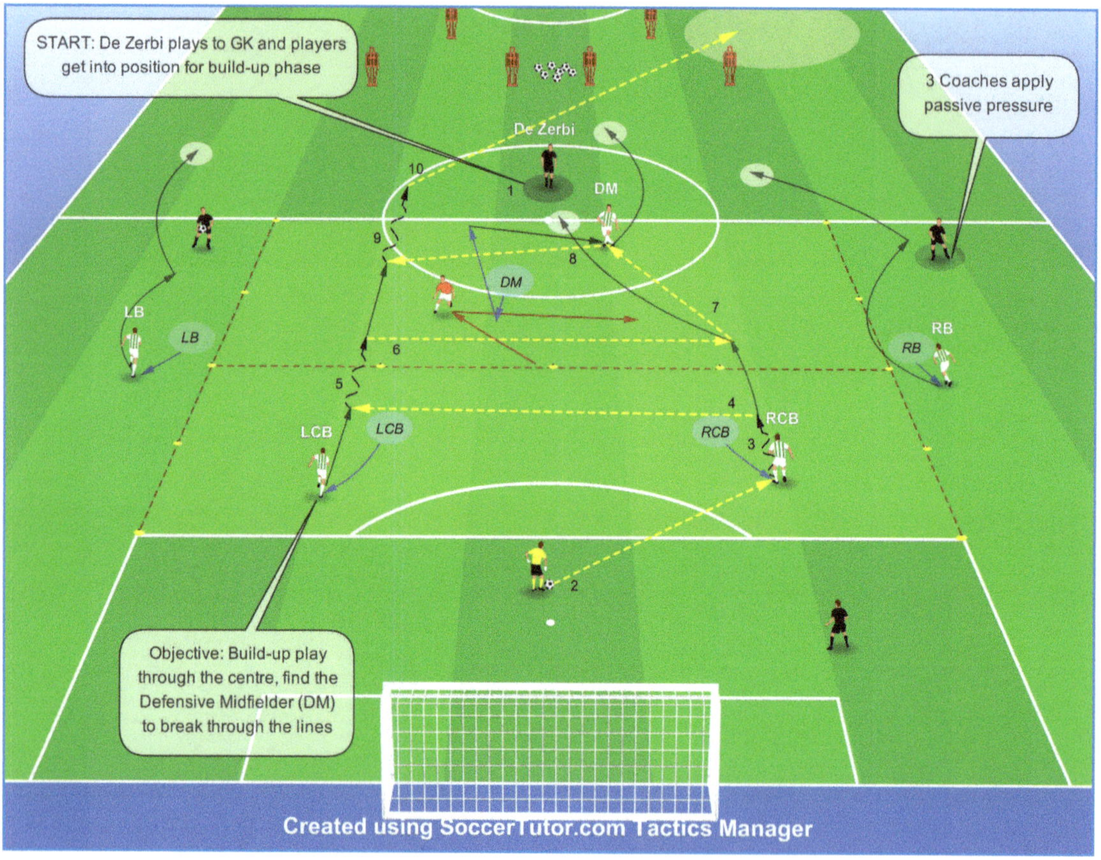

START: De Zerbi plays to GK and players get into position for build-up phase

3 Coaches apply passive pressure

Objective: Build-up play through the centre, find the Defensive Midfielder (DM) to break through the lines

Created using SoccerTutor.com Tactics Manager

The blue circles show the starting positions.

Practice Description

1-6. De Zerbi starts by playing an aerial pass to the **GK**. The **GK** passes to the right centre back (**RCB**). He passes across to the left centre back (**LCB**), who carries the ball forward into the second central zone. The red player blocks the forward pass, so **LCB** passes back across for the oncoming **RCB**, who also now enters the second central zone.

7-8. RCB is pressed by the red player and passes to the defensive midfielder (**DM**), who shifts across to receive and passes for the oncoming **LCB**.

9-10. LCB passes diagonally into the space in between the full back and centre back mannequin (through pass).

Note: The full backs make supporting movements throughout. They are involved in the 5+GK v2 variation, which follows in this section.

Source: Roberto De Zerbi's Sassuolo Calcio preseason training session in Vipiteno, Italy - 16th July 2019

2. Centre Backs Build-up Through the Centre with Vertical Movements + Final Vertical Through Pass (5+GK v1)

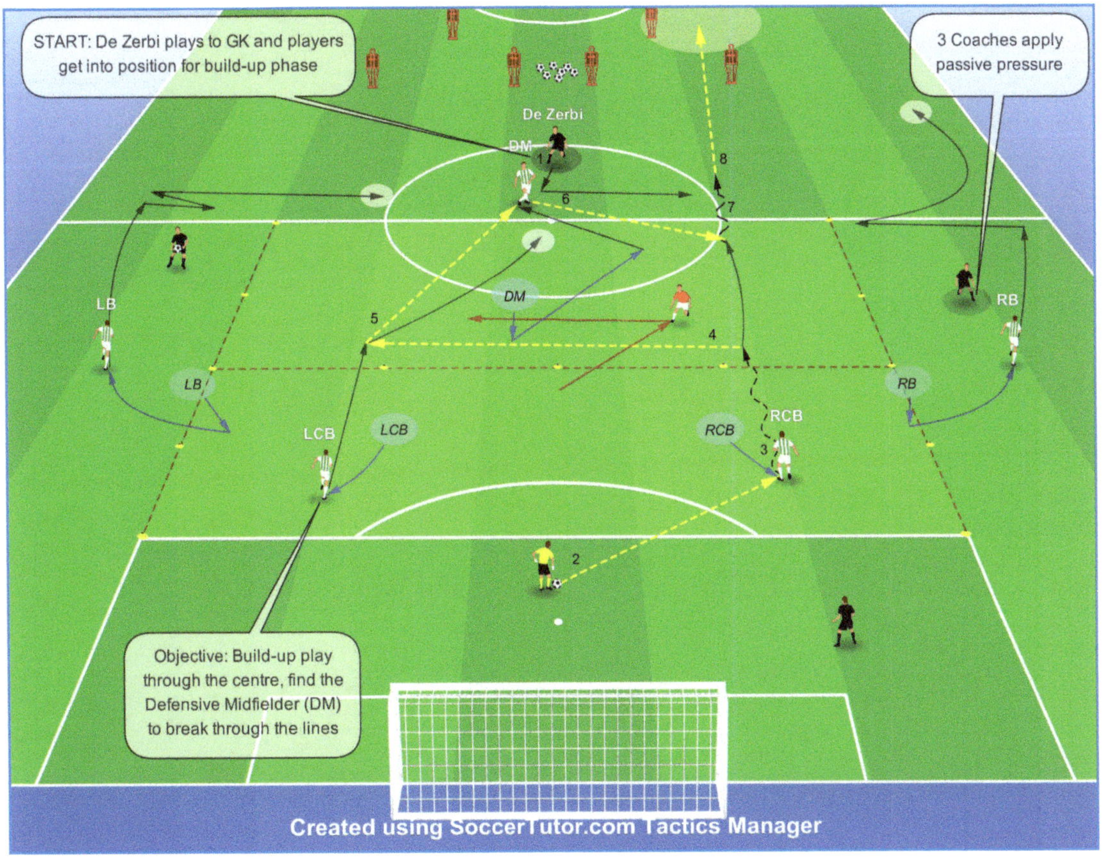

START: De Zerbi plays to GK and players get into position for build-up phase

3 Coaches apply passive pressure

Objective: Build-up play through the centre, find the Defensive Midfielder (DM) to break through the lines

Created using SoccerTutor.com Tactics Manager

The blue circles show the starting positions.

Practice Description

1-5. **De Zerbi** starts by playing an aerial pass to the **GK**. The **GK** passes to the right centre back (**RCB**). He carries the ball into the second central zone and the red player blocks the forward pass, so he passes across to the left centre back (**LCB**), who has moved forward to receive. **LCB** passes to the defensive midfielder (**DM**) in the centre.

6-7. **DM** has shifted across to receive (back to goal) and lays the ball off for the oncoming **RCB**, who carries the ball past the halfway line.

8. **LCB** passes forward into the space in between the full back and centre back mannequin (through pass).

Note: The full backs make supporting movements throughout. They are involved in the 5+GK v2 variation, which follows in this section.

Source: Roberto De Zerbi's Sassuolo Calcio preseason training session in Vipiteno, Italy - 16th July 2019

3a. Pressing Movements + Reset Positioning for Build-up Play from the GK (5+GK v2)

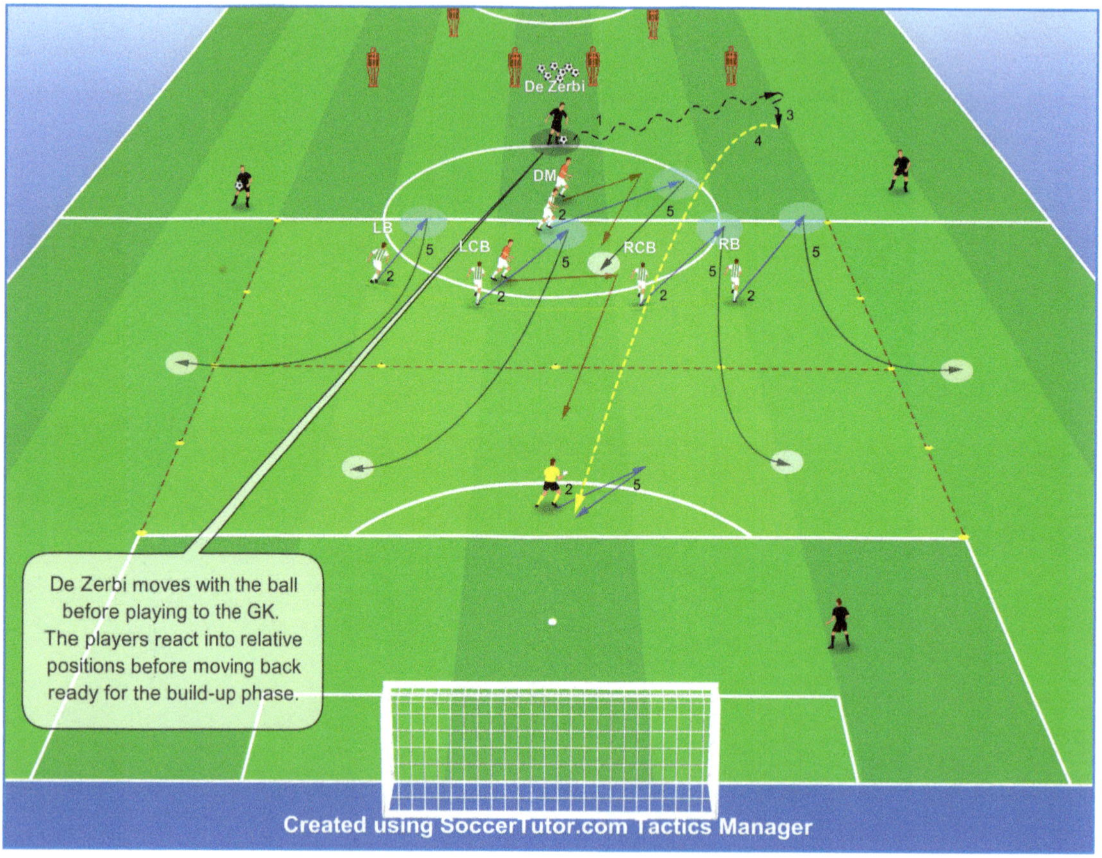

De Zerbi moves with the ball before playing to the GK. The players react into relative positions before moving back ready for the build-up phase.

Created using SoccerTutor.com Tactics Manager

Practice Description

1-2. **De Zerbi** starts by dribbling the ball back towards one side of the pitch. The white players all make pressing movements in relation to the ball position (see blue arrows & circles). The red players shift across as if to provide passing options.

3-4. **De Zerbi** then turns to move forward with the ball and plays an aerial pass to the **GK**.

5. The **GK** receives, and the white players drop back into positions ready to build up play from the **GK**. The 2 red players move forward ready to disrupt the build-up play.

→ The build-up pattern/sequence follows on the next page (3b).

Note: The centre backs drop back into deep positions either side of the GK and the full backs are in more wide positions just outside the area, as shown.

Source: Roberto De Zerbi's Sassuolo Calcio preseason training session in Vipiteno, Italy - 16th July 2019

3b (1). Bait the Press and Find the Right Moment to Advance Build-up Play vs Forward Pressing High (5+GK v2)

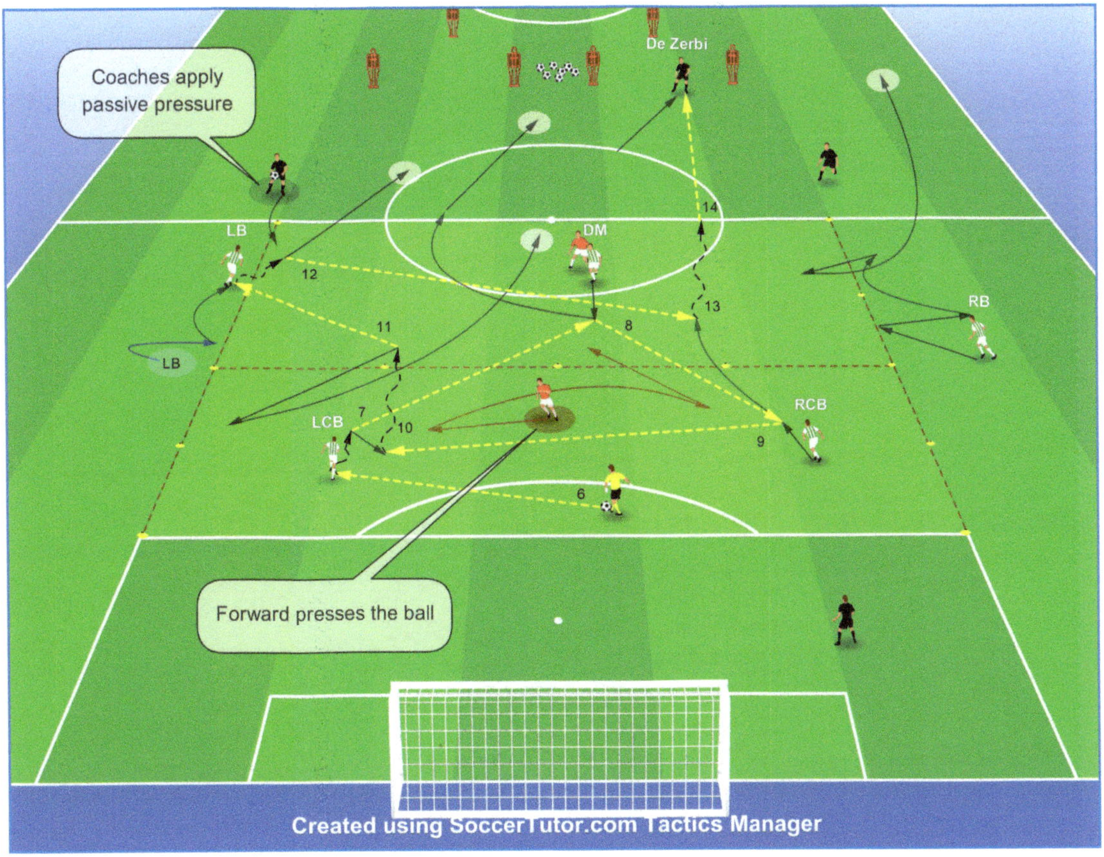

Practice Description (Continued...)

6-8. The **GK** passes to the left centre back (**LCB**), who takes a touch forward and passes to the defensive midfielder (**DM**), who is marked from behind by the red midfielder. **DM** drops to receive and pass back to the right centre back (**RCB**).

9-12. **RCB** passes to **LCB**, who is pressed by the red forward, receives, moves forward with the ball into the 2nd central zone and passes to the left back (**LB**). **LB** moves forward to receive, takes a touch and passes back diagonally across the pitch for the oncoming **RCB**.

13-14. **RCB** dribbles forward up to the halfway line and passes to **De Zerbi**, which completes the pattern/sequence.

Note: The other players all make movements to push the team forward within the formation and support the attack with different passing options.

Source: Roberto De Zerbi's Sassuolo Calcio preseason training session in Vipiteno, Italy - 16th July 2019

3b (2). Bait the Press and Find the Right Moment to Advance Build-up Play vs Forward Dropping Off (5+GK v2)

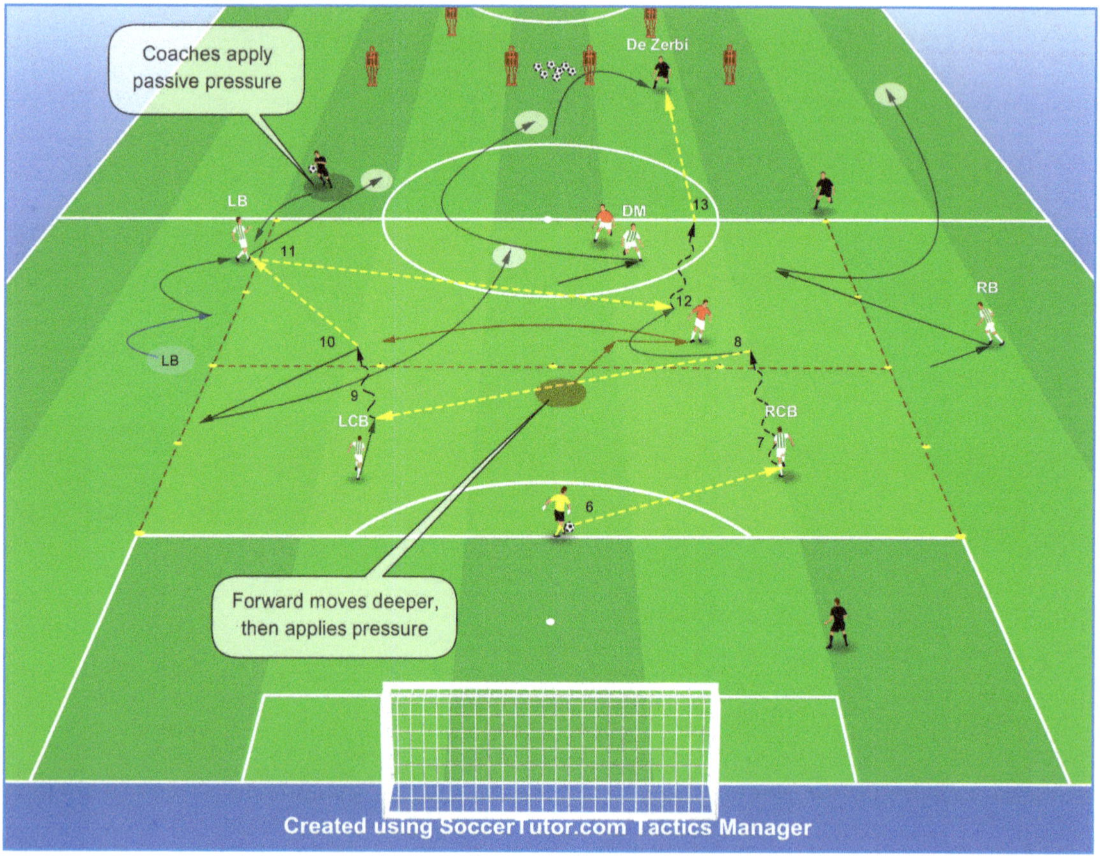

Practice Description (Variation)

6-8. The **GK** passes to the right centre back (**RCB**), who has no opponent near him. He dribbles into the second central zone, where he is then closed down by the red forward. At that point, he passes across and back to the left centre back (**LCB**).

9-10. LCB also dribbles into the second central zone, and then passes to the left back (**LB**), who has made 2 previous forward movements, as shown.

11. LB passes back diagonally across the pitch for the oncoming **RCB**.

12-13. RCB dribbles forward up to the halfway line and passes to **De Zerbi**, which completes the pattern/sequence.

Note: The other players all make movements to push the team forwards within the formation and support the attack with different passing options.

Source: Roberto De Zerbi's Sassuolo Calcio preseason training session in Vipiteno, Italy - 16th July 2019

4. De Zerbi's Specific Coached Patterns to Play Out from Back Through First and Second Lines of Pressure (8+GK v6)

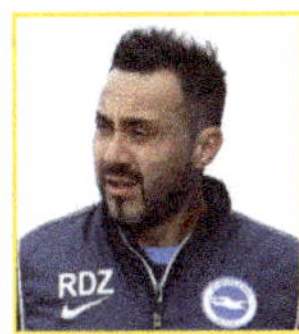

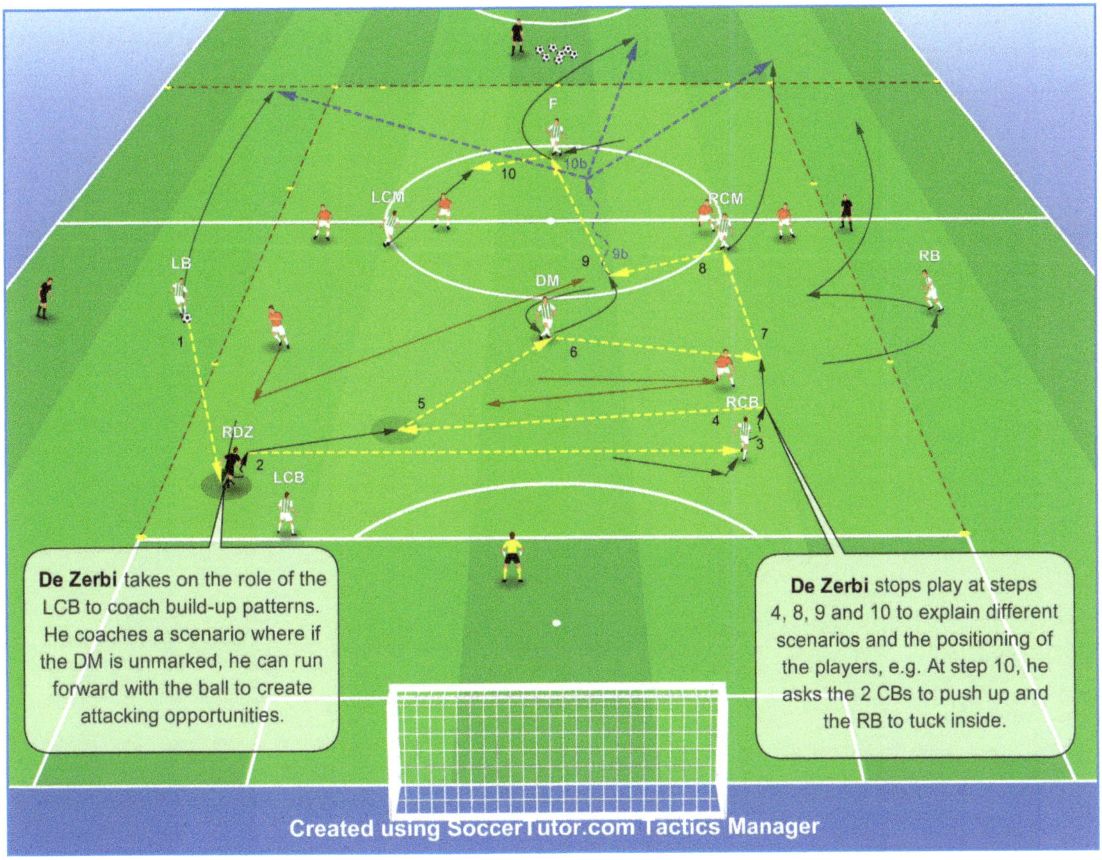

F
10b
10
LCM
RCM
LB
9
9b
8
RB
DM
1
7
6
5
RCB
RDZ
4
3
2
LCB
De Zerbi takes on the role of the LCB to coach build-up patterns. He coaches a scenario where if the DM is unmarked, he can run forward with the ball to create attacking opportunities.
De Zerbi stops play at steps 4, 8, 9 and 10 to explain different scenarios and the positioning of the players, e.g. At step 10, he asks the 2 CBs to push up and the RB to tuck inside.
Created using SoccerTutor.com Tactics Manager

Practice Description

1. The left back (**LB**) passes to **De Zerbi** (**RDZ**), who takes over the role of left centre back (**LCB**) to coach the players.

2-6. **RDZ** passes across to the right centre back (**RCB**), who is pressed by the red forward as he takes a forward touch. **RCB** passes back across to **RDZ**. **RDZ** moves inside to meet the pass and pass to the defensive midfielder (**DM**), who sets the ball back for the oncoming **RCB**.

7-10. **RCB** passes to the right central midfielder (**RCM**) who is marked from behind, so sets the ball back for **DM** to receive again. **DM** passes to the forward (**F**), who has his back to goal, and sets the ball back for the oncoming left central midfielder (**LCM**).

Variation (9b-10b). Instead of passing to the **F**, **DM** can dribble the ball forward and then play a through pass beyond the marked out end line.

Source: Roberto De Zerbi's Sassuolo Calcio preseason training session in Vipiteno, Italy - 18th July 2018

5. Build-up from GK to Forward with Lay-off for DM's Third Man Run to Break the Midfield Line (8+GK v6)

RDZ

De Zerbi passes to the GK, and players move into position to begin the build-up
Under pressure, RCB implements a RBZ pattern to play out from the back
Created using SoccerTutor.com Tactics Manager

Practice Description

Start. **De Zerbi** passes to the **GK**, and the players move into position for build-up.

1-5. The **GK** passes to the right centre back (**RCB**), who takes a forward touch under pressure from the red forward. He is able to pass to the **DM**, who is marked and passes back to **LCB** in space.

5-7. **LCB** moves forward with the ball and passes to the left central midfielder (**LCM**), who must turn and evade the red midfielder behind him.

8-9. **LCM** is able to then pass to the forward (**F**), who plays with his back to goal, and sets the ball back for the oncoming **DM's** deep run.

10-11. **DM** moves forward with the ball and passes beyond the marked out end line for the curved run of **F** in behind.

Source: Roberto De Zerbi's Sassuolo Calcio preseason training session in Vipiteno, Italy - 18th July 2018

6. Build-up from GK to Forward on the Right Side with the Central Midfielder's Third Man Run in Behind (8+GK v6)

Practice Description

Start. De Zerbi passes to the **GK**, and the players move into position for build-up.

1-2. The **GK** passes to the right centre back (**RCB**), who **advances with the ball because he is not pressed by the red forward**.

3-4. RCB passes to the right back (**RB**), who passes inside to the defensive midfielder (**DM**).

5. DM had shifted across to the right side to receive and then plays a pass through the red midfield line for the forward (**F**), who also shifts across to the right side.

6. The right central midfielder (**RCM**) makes a third man run beyond the marked out line to receive a wall pass from **F** in behind the defensive line.

Source: Roberto De Zerbi's Sassuolo Calcio preseason training session in Vipiteno, Italy - 18th July 2018

7. Build-up from GK and Patience to Break Through Lines with Double Switch and Quick Support Play (8+GK v6)

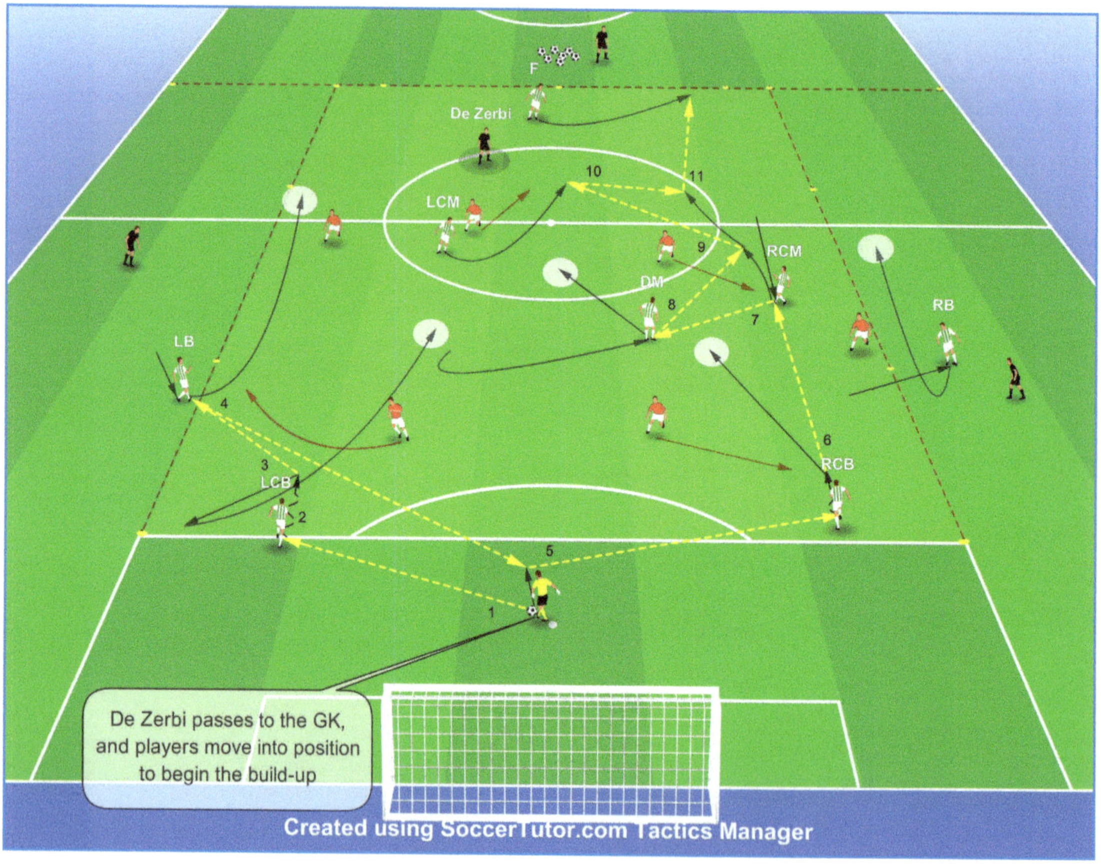

De Zerbi passes to the GK, and players move into position to begin the build-up

Created using SoccerTutor.com Tactics Manager

Practice Description

Start. **De Zerbi** passes to the **GK**, and the players move into position for build-up.

1-4. The **GK** passes to the left centre back (**LCB**), who takes a forward touch and passes to the left back (**LB**), who passes back to the **GK** when pressed by the red forward.

5. The **GK** then passes to the right centre back (**RCB**), who is pressed by the other red forward as he takes a forward touch.

6-8. **RCB** passes to the right central midfielder (**RCM**), who drops back to receive. **RCM** plays a quick one-two with the defensive midfielder (**DM**) to get past the red opponent.

9-10. **RCM** plays another one-two with the left central midfielder (**LCM**), who makes a forward movement past his opponent.

11. **RCM** finishes the sequence with a pass for the movement of the forward (**F**) towards the right side.

Source: Roberto De Zerbi's Sassuolo Calcio preseason training session in Vipiteno, Italy - 18th July 2018

8. Build-up from GK with One-Two to Break Midfield Line, and Play into Path of Forward's Movement (8+GK v6)

De Zerbi passes to the GK, and players move into position to begin the build-up

Created using SoccerTutor.com Tactics Manager

Practice Description

Start. **De Zerbi** passes to the **GK**, and the players move into position for build-up.

1-2. The **GK** passes to the right centre back (**RCB**), who takes a forward touch and passes across to the left centre back (**LCB**). The red forward applies pressure.

3-4. **LCB** passes to the left back (**LB**), who passes to the defensive midfielder (**DM**) dropping back to provide support.

5-7. **DM** passes back to **LCB**, who receives and passes back across to **RCB**.

8-9. **RCB** passes to the right central midfielder (**RCM**), who plays inside under pressure from red opponents, to **DM**, who makes an extensive shift across the pitch to provide support.

10-11. **DM** plays the return pass (give & go) for **RCM** to break the midfield line and finishes the sequence with a pass for the movement of the forward (**F**).

Source: Roberto De Zerbi's Sassuolo Calcio preseason training session in Vipiteno, Italy - 18th July 2018

9. Build-up from Throw-in on Left Side with Centre Back Exploiting Space to Receive and Drive Forward (8+GK v6)

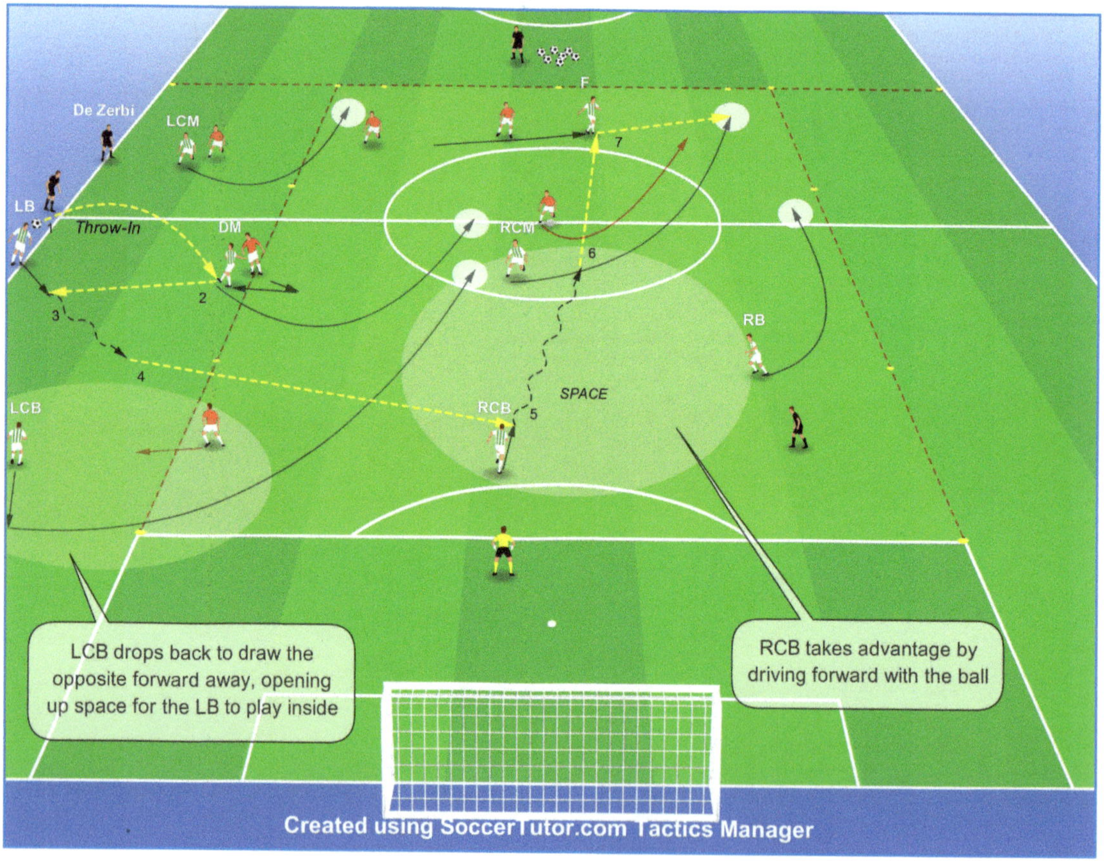

LCB drops back to draw the opposite forward away, opening up space for the LB to play inside

RCB takes advantage by driving forward with the ball

Created using SoccerTutor.com Tactics Manager

Practice Description

1. The left back (**LB**) takes a throw-in to the defensive midfielder (**DM**), who is marked from behind.

2-4. **DM** passes back to **LB**, who carries the ball backwards and passes into the central space to the right centre back (**RCB**). The left centre back (**LCB**) had dropped back to draw the opposing red forward away from the ball, and to open up space for **LB** to play inside.

5. **RCB** takes advantage of the large amount of space (highlighted) in the centre to dribble the ball forward.

6-7. To draw away the red defender and create space for **RCB**, the right central midfielder (**RCM**) moves high and wide which takes his marker with him. **RCB** passes to the forward (**F**), who shifts across away from his marker, and passes for the third man movement of **RCM** to complete the sequence.

Source: Roberto De Zerbi's Sassuolo Calcio preseason training session in Vipiteno, Italy - 18th July 2018

10. Build-up from Throw-in on Right Side with Centre Back Exploiting Space to Receive and Drive Forward (8+GK v6)

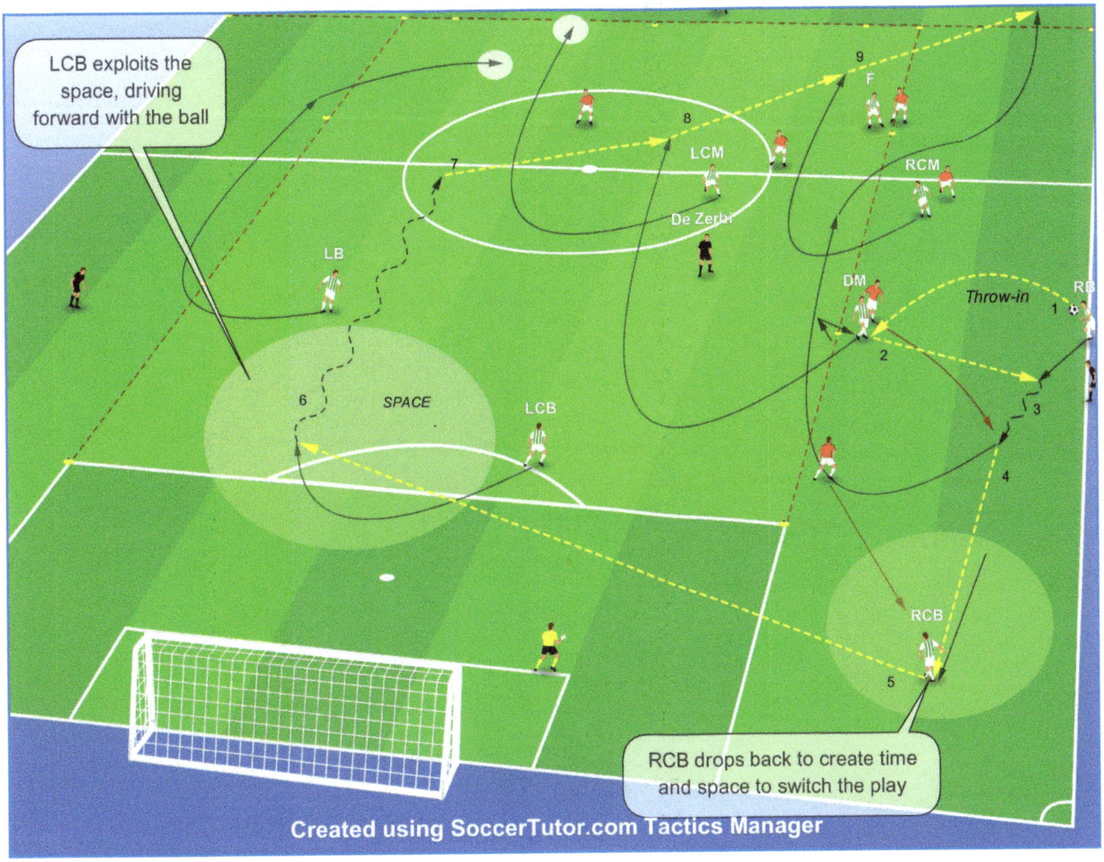

Practice Description

1. The right back (**RB**) takes a throw-in to the defensive midfielder (**DM**), who is marked from behind.

2-5. **DM** passes back to **RB**, who receives and passes backwards to the right centre back (**RCB**) as he is put under pressure. **RCB** had dropped back to create time and space to receive, and then switch the play to the left centre back (**LCB**), who opens up towards the left side.

6. **LCB** takes advantage of the large amount of space (highlighted) to dribble the ball forward. All of the players make forward runs to support the play.

7-8. **LCB** passes inside to the oncoming **DM**, who passes to the right central midfielder (**RCM**).

9. The final pass is from **RCM** to **RB**, who has made a long run from deep to receive beyond the end line on the overlap, which completes the sequence.

Source: Roberto De Zerbi's Sassuolo Calcio preseason training session in Vipiteno, Italy - 18th July 2018

11. 5v3 Build-up Play in the Centre of the Pitch to Play Through and Finish in Small Goals

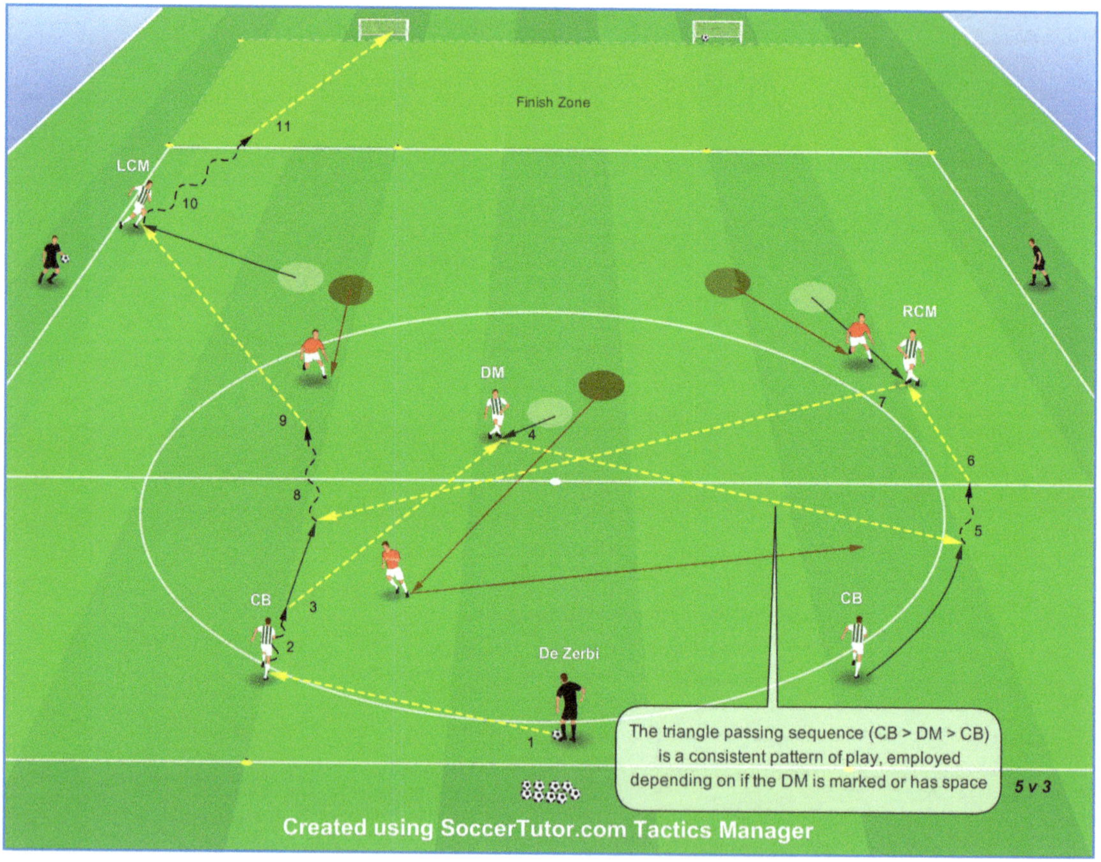

Finish Zone
LCM
RCM
DM
CB
CB
De Zerbi
The triangle passing sequence (CB > DM > CB) is a consistent pattern of play, employed depending on if the DM is marked or has space
5 v 3
Created using SoccerTutor.com Tactics Manager

Practice Description

Start. The white team have 2 centre backs and 3 central midfielders. The reds have 3 central midfielders. Their respective starting positions are shown by the highlighted circles. The aim is to build up play, break the midfield line with a pass to either **LCM** or **RCM**, and then score in one of the small goals.

1. **De Zerbi** passes to a centre back (**CB**) and the players use different combinations.

2-4. This triangle passing sequence is most commonly used (**CB → DM → CB**), depending on whether the defensive midfielder (**DM**) is marked or in space.

5-7. **CB** takes a forward touch and passes to the right central midfielder (**RCM**), who is put under pressure. **RCM** passes across for the oncoming **CB**.

8-11. **CB** moves forward and is closed down by the red midfielder. He passes to **LCM**, who dribbles into "Finish Zone" to score.

Source: Roberto De Zerbi's Sassuolo Calcio preseason training session in Vipiteno, Italy - 23rd July 2019

12. Possession, Switching Play, and Wing Play Positional 10v6 (+4) Build-up to Finish

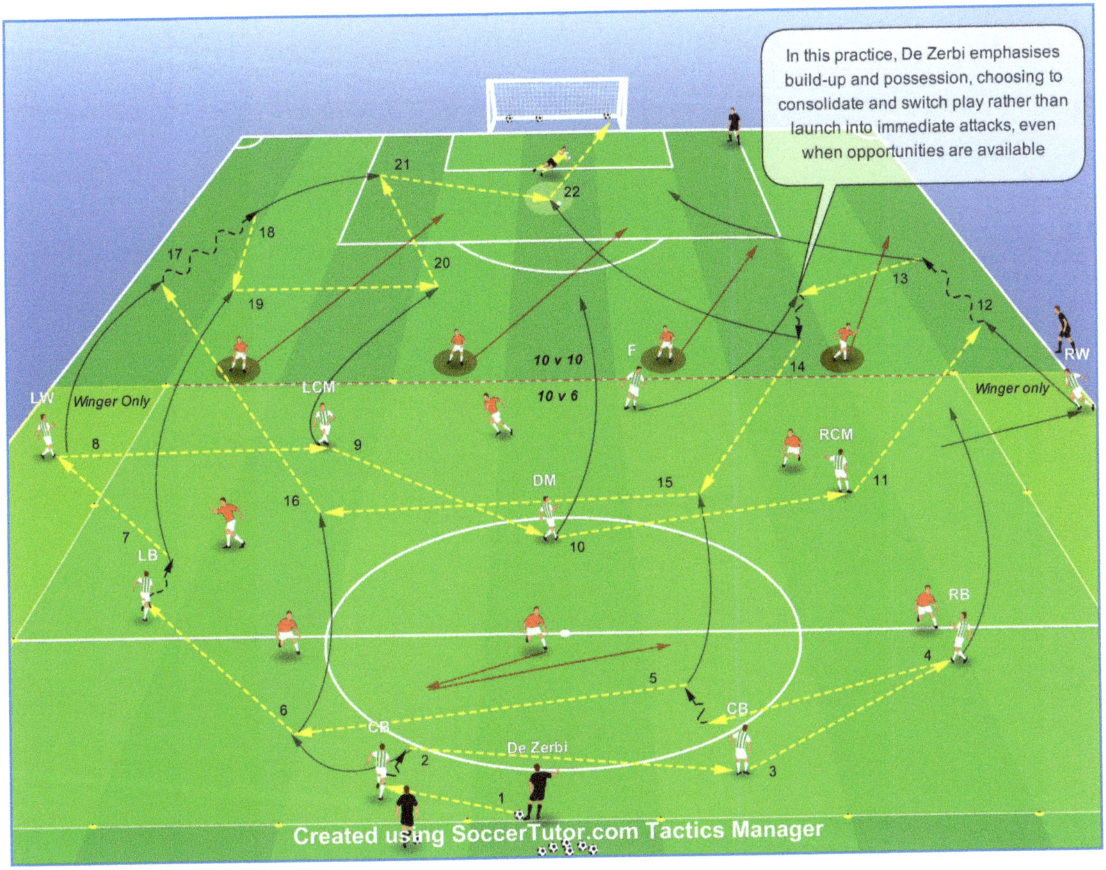

In this practice, De Zerbi emphasises build-up and possession, choosing to consolidate and switch play rather than launch into immediate attacks, even when opportunities are available

Created using SoccerTutor.com Tactics Manager

Practice Description

- The white team have 10 outfield players in a 4-3-3 formation. The reds defend with a 4-3-3 shape + GK. There are 2 main zones divided by the red line and there are also 2 *"Winger Only"* zones marked out within the low zone.
- The aim is to build up play into the end zone and score. However, **De Zerbi and the coaches' focus is also on keeping possession and switching play**.
- The players therefore do not launch into immediate attacks before consolidating possession first or switching play, even when opportunities are available.
- In this example, there is a double switch of play from one winger to the other.
- Once the ball is played with intent into the end zone, the 4 red defenders become active and drop back to defend their goal. The white players use quick combination play to try and score.

Source: Roberto De Zerbi's Sassuolo Calcio preseason training session in Vipiteno, Italy - 23rd July 2019

13. Positional Build-up to Break Through Lines and Finish in a Positional 10v6 Practice

Practice Description

- Within the marked out low zone, the blues have their back 4, 2 defensive midfielders, and 1 attacking midfielder vs 6 red opponents. The 2 wingers and the forward are in their typical positions higher up the pitch where there are 4 mannequins positioned to represent the red's team's defensive line (back 4).
- Each player's starting position is next to their respective cone/marker. **De Zerbi** passes the ball in to start.
- The blues must keep possession and move the ball to the forward (**F**), as shown. **F** lays the ball off for an oncoming blue player (**AM** in diagram).
- From this point, all the blue players except the centre backs move forward to join the attack. The aim is to finish quickly with 4 red opponents tracking back to defend the goal.
- In the diagram, **AM** plays to the right winger (**RW**), who dribbles forward and delivers a low cross for **LW** to score.

Source: Roberto De Zerbi's Brighton training session at Elite Football Performance Centre - 19th December 2022

SOCCER
TUTOR
.COM

14. Build-up Through the 3 Zones with Overloads in a Positional 10v9 Game

RDZ

Situation = 10 v 9
AM can create a 7v4 advantage within the 1st zone if he chooses
Reds aim to win the ball and score through any of the 3 red pole gates
Blues build up and try to score through any the 3 yellow pole gates
6+1 v 4
Created using SoccerTutor.com Tactics Manager

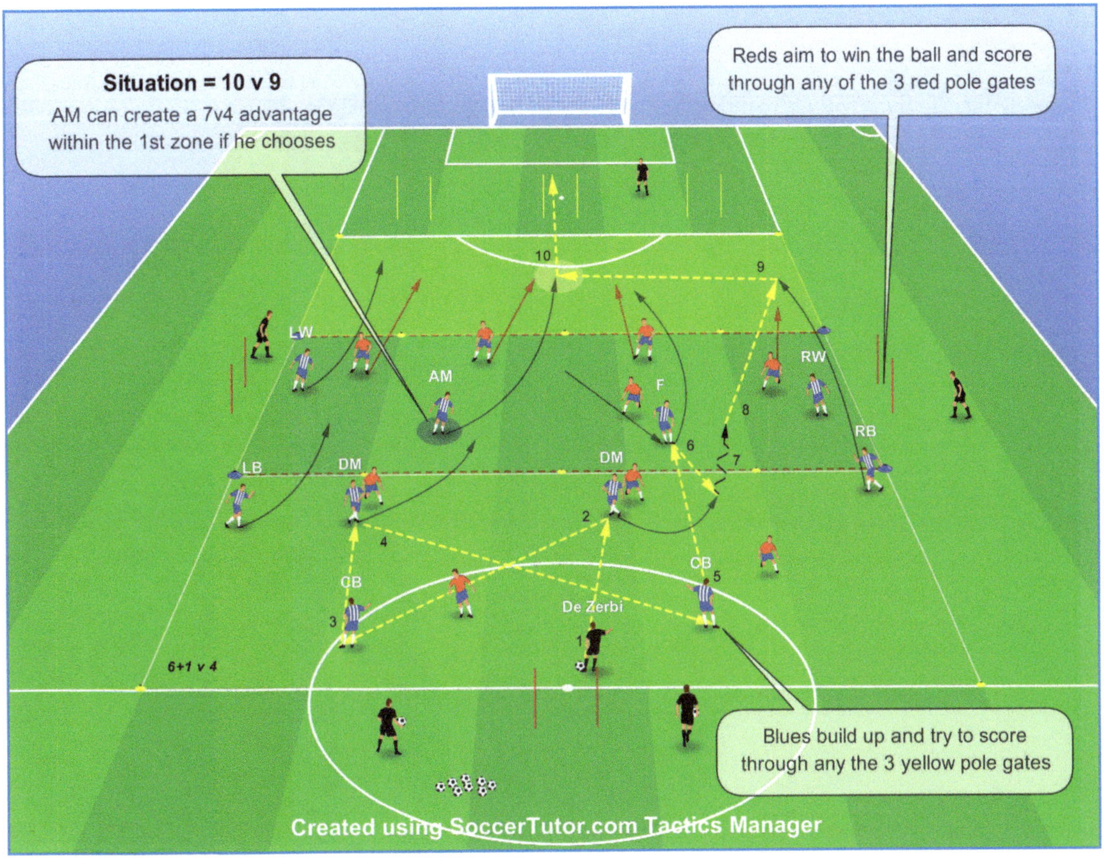

Practice Description

- There are 3 zones marked out as shown with a total situation of 10v9. We have 6v4 in Zone 1 and 4v5 in Zone 2.
- The blues aim to build up play through Zones 1 and 2, play a through pass for a runner into Zone 3, and then score through any of the 3 yellow pole gates.
- The red players remain in their zone except the 4 defenders, who can drop back once the ball is played into Zone 3.
- The attacking midfielder (**AM**) can drop into Zone 1 to create a 7v4 advantage to help the initial build-up. Once the ball is in Zone 2, the blue Zone 1 players can all move forward (except the **CBs**).
- In the diagram, the blues consolidate possession in Zone 1, the defensive midfielder (**DM**) receives a lay-off from the forward (**F**) in Zone 2, and the right back (**RB**) makes a deep run to receive and pass for **AM** to finish in Zone 3.

Source: Roberto De Zerbi's Brighton training session at AMEX Stadium - 11th April 2023

Attacking Positional Patterns of Play

Direct from
Roberto De Zerbi's
Training Sessions

"Everyone knows what we have to do in our position, and he expects different things from each position. He gives you enough information to choose the right decision for you. That is good as a player. You can see which decision fits."

Alexis Mac Allister

Liverpool, Argentina, and former Brighton Midfielder

ROBERTO DE ZERBI'S SASSUOLO 4-3-3 FORMATION

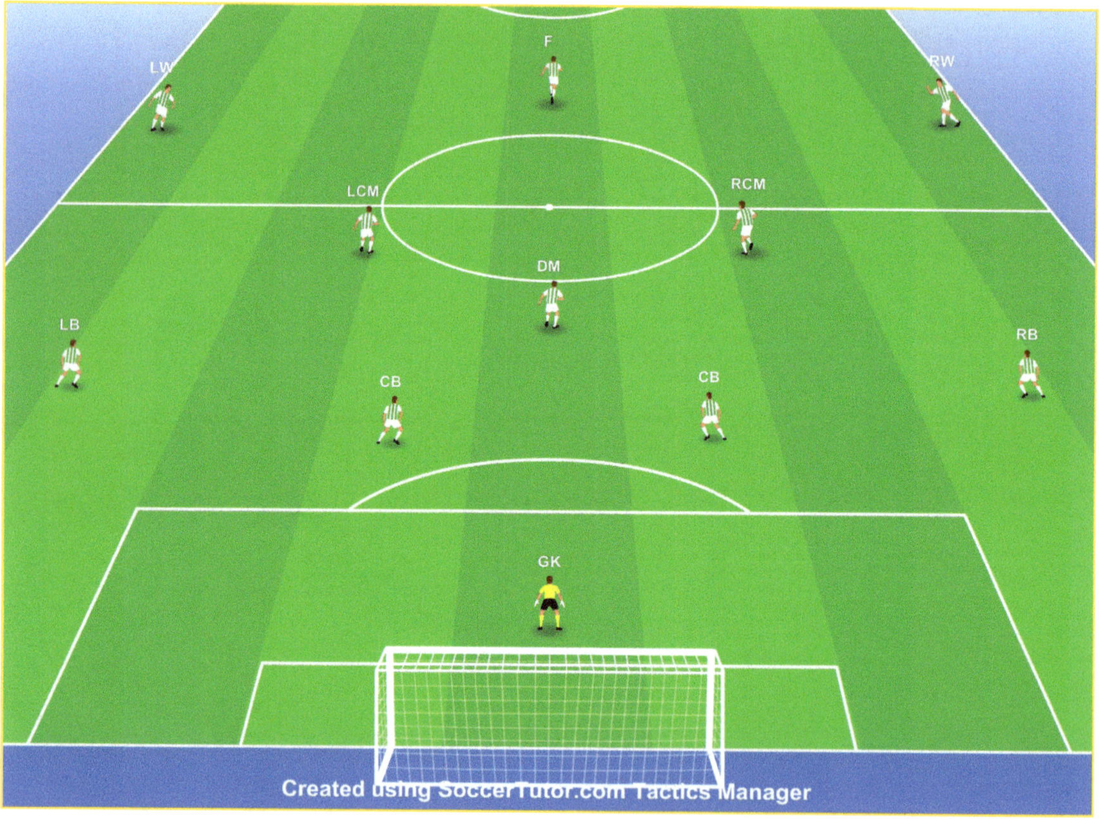

- **GK:** Goalkeeper
- **CB:** Left Centre Back
- **CB:** Right Centre Back
- **LB:** Left Back
- **RB:** Right Back
- **DM:** Defensive Midfielder
- **LCM:** Left Central Midfielder
- **RCM:** Right Central Midfielder
- **LW:** Left Winger
- **RW:** Right Winger
- **F:** Forward

ROBERTO DE ZERBI'S 2-3-2-3 ATTACKING PHASE FORMATION

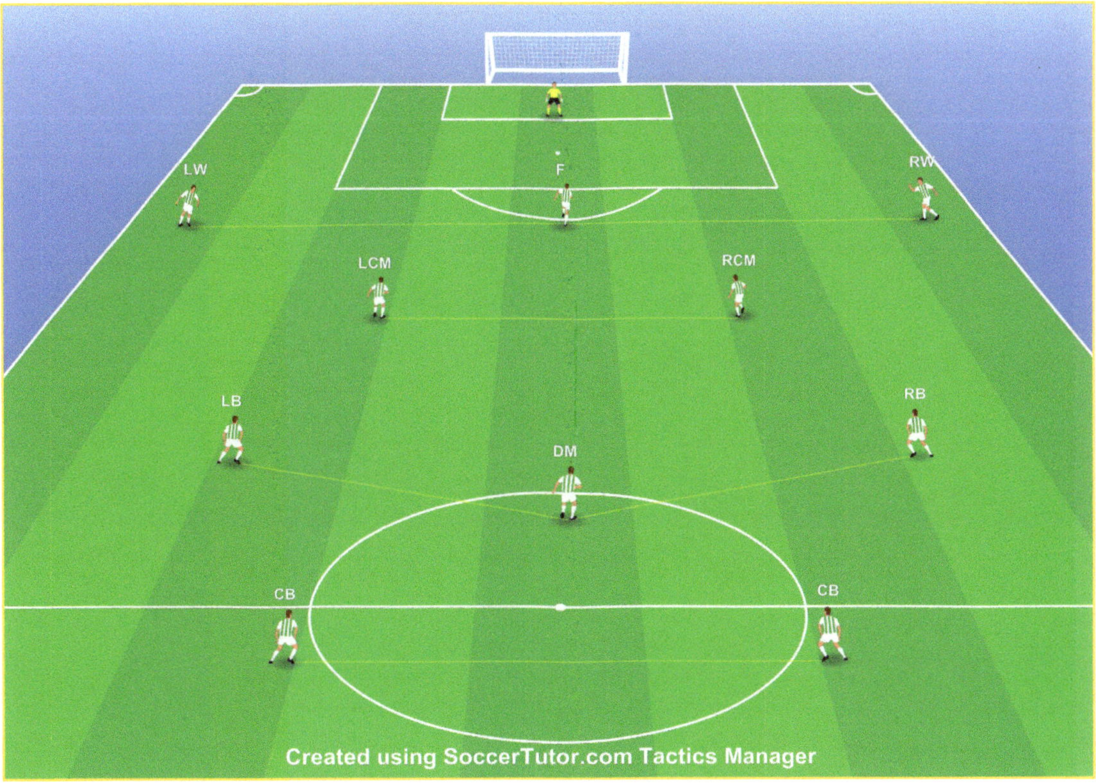

Created using SoccerTutor.com Tactics Manager

Roberto De Zerbi has adapted his style of play during his career but has used variations of this 2-3-2-3 attacking phase shape throughout. The examples to follow in this section are from his early training sessions with Sassuolo using the 4-3-3.

DEFENDERS: The **centre backs** (**CB**) provide defensive stability. The **full backs** (**LB** & **RB**) help form the second line and build-up play in central areas, but also move out of these positions (forward runs) to provide width and deliver crosses.

MIDFIELDERS: The **defensive midfielder** (**DM**) is deep in the second line with a crucial role in maintaining possession, ball circulation, and build-up play through the centre of the pitch. The **central midfielders** (**LCM** & **RCM**) in the third line play a key role in receiving between the lines, linking the second line with the attackers and creating goal scoring opportunities.

WINGERS: The **wingers** (**LW** & **RW**) occupy wide positions in the front 3 to stretch the opposition, deliver crosses, and cut inside to create goal scoring chances.

FORWARD: The **forward** (**F**) has a central role with hold up play, linking wingers and central midfielders, and scoring goals.

PATTERNS OF PLAY TRAINING SET-UP 1 (3-2-3 ATTACKING PHASE SHAPE)

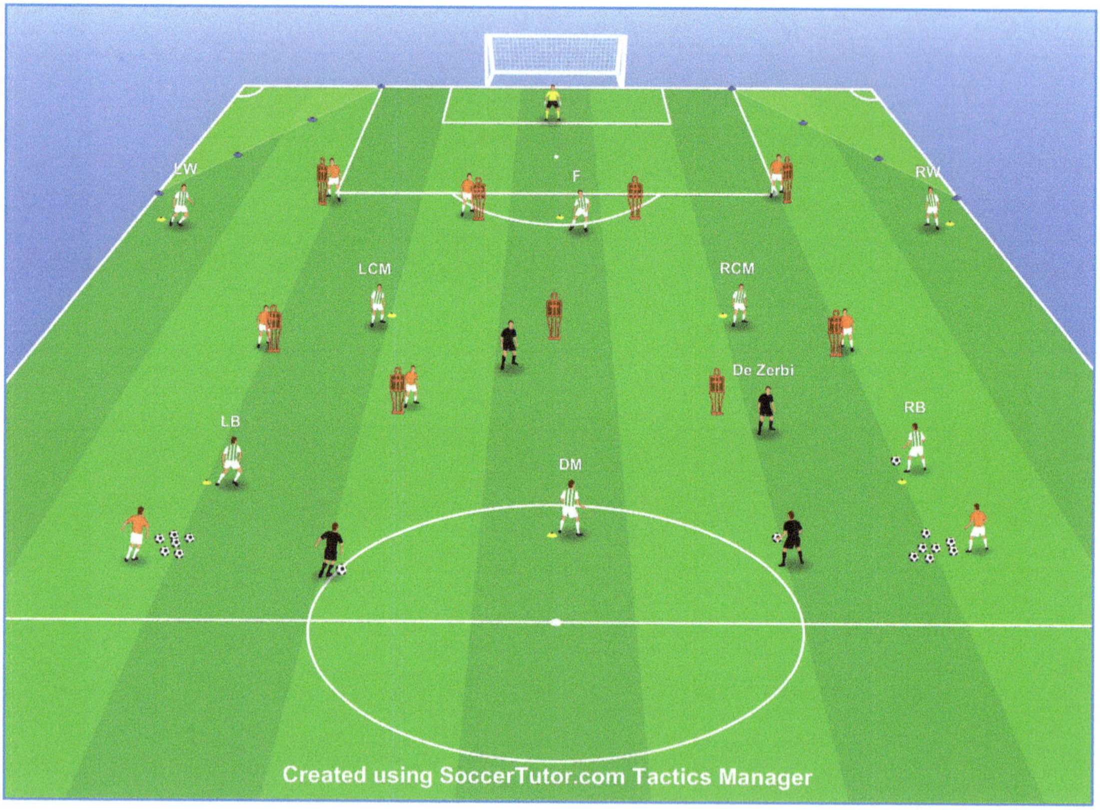

- This diagram shows Roberto De Zerbi's set-up for practicing **attacking positional patterns of play with Sassuolo** using 9 players (no centre backs).
- There are coaches in different positions. Their role is to play new balls in and close down players/apply pressure to block passing lanes at certain points to help make the patterns of play game realistic, with some defensive resistance.
- There are 2 positions where there are a number of balls to restart with.
- There are 9 red mannequins which represent the opposition in a compact 4-5 defensive formation.
- In each position, there are 2 players (extras in orange bibs), who form 2 teams of 10 outfield players to practice patterns.
- The 2 teams **run the patterns outlined by De Zerbi** alternately. As soon as one team finishes, they jog back to their positions and the next team goes.

Source: Roberto De Zerbi's Sassuolo Calcio preseason training session in Vipiteno, Italy - 16th July 2019

"The tougher the pressure, the more vertical development. The less pressure, the greater our control of the match and possession of the ball will be."

1. Switch of Play to Winger and Full Back's Underlapping Run in Behind into the Box

Practice Description

1. The right back (**RB**) takes a touch forward with the ball, is put under pressure by De Zerbi, and then passes to the right central midfielder (**RCM**).

2-3. **RCM** plays back to the defensive midfielder (**DM**). The **DM** is put under pressure by the Coach, takes a touch to his left, and passes diagonally to the left central midfielder (**LCM**).

4. **LCM** receives and passes out wide to the advanced left winger (**LW**).

5. **LW** receives and passes into the box for the left back (**LB**), who makes a long deep underlapping run on the inside of the full back mannequin to receive in behind the defensive line.

6-7. The opposite winger (**RW**) has made a well timed run off the flank. **LB** delivers a low cross across the box for him to score. Both central midfielders (**LCM** and **RCM**) and the forward (**F**) also make runs into different areas of the box to provide alternative options.

Source: Roberto De Zerbi's Sassuolo Calcio preseason training session in Vipiteno, Italy - 16th July 2019

2. Switch of Play to Winger and Full Back's Overlapping Run in Behind and into the Box

Practice Description

1. The right back (**RB**) moves forward with the ball, is put under pressure by De Zerbi, and then passes to the right central midfielder (**RCM**).
2. **RCM** first checks away, then drops back to receive, and passes back to the defensive midfielder (**DM**).
3. **DM** is put under pressure by the Coach and passes diagonally to the left central midfielder (**LCM**), who has checked up and dropped back to receive.
4. **LCM** receives and passes out wide to the advanced left winger (**LW**).

5-6. **LW** receives, drives inside at the full back mannequin, and then passes into the box for the deep overlapping run of the left back (**LB**).

7-8. The forward (**F**) makes a well timed run to the near post. **LB** cuts the ball back for him to score. Both central midfielders (**LCM** and **RCM**) and the opposite winger (**RW**) also make runs into the box to provide alternative options.

Source: Roberto De Zerbi's Sassuolo Calcio preseason training session in Vipiteno, Italy - 16th July 2019

3. Switch of Play to Winger, Central Midfielder's Penetrating Run in Behind to Receive + Cut Back

Practice Description

1. The left back (**LB**) moves forward with the ball, is put under pressure by De Zerbi, and then passes to the left central midfielder (**LCM**), who drops to receive.
2. **LCM** passes back to the defensive midfielder (**DM**), who checks before moving to receive in the centre.
3. **DM** is put under pressure by the Coach and passes diagonally to the right central midfielder (**RCM**), who has moved to receive on the half-turn.
4. **RCM** passes out wide to the advanced right winger (**RW**).

5-6. **RW** receives, drives inside at the full back mannequin, and then passes into the box for the penetrating run of the (**RCM**) in behind and into the box.

7-8. **RCM** cuts the ball back for **LCM**, who makes a well timed run to the penalty spot area and scores. The opposite winger (**LW**) and forward (**F**) also make runs into the box and the **DM** moves into position at the edge of the box

Source: Roberto De Zerbi's Sassuolo Calcio preseason training session in Vipiteno, Italy - 16th July 2019

4. Switch of Play with Central Midfielder Dropping to Receive when 2 Passing Lanes are Blocked

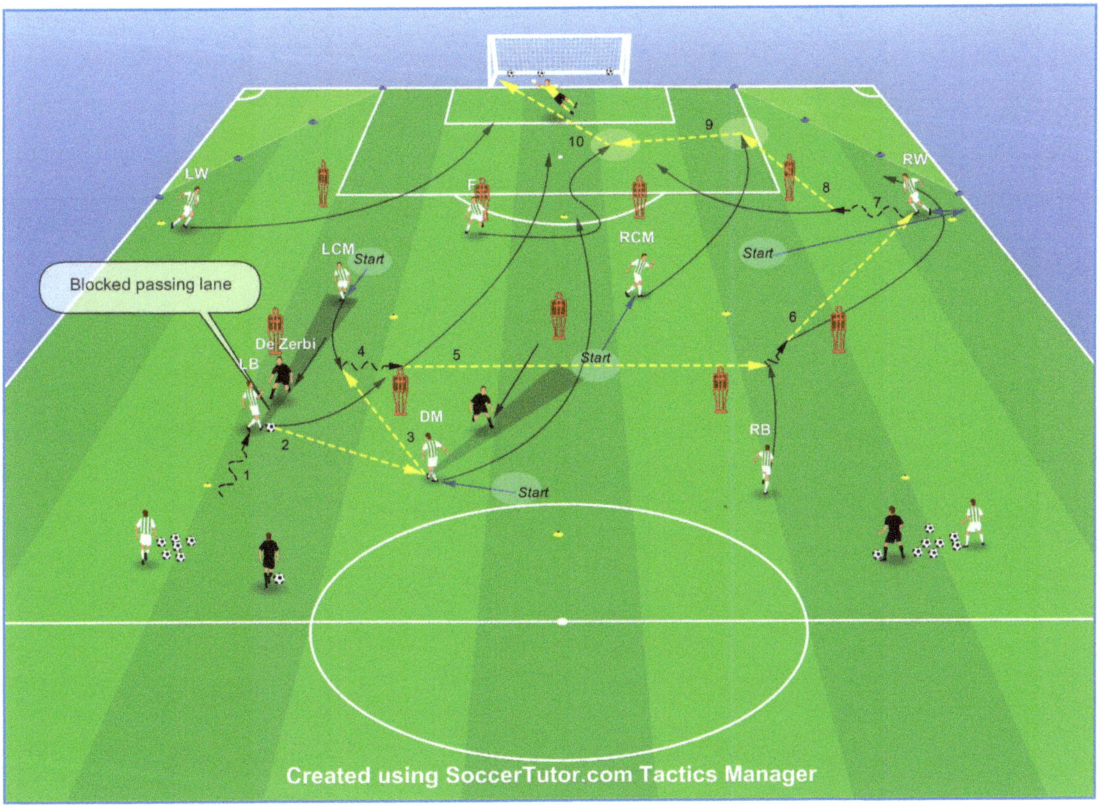

Blocked passing lane

Created using SoccerTutor.com Tactics Manager

Practice Description

1-2. The left back (**LB**) moves forward with the ball and is **pressed by De Zerbi**, who blocks the forward pass. **LB** therefore passes back to the defensive midfielder (**DM**), who shifts across.

3. The defensive midfielder (**DM**) passes forward to the left central midfielder (**LCM**), who drops back to receive.

4-5. LCM moves inside with the ball and passes across for the forward run of the right back (**RB**) beyond the mannequin.

6. RB receives and passes to the right winger (**RW**), who has moved wide from an inside start position.

7-8. RW receives, drives inside at the full back mannequin, and then passes into the box for the penetrating run of the right central midfielder (**RCM**) in behind and into the box.

9-10. RCM passes across for the forward (**F**), who makes a well timed run to score. Both wingers (**LW** and **RW**) also make runs into the box and the **DM** moves into position at the edge of the box.

Source: Roberto De Zerbi's Sassuolo Calcio preseason training session in Vipiteno, Italy - 16th July 2019

5. Combination Play in Centre with Supporting Runs, and Through Pass in Behind to the Winger

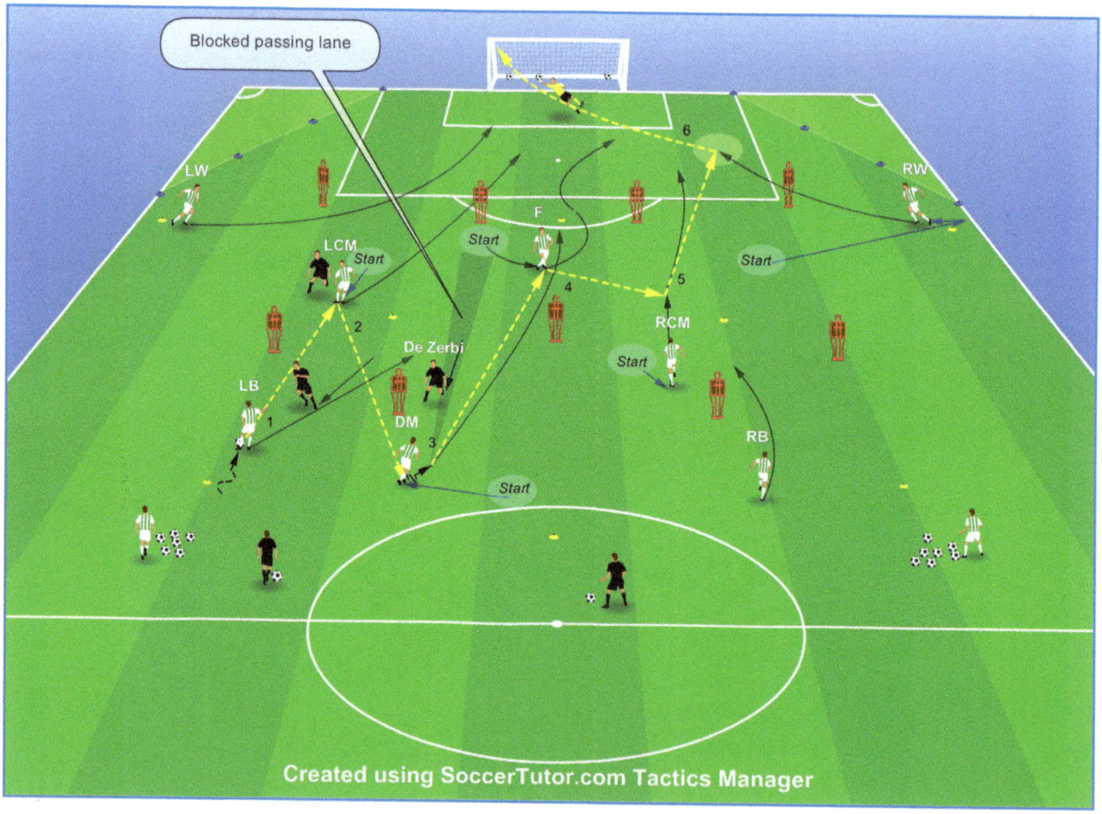

Practice Description

1. The left back (**LB**) moves forward with the ball, is put under pressure by the Coach, but still manages to pass forward to the left central midfielder (**LCM**), although he is marked by another Coach.
2. As he is marked closely, **LCM** passes back to the defensive midfielder (**DM**).
3. **DM** is put under pressure by De Zerbi, so the forward (**F**) moves across into the open passing lane to receive the next pass.
4. **F** sets the ball back for the oncoming right central midfielder (**RCM**).
5. **RCM** plays a through pass into the box for the well timed run of the right winger (**RW**) off the flank.
6. **RW** shoots across the goal to try and score. Both central midfielders (**LCM** and **RCM**), **F**, and the opposite winger (**LW**) make runs into the box. The **DM** moves into position at the edge of the box.

Source: Roberto De Zerbi's Sassuolo Calcio preseason training session in Vipiteno, Italy - 16th July 2019

6. Combination Play in the Left Central Area with Forward's Lay-off and Spin in Behind to Score (Give & Go)

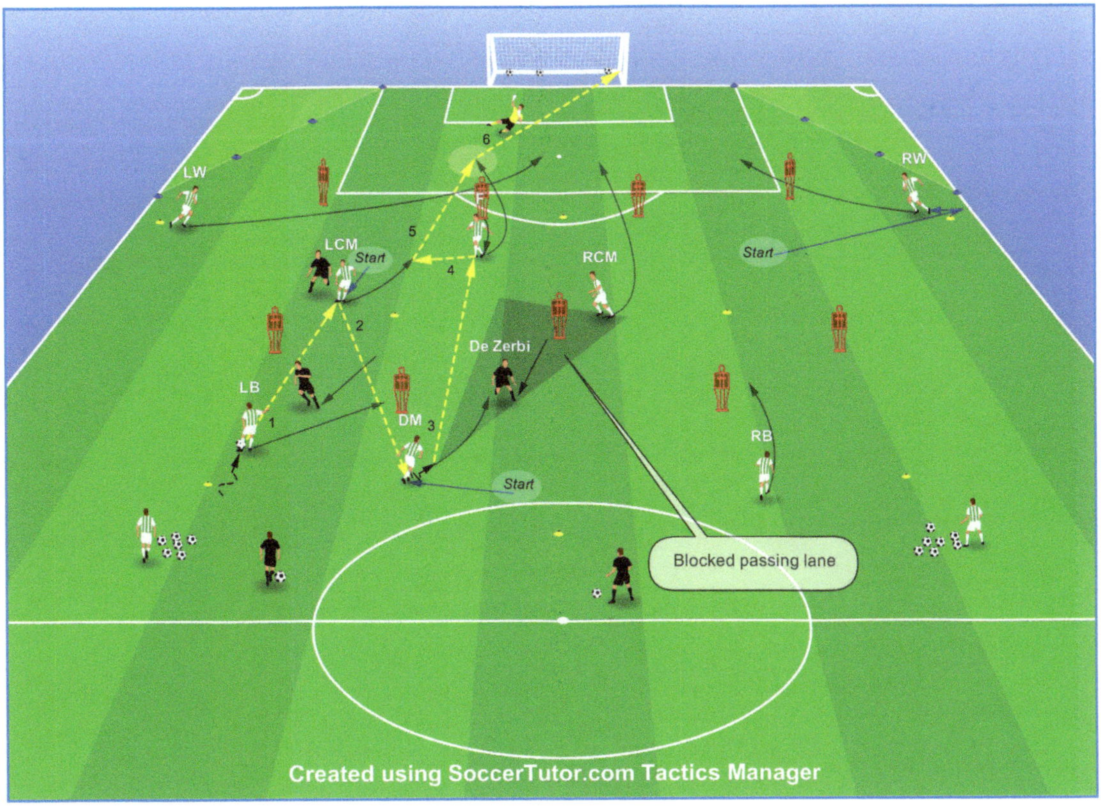

Practice Description

1. The left back (**LB**) moves forward with the ball, is put under pressure by the Coach, but still manages to pass forward to the left central midfielder (**LCM**), although he is marked by another Coach.
2. As he is marked closely, **LCM** passes back to the defensive midfielder (**DM**).
3. **DM** is pressed by De Zerbi who blocks a pass to **RCM** but leaves a vertical pass to the forward (**F**) open, who receives in front of the centre back mannequin.

4-5. **F** sets the ball back for the oncoming left central midfielder (**LCM**), who spins away from his marker. **LCM** plays a through pass into the box for the well timed run of the forward (**F**), who spins around the centre back mannequin to receive the return for the give & go.

6. **F** tries to score 1v1 against the GK. Both wingers (**LW** and **RW**) and the other central midfielder (**RCM**) make runs into the box.

Source: Roberto De Zerbi's Sassuolo Calcio preseason training session in Vipiteno, Italy - 16th July 2019

7. Combination Play in the Right Central Area with Forward's Lay-off and Spin in Behind to Score (Give & Go)

Practice Description

1. The right back (**RB**) moves forward with the ball, is put under pressure by the Coach, but still manages to pass forward to the right central midfielder (**RCM**), although he is marked by another Coach.
2. As he is marked closely, **RCM** passes back to the defensive midfielder (**DM**).
3. **DM** is pressed by De Zerbi who blocks a pass to **LCM** but leaves a pass to the forward (**F**) open, who drops back and across to receive.

4-5. **F** sets the ball back for the oncoming right central midfielder (**RCM**), who spins away from his marker. **RCM** plays a through pass into the box for the well timed run of **F** in between the 2 centre back mannequins to receive the return for the give & go.

6. **F** tries to score 1v1 against the GK. Both wingers (**LW** and **RW**) and the other central midfielder (**LCM**) make runs into the box.

Source: Roberto De Zerbi's Sassuolo Calcio preseason training session in Vipiteno, Italy - 16th July 2019

PATTERNS OF PLAY TRAINING SET-UP 2 (3-2-3 ATTACKING PHASE SHAPE)

- This diagram shows Roberto De Zerbi's second variation for the set-up of **attacking positional patterns of play with Sassuolo** using 9 players (no centre backs). The different positions of the cones create different start positions.
- There are coaches in different positions. Their role is to play new balls in and close down players/apply pressure to block passing lanes at certain points to help make the patterns of play game realistic, with some defensive resistance.
- There are 2 positions where there are a number of balls to restart with. There are 9 red mannequins which represent the opposition in a compact 4-5 defensive formation.
- In each position, there are 2 players (extras in orange bibs), who form 2 teams of 10 outfield players to practice patterns. The 2 teams **run the patterns outlined by De Zerbi** alternately. As soon as one team finishes, they jog back to their positions and the next team goes.

Source: Roberto De Zerbi's Sassuolo Calcio preseason training session in Vipiteno, Italy - 23rd July 2019

1. Possession on Strong Side Before Switching Point of Attack to Winger with Full Back's Overlapping Run

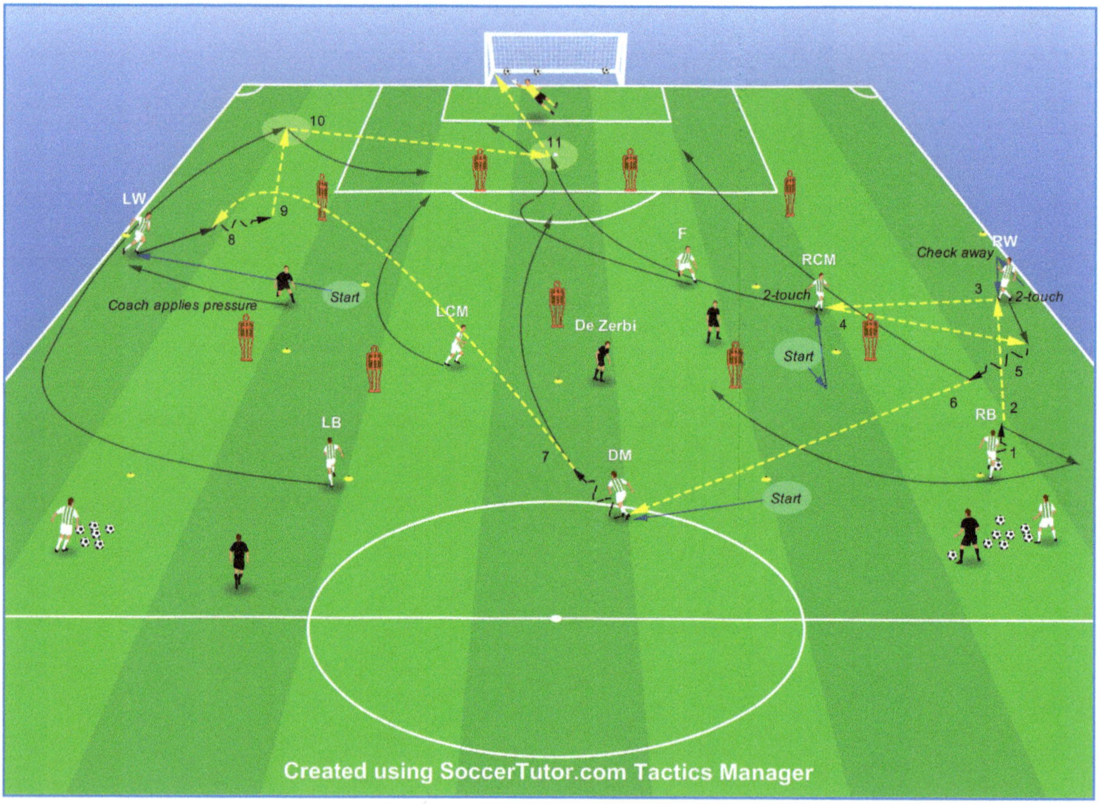

Created using SoccerTutor.com Tactics Manager

Practice Description

1-2. The right back (**RB**) moves forward with the ball and passes forward to the right winger (**RW**).

3. **RW** passes inside to the right central midfielder (**RCM**).

4-5. **RCM** sets the ball back for **RW**, who drops to receive and carries the ball inside.

6. **RW** passes back to the defensive midfielder (**DM**) in the centre.

7. **DM** receives and moves forward with the ball, and then plays an aerial pass to switch the play to the advanced left winger (**LW**).

8-9. **LW** drives inside and passes for the well timed deep run of the left back (**LB**) on the overlap.

10-11. **LB** passes across the box to the forward (**F**), who makes a run into the centre of the box to score. Both central midfielders and both wingers also make runs into the box.

Source: Roberto De Zerbi's Sassuolo Calcio preseason training session in Vipiteno, Italy - 23rd July 2019

2. Possession on Strong Side + Switch Point of Attack to Winger with Central Midfielder's Penetrating Run in Behind

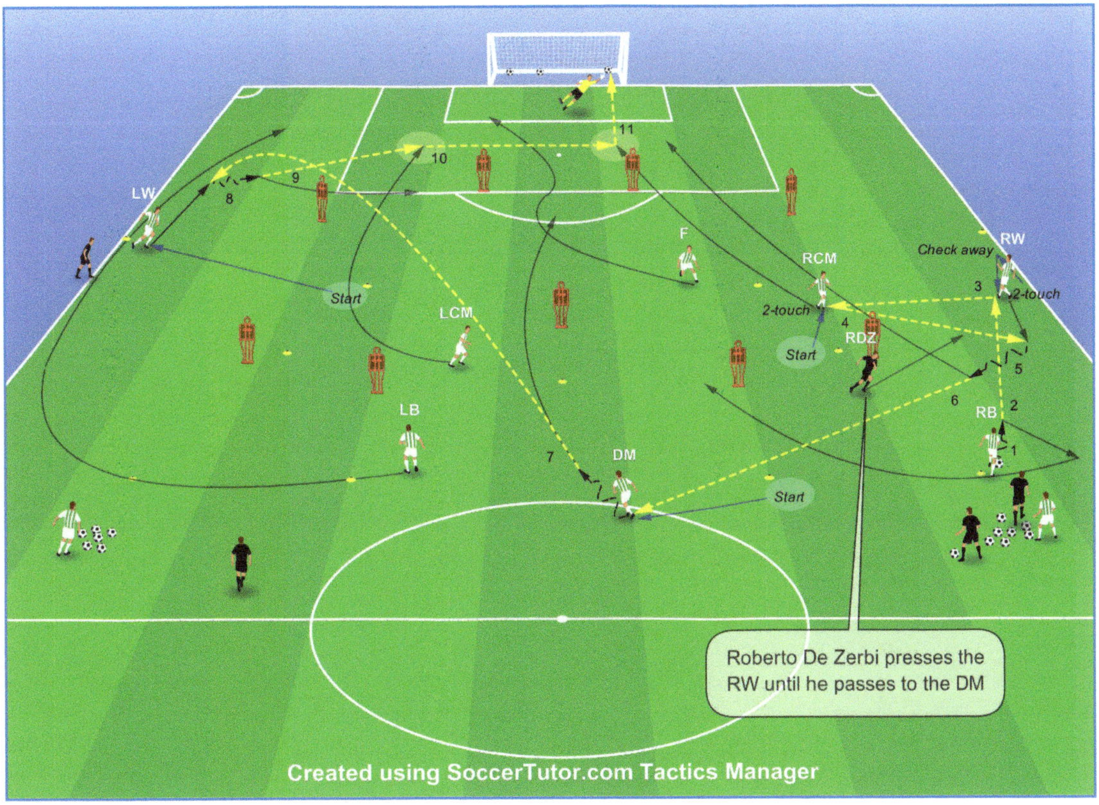

Roberto De Zerbi presses the RW until he passes to the DM

Created using SoccerTutor.com Tactics Manager

Practice Description

1-2. The right back (**RB**) moves forward with the ball and passes forward to the right winger (**RW**).

3. RW passes inside to the right central midfielder (**RCM**).

4-5. RCM sets the ball back for **RW**, who drops to receive and carries the ball inside.

6. De Zerbi presses the **RW**, who passes back to the defensive midfielder (**DM**) in the centre.

7. DM receives and moves forward with the ball, and then plays an aerial pass to switch the play to the advanced left winger (**LW**).

8-9. LW drives inside and passes into the box for the well timed penetrating run of the left central midfielder (**LCM**).

10-11. LCM passes across the box to **RCM**, who makes a run into the box to score. The forward (**F**) and **RW** also make runs into the box.

Source: Roberto De Zerbi's Sassuolo Calcio preseason training session in Vipiteno, Italy - 23rd July 2019

3. Possession on Strong Side + Switch Point of Attack to Winger with Lay-Off and Full Back's Overlapping Run

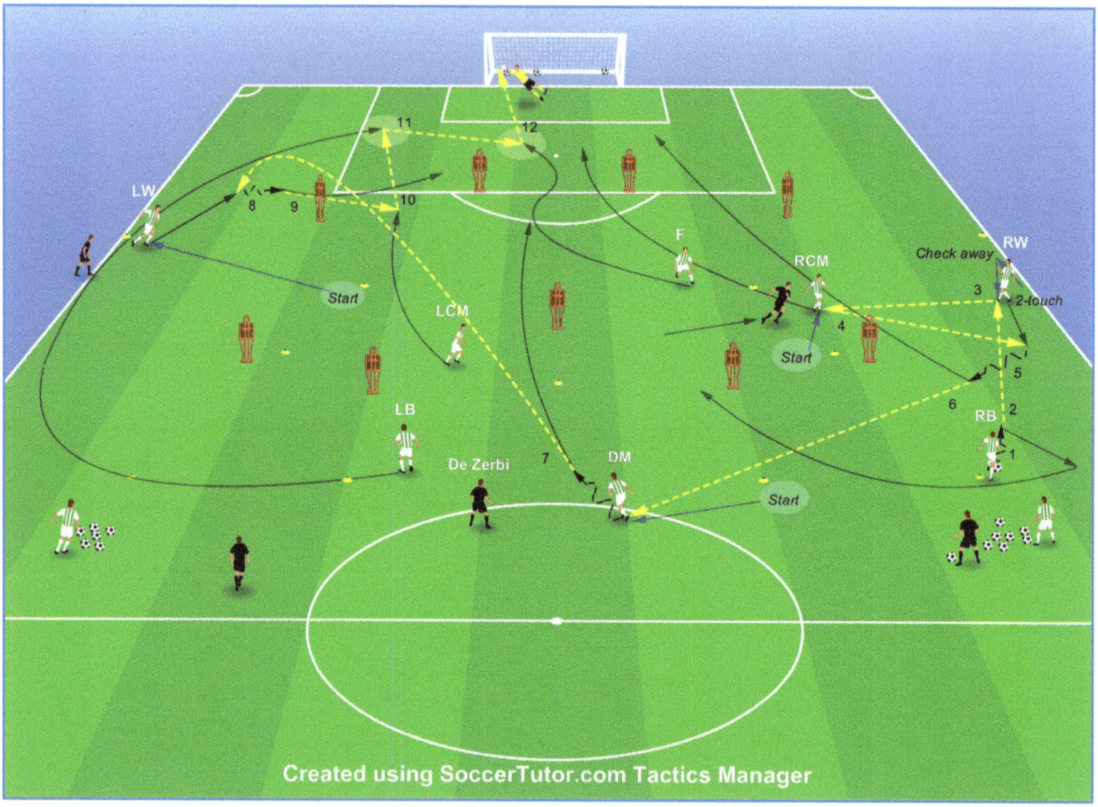

Practice Description

1-2. The right back (**RB**) moves forward with the ball and passes forward to the right winger (**RW**).

3. **RW** passes inside to the right central midfielder (**RCM**).

4-5. **RCM** sets the ball back for **RW**, who drops to receive and carries the ball inside.

6. **RW** passes back to the defensive midfielder (**DM**) in the centre.

7. **DM** receives and moves forward with the ball, and then plays an aerial pass to switch the play to the advanced left winger (**LW**).

8-9. **LW** takes a touch inside and passes across for the oncoming left central midfielder (**LCM**).

10-12. **LCM** passes into the box for the deep overlapping run of the left back (**LB**) in behind. **LB** cuts the ball back for the forward (**F**) to score. **RCM**, **RW**, and **LW** also make runs into the box to provide alternative options.

Source: Roberto De Zerbi's Sassuolo Calcio preseason training session in Vipiteno, Italy - 23rd July 2019

4. Possession in Centre + Forward's Lay-off for Central Midfielder's Through Pass to Winger on Strong Side

Practice Description

1. The left back (**LB**) passes back to the defensive midfielder (**DM**).

2. **DM** is pressed by De Zerbi and passes forward to the left central midfielder (**LCM**), who drops back to receive.

3-4. **LCM** passes inside to the other central midfielder (**RCM**), who shifts across and sets the ball back for the **DM**.

5-6. **DM** passes to the forward (**F**), who sets the ball for the oncoming **LCM**.

7. **LCM** plays a through pass in between the full back and centre back mannequins for the run of the left winger (**LW**), who makes a sharp diagonal movement off the flank.

8. **LW** shoots across the GK to try and score. **F**, **RCM**, and the right winger (**RW**) all make runs into the box to provide support and a possible final passing option.

Source: Roberto De Zerbi's Sassuolo Calcio preseason training session in Vipiteno, Italy - 23rd July 2019

5. Possession in Centre + Forward's Lay-off for Central Midfielder's Through Pass to Winger on Weak Side

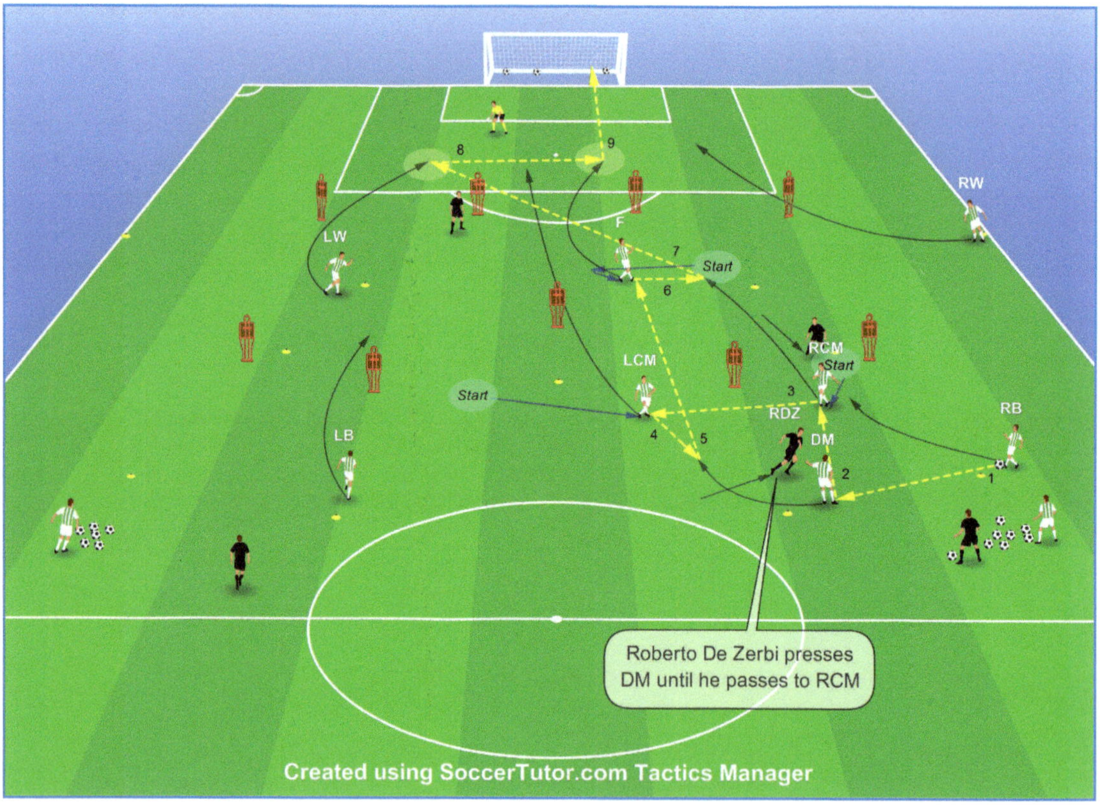

Practice Description

1. The right back (**RB**) passes to the defensive midfielder (**DM**).

2. **DM** is pressed by De Zerbi and passes forward to the right central midfielder (**RCM**), who drops back to receive under pressure from the Coach.

3-4. **RCM** passes inside to the other central midfielder (**LCM**), who shifts across and sets the ball for the movement of **DM**.

5-6. **DM** passes to the forward (**F**), who sets the ball for the oncoming **RCM**.

7. **RCM** plays a diagonal through pass in between the 2 centre back mannequins for the run of the left winger (**LW**), who makes a movement inside the full back mannequin.

8-9. **LW** passes the ball across the box for **F** to score. **LCM** and the right winger (**RW**) make runs into the box to provide support and a different final passing option.

Source: Roberto De Zerbi's Sassuolo Calcio preseason training session in Vipiteno, Italy - 23rd July 2019

6. Possession in Centre + Forward's Turn and Through Pass for Winger in Behind

Roberto De Zerbi presses DM until he passes to F

Created using SoccerTutor.com Tactics Manager

Practice Description

1. The right back (**RB**) passes inside to the defensive midfielder (**DM**).
2. **DM** is pressed by De Zerbi and passes forward to the right central midfielder (**RCM**), who drops back to receive under pressure from the Coach.

3-4. **RCM** passes inside to the other central midfielder (**LCM**), who shifts across and sets the ball for the movement of **DM**.

5-6. **DM** passes to the forward (**F**), who receives, turns, and moves forward.

7. **F** plays a diagonal through pass in between the 2 centre back mannequins for the run of the left winger (**LW**), who makes a movement in between the full back and centre back mannequins.
8. In this example, **LW** shoots at goal. **F**, **LCM**, **RCM**, and the right winger (**RW**) all make runs into the box to provide support and a passing option in case **LW** wants to use them.

Source: Roberto De Zerbi's Sassuolo Calcio preseason training session in Vipiteno, Italy - 23rd July 2019

7. Short Combination, Break the Line, Forward's Lay-off for Central Midfielder's Through Pass, and Winger's Cut Back

Coach presses DM until he passes to F

Created using SoccerTutor.com Tactics Manager

Practice Description

1. The right back (**RB**) passes inside to the defensive midfielder (**DM**).
2. **DM** is pressed by De Zerbi and passes forward to the right central midfielder (**RCM**), who drops back to receive.

3-4. **RCM** passes inside to the other central midfielder (**LCM**), who shifts across and sets the ball back for the movement of the **DM** around De Zerbi.

5-6. **DM** passes to the forward (**F**), who sets the ball for the oncoming **LCM**.

7. **LCM** plays a diagonal through pass in between the full back and centre back mannequins for the run of the left winger (**LW**) into the box.

8-9. **LW** passes across the box for **F** to score. **RCM** and the right winger (**RW**) make runs into the box to provide support and a different final passing option.

Source: Roberto De Zerbi's Sassuolo Calcio preseason training session in Vipiteno, Italy - 23rd July 2019

8. Switch Play to Full Back on Overlap, Reset when Blocked + CM's Give & Go to Receive in Behind

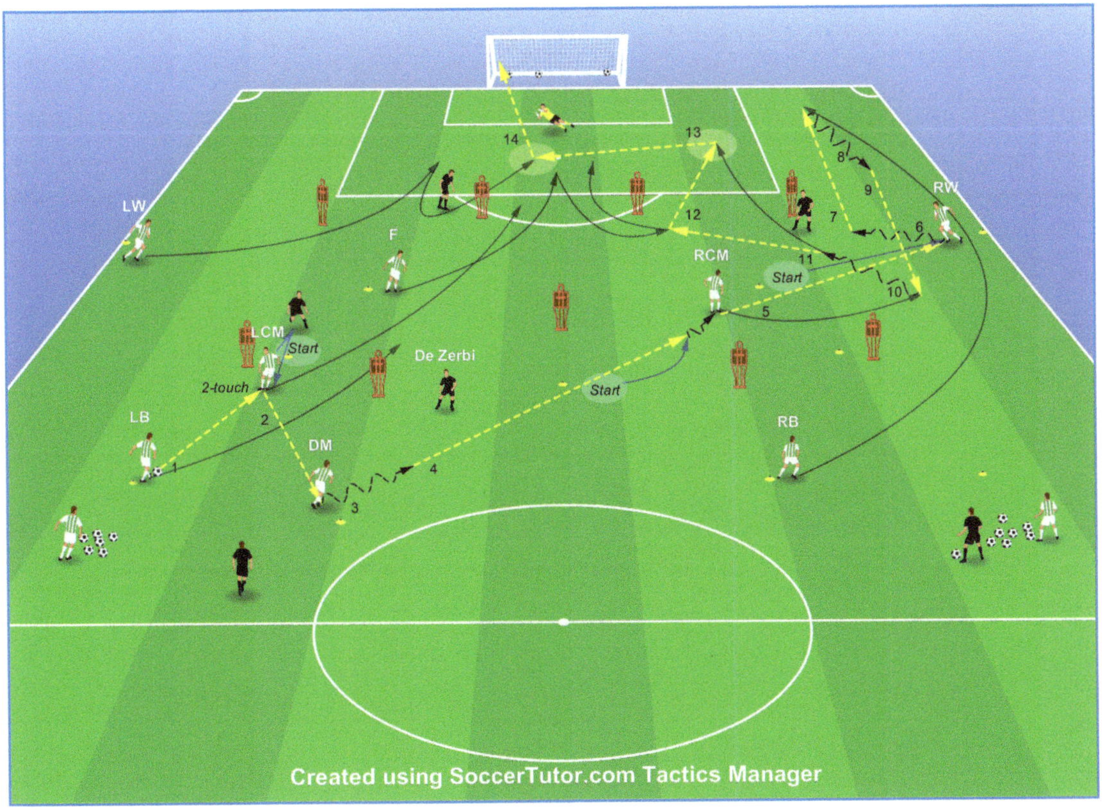

Practice Description

1. The left back (**LB**) passes to the left central midfielder (**LCM**), who drops to receive under pressure from the Coach.

2-3. **LCM** passes back to the defensive midfielder (**DM**), who moves forward and inside with the ball.

4. **DM** passes diagonally to the right central midfielder (**RCM**), who receives and opens up to play forward.

5. **RCM** passes out wide to the advanced right winger (**RW**).

6-7. **RW** receives, drives inside at the full back mannequin, and then passes to the right back (**RB**) on the overlap.

8-9. **RB** turns, carries the ball backwards, and then passes to **RCM**, who shifts towards the sideline.

10-12. **RCM** dribbles towards the box and then plays a give & go with the forward (**F**) to receive inside the box.

13-14. **RCM** cuts the ball back for **LW** to score. **F** and **RCM** also move into the box in support.

Source: Roberto De Zerbi's Sassuolo Calcio preseason training session in Vipiteno, Italy - 23rd July 2019

9. Switch Play to Right Back on Overlap, Reset, and Central Midfielder's Lofted Pass into the Box

Practice Description

1-2. The left back (**LB**) passes forward to the left central midfielder (**LCM**). **LCM** checks away, drops to receive under pressure from the Coach, and passes back to the defensive midfielder (**DM**).

3-4. DM moves forward and inside with the ball and then passes diagonally to the right central midfielder (**RCM**), who receives and opens up to play forward.

5. RCM passes out wide to the advanced right winger (**RW**).

6-7. RW receives, drives inside at the full back mannequin, and then passes to the right back (**RB**) on the overlap.

8-9. RB turns, carries the ball backwards, and then passes to **RCM**, who shifts towards the sideline.

10-11. RCM receives and then plays a diagonal aerial pass inside the box for the movement of the left winger (**LW**) who tries to score. **F**, **LCM**, and **RW** also make movements into the box to provide support.

Source: Roberto De Zerbi's Sassuolo Calcio preseason training session in Vipiteno, Italy - 23rd July 2019

10. Switch Play to Left Back on Overlap, Reset when Blocked, and Central Midfielder's Lofted Pass into the Box

Practice Description

1. The right back (**RB**) passes forward to the right central midfielder (**RCM**), who is put under pressure by the Coach.

2. **RCM** passes back to the defensive midfielder (**DM**).

3-4. **DM** moves forward and inside with the ball and then passes diagonally to the left central midfielder (**LCM**), who receives and opens up to play forward.

5. **LCM** passes out wide to the advanced left winger (**LW**).

6-7. **LW** receives, drives inside at the full back mannequin, and then passes to the left back (**LB**) on the overlap.

8-9. **LB** turns, carries the ball backwards, and then passes to **LCM**, who shifts towards the sideline.

10-11. **LCM** receives and then plays a diagonal aerial pass inside the box for the movement of the **RCM** to score. The forward (**F**) and both wingers (**LW** and **RW**) also make movements into the box to provide support.

Source: Roberto De Zerbi's Sassuolo Calcio preseason training session in Vipiteno, Italy - 23rd July 2019

PATTERNS OF PLAY TRAINING SET-UP 3 (2-3-2-3 ATTACKING PHASE SHAPE)

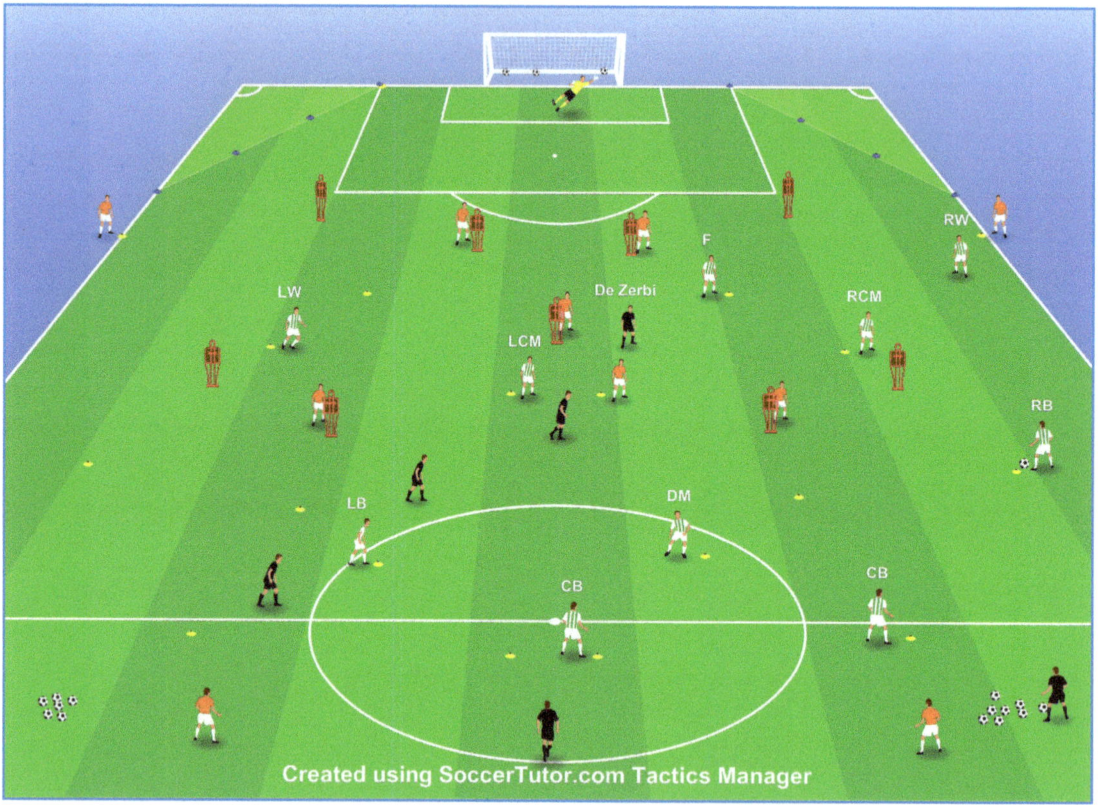

- This diagram shows Roberto De Zerbi's set-up for practicing **attacking positional patterns of play with the 10 Sassuolo outfield players (4-3-3)**.
- There are coaches in different positions. Their role is to play new balls in and also close down the players to block passing lanes at certain points to help make the patterns of play game realistic, with some defensive resistance.
- There are 2 positions where there are a number of balls to restart with.
- There are 9 red mannequins which represent the opposition in a compact 4-5 defensive formation.
- In each position, there are 2 players (extras in orange bibs), who form 2 teams of 10 outfield players to practice patterns.
- The 2 teams **run the patterns outlined by De Zerbi** alternately. As soon as one team finishes, they jog back to their positions and the next team goes.

Source: Roberto De Zerbi's Sassuolo Calcio preseason training session in Vipiteno, Italy - 20th July 2019

"I love the winger who tries to beat his man. I love those players who live between the lines. I love the centre back who tries to command the play."

1. Combination Play Wide, Reset to Centre Back, and Attack Through the Flank

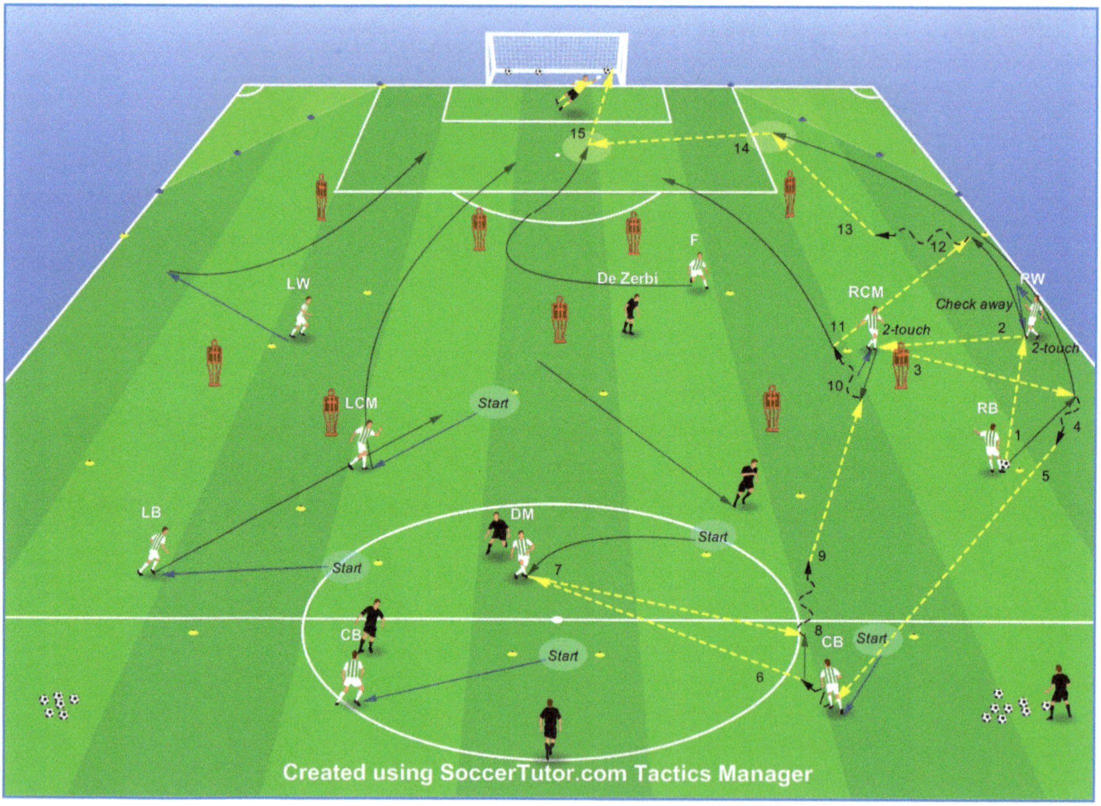

Practice Description

1-2. The right back (**RB**) passes forward to the right winger (**RW**), who passes inside to the right central midfielder (**RCM**).

3-5. **RCM** passes to **RB**, who turns and passes back to the centre back (**CB**) to reset.

6-7. **CB** plays a on-two with the defensive midfielder (**DM**), who is put under pressure by the Coach behind him.

8-10. **DM** moves forward with the ball and passes to **RCM**, who receives and turns.

11. **RCM** passes wide to **RW**, who makes a forward movement to receive.

12-13. **RW** drives inside and then passes in behind for the deep overlapping run of the right back (**RB**).

14. **RB** cuts the ball back for the forward (**F**) to score in the centre. Both central midfielders (**LCM** and **RCM**) and the opposite winger (**LW**) also make runs into different areas of the box to provide alternative options.

Source: Roberto De Zerbi's Sassuolo Calcio preseason training session in Vipiteno, Italy - 20th July 2019

2. Combination Play Wide, Reset to Centre Back, and Attack Through the Centre with Forward as Target Man

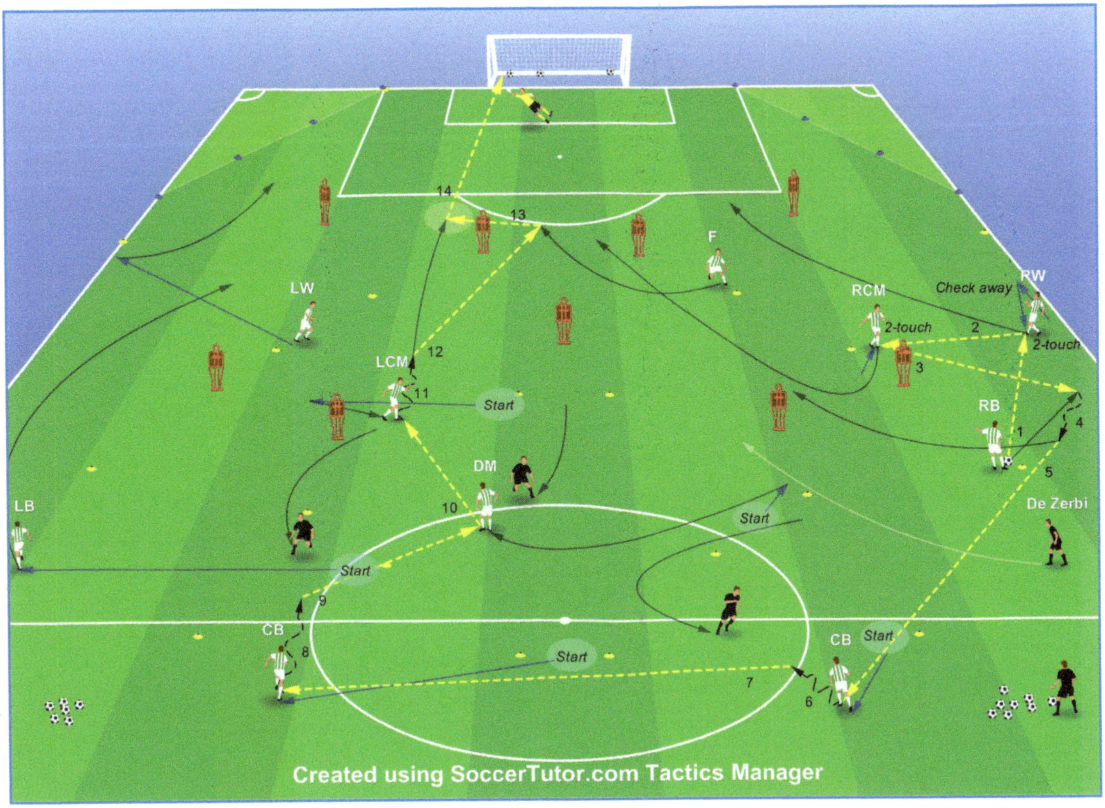

Created using SoccerTutor.com Tactics Manager

Practice Description

1-2. The right back (**RB**) passes forward to the right winger (**RW**), who passes inside to the right central midfielder (**RCM**).

3-5. **RCM** passes to **RB**, who turns and passes back to the centre back (**CB**) to reset.

6-7. **CB** takes a touch under pressure from the Coach and passes across to the other centre back.

8-9. The other **CB** moves forward and is pressed by the Coach, so passes to **DM**.

10. **DM** is also pressed and passes forward to the left central midfielder (**LCM**).

11-12. **LCM** turns to face forward and passes in between the 2 centre back mannequins for the movement of the forward (**F**).

13-14. **F** sets the ball for the oncoming **LCM** to complete the one-two combination. **LCM** shoots at goal.

Source: Roberto De Zerbi's Sassuolo Calcio preseason training session in Vipiteno, Italy - 20th July 2019

3. Reset to Centre Back and Attack Through the Centre with Central Midfielder's Through Pass to Winger

Created using SoccerTutor.com Tactics Manager

Practice Description

1-2. The right back (**RB**) passes to the right central midfielder (**RCM**). He passes back to the defensive midfielder (**DM**), who is marked by the Coach.

3-4. **DM** passes to **RB**, who drops to receive, and then passes back to the centre back (**CB**) to reset.

5-6. **CB** takes a touch under pressure from the Coach and passes to the **DM**, who makes an extensive movement to receive in a deep central position.

7. **DM** passes back to the other centre back.

8-9. **CB** moves forward with the ball, is pressed by the Coach, and passes to the right central midfielder (**RCM**).

11. **RCM** turns to face forward and passes in between the full back and centre back mannequins for the run of the right winger (**RW**) in behind and into the box.

12. **RW** shoots across the GK to try and score. The forward (**F**), left central midfielder (**LCM**), and left winger (**LW**) all make runs into the box for support.

Source: Roberto De Zerbi's Sassuolo Calcio preseason training session in Vipiteno, Italy - 20th July 2019

4. Quick Combination and Switch of Play via Both Centre Backs to the Winger with Overlapping Full Back

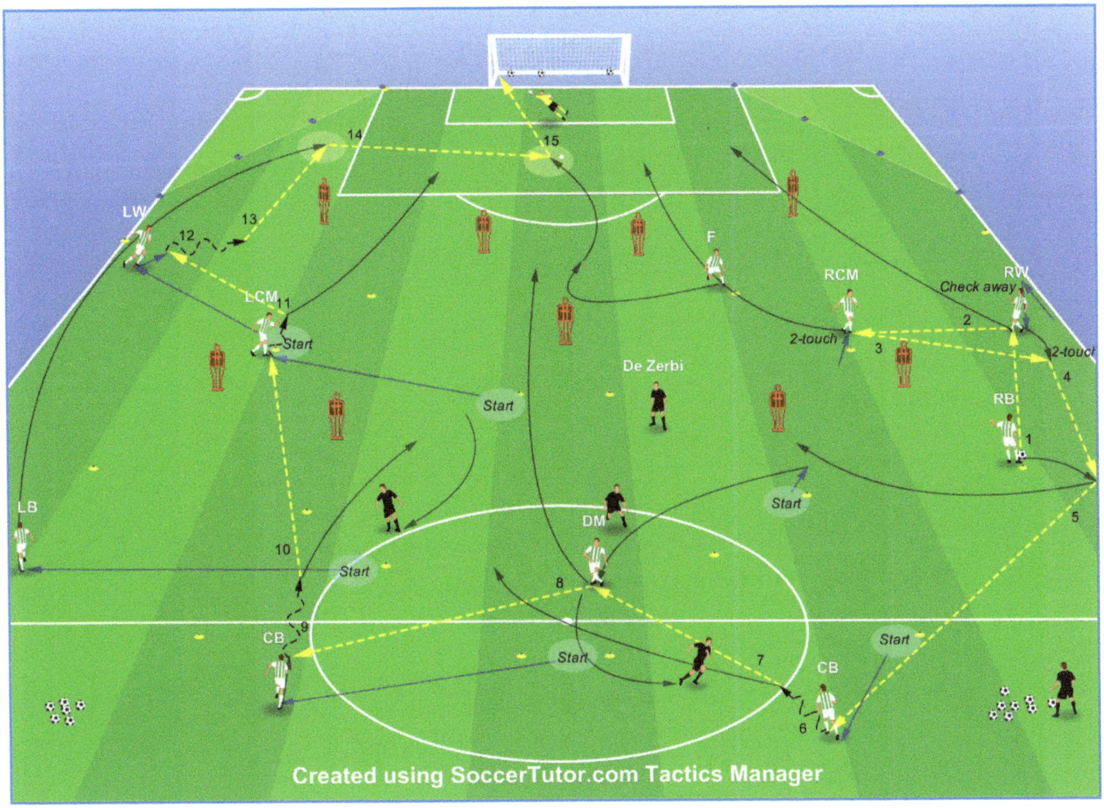

Created using SoccerTutor.com Tactics Manager

Practice Description

1-2. The right back (**RB**) passes forward to the right winger (**RW**), who passes inside to the right central midfielder (**RCM**).

3-4. RCM passes to **RW**. He passes back to the right back (**RB**), who must drop to receive.

5. RB passes back to the centre back (**CB**) to reset, who is pressed by the Coach.

6-7. CB takes a touch forward and passes to the defensive midfielder (**DM**), who drops to receive in a deep position.

8-10. DM passes back to the other centre back (**CB**), who receives on the move and carries the ball forward before passing to the left central midfielder (**LCM**).

11-13. LCM turns to face forward and passes to the left winger (**LW**), who drives inside and passes in behind for the overlapping run of the left back (**LB**).

14-15. LW cuts the ball back for the forward (**F**) to score. Both central midfielders (**LCM** & **RCM**) and the opposite winger (**RW**) also make runs into the box.

Source: Roberto De Zerbi's Sassuolo Calcio preseason training session in Vipiteno, Italy - 20th July 2019

5. Quick Combination and Switch of Play via the Centre Back to the Winger with Overlapping Full Back

Practice Description

1-4. In a triangle, the 2-touch *(receive and pass)* goes from the left back (**LB**) to the defensive midfielder (**DM**), to the left central midfielder (**LCM**), and back to the **DM**, who drops away from his marker to receive the fourth pass in the sequence.

5-7. **DM** passes across to the centre back (**CB**), who has moved forward past the halfway line to receive, carry the ball forward and pass to the advanced right winger (**RW**) positioned on the sideline.

8-10. **RW** receives, drives inside, and then plays a give & go with the right central midfielder (**RCM**), who has moved forward.

11. **RW** receives in behind and passes the ball across the box towards the far post for the forward (**F**) to score. **RCM** and **LW** also make runs into the box to provide support and alternative options.

Source: Roberto De Zerbi's Sassuolo Calcio preseason training session in Vipiteno, Italy - 20th July 2019

6. Quick Combination and Switch of Play via the Defensive Midfielder to the Winger with Overlapping Full Back

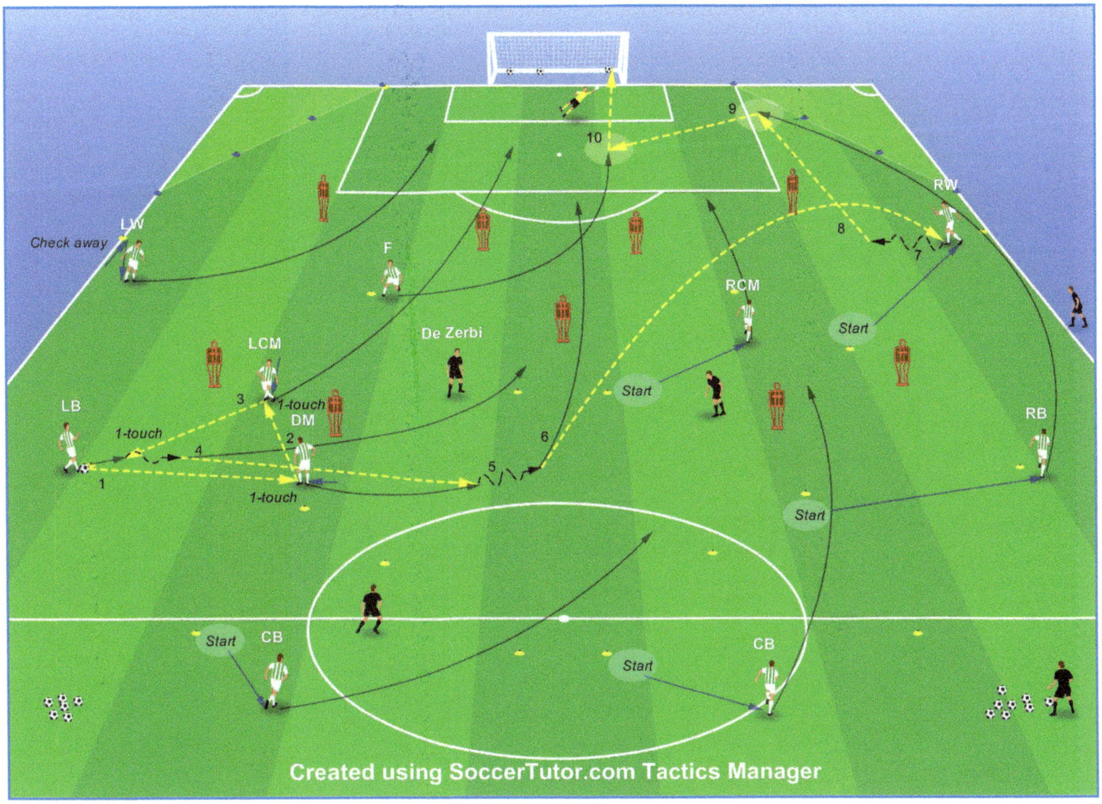

Practice Description

1-4. In a triangle, the one-touch passes go from the left back (**LB**) to the defensive midfielder (**DM**), to the left central midfielder (**LCM**), and back to the **DM**, who opens up and lets the ball run across him into space to receive the fourth pass in the sequence.

5-6. **DM** switches the play to the advanced right winger (**RW**) positioned on the sideline with an aerial pass. All the other players make supporting movements.

7-8. **RW** receives, drives inside, and then passes in behind for the deep overlapping run of the right back (**RB**).

9-10. **RB** cuts the ball back for the forward (**F**) to score. Both central midfielders (**LCM** & **RCM**) and the opposite winger (**LW**) also make runs into the box to provide support and alternative options.

Source: Roberto De Zerbi's Sassuolo Calcio preseason training session in Vipiteno, Italy - 20th July 2019

PATTERNS OF PLAY TRAINING SET-UP 4 (2-3-2-3 ATTACKING PHASE SHAPE)

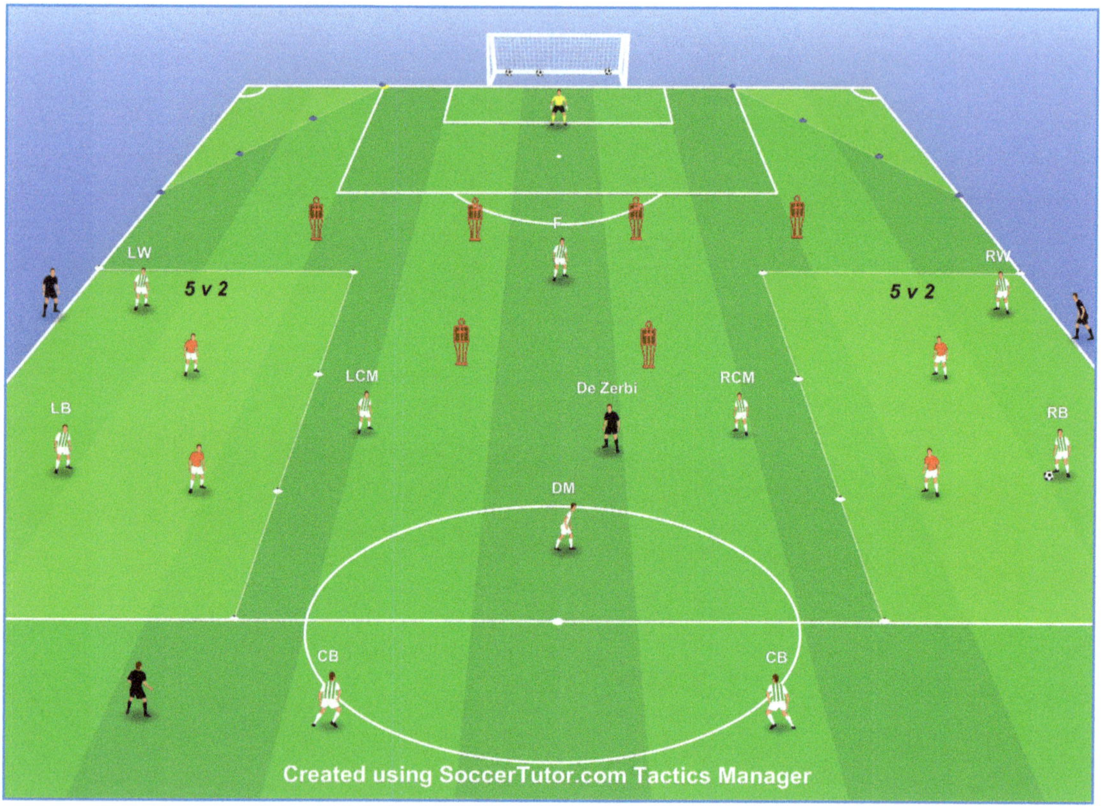

- This diagram shows Roberto De Zerbi's set-up for practicing **attacking positional patterns of play (4-3-3 formation)** at Sassuolo with 5v2 wide zones.
- There are 6 red mannequins which represent the opposition's back 4 and 2 central midfielders. In addition, there are 2 active red full backs + wingers. This creates a 4-4-2 defensive formation.
- The **wide zones are marked as 5v2** as the red wide players must remain within these zones and a maximum of 5 white/green players are allowed to enter at one time e.g. left back (**LB**), left winger (**LW**), left central midfielder (**LCM**), defensive midfielder (**DM**), and centre back (**CB**) in the first example on the next page.
- The **players run different patterns, which are coached by De Zerbi** - on the following pages, there are 7 observed examples for this practice set-up from a Sassuolo training session.

Source: Roberto De Zerbi's Sassuolo Calcio preseason training session in Vipiteno, Italy - 20th July 2018

"It is one of the teams I try to learn a lot. It is unique like a Michelin star restaurant – in Catalonia, the best cook for many, many years, he changed completely the cuisine and I think Brighton is playing something unique, special."

Pep Guardiola

1. Double Switch of Play via the Centre Back and Defensive Midfielder with 5v2 Wide Zones

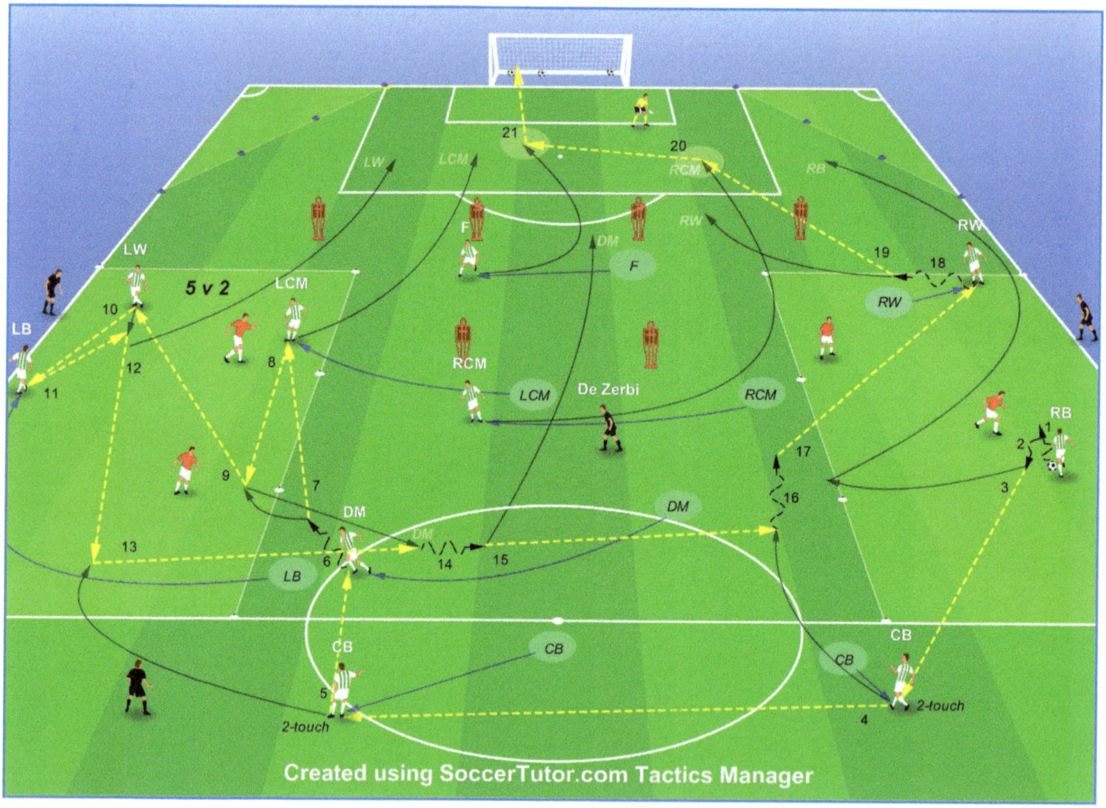

The blue circles show the starting positions.

Practice Description

1-4. The right back (**RB**) moves forward, back, and passes to the centre back (**CB**), who passes to the other centre back.

5-8. **CB** passes to **DM**, who receives, turns, and passes to **LCM** (central midfielder), then moves to receive the return.

9-13. **DM** passes to the winger (**LW**), who plays a one-two with the left back (**LB**). **CB** moves wide into the 5v2 zone to receive the next pass, then pass to **DM**.

14-17. **DM** opens up and passes to **CB**, who moves forward past the halfway line to receive on the move before passing wide to the right winger (**RW**).

18-19. **RW** drives inside and passes in behind for the curved run of the right central midfielder (**RCM**).

20-21. **RCM** passes across the box for the forward (**F**) to score in the centre. The other central midfielder (**LCM**) and the opposite winger (**LW**) also make runs into the box to provide options.

Source: Roberto De Zerbi's Sassuolo Calcio preseason training session in Vipiteno, Italy - 20th July 2018

2. Possession Play on the Right Flank (5v2 Wide Zone) and Finish Attack with Through Pass to Forward in Behind

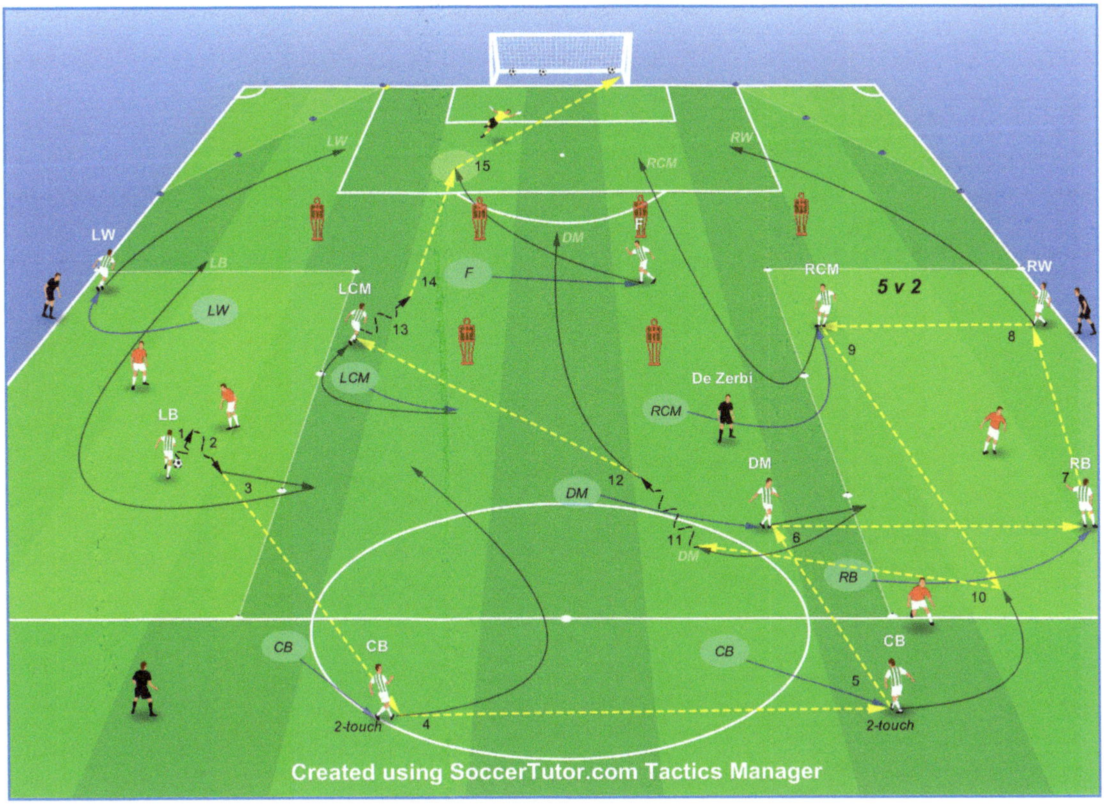

The blue circles show the starting positions.

Practice Description

1-4. The left back (**LB**) moves forward, back, and passes to the centre back (**CB**), who passes to the other centre back.

5-9. **CB** passes to **DM**, who moves across to receive. He passes to the right back (**RB**), who passes to the right winger (**RW**). **RW** passes inside to the right central midfielder (**RCM**), who makes a curved movement across and forward. **RCM** passes back to **CB** to reset again.

10-13. **CB** passes to **DM**, who receives on the half-turn and carries the ball forward. He then passes diagonally to the left central midfielder (**LCM**), who receives on the back foot facing forward.

14-15. **LCM** passes in behind for the run of the forward (**F**) in between the 2 centre back mannequins. Both wingers (**LW** and **RW**) and **RCM** make runs into the box to provide support and a possible passing option.

Source: Roberto De Zerbi's Sassuolo Calcio preseason training session in Vipiteno, Italy - 20th July 2018

3. Possession Play on the Left Flank (5v2 Wide Zone) and Finish Attack with Through Pass to Forward in Behind

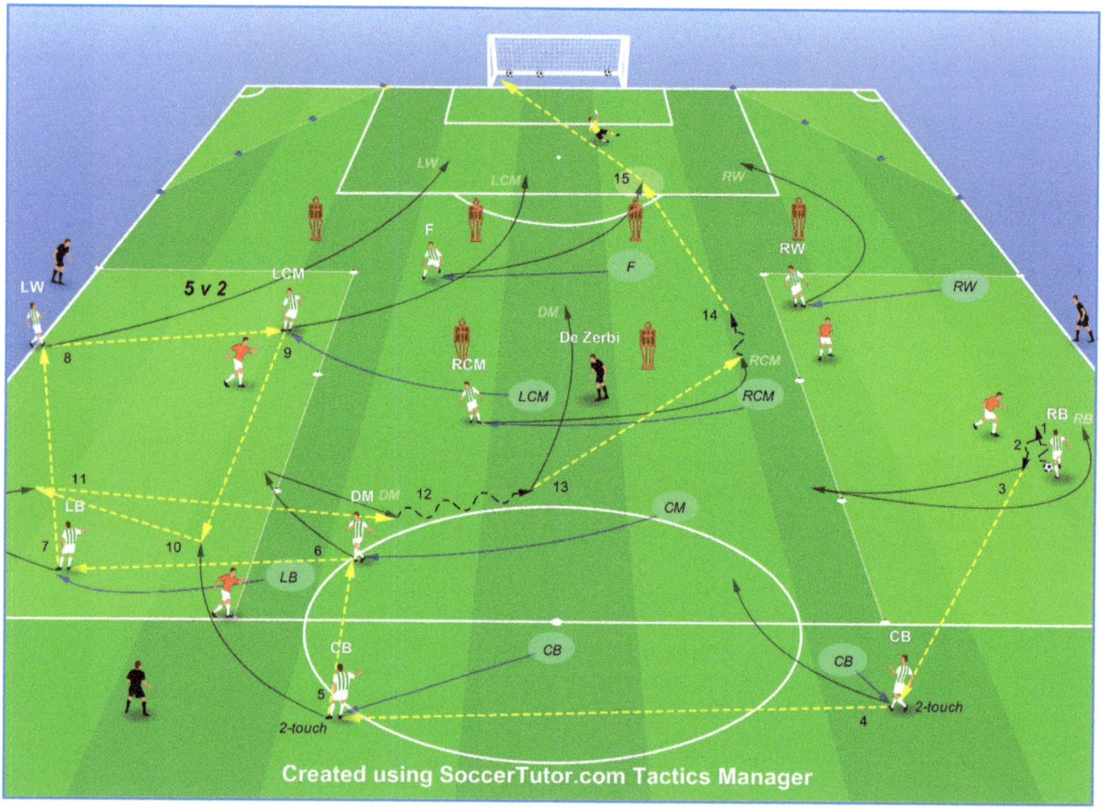

The blue circles show the starting positions.

Practice Description

1-4. The right back (**RB**) moves forward, back, and passes to the centre back (**CB**), who passes to the left centre back.

5-7. **CB** passes to **DM**, who passes wide to the left back (**LB**). **LB** then passes to the left winger (**LW**) on the sideline.

8-11. **LW** passes inside to the **LCM**, who has moved from the centre into the 5v2 wide zone. **LCM** passes back to **CB**, who passes to **LB**. **LB** passes inside to **DM**.

12-13. **DM** opens up and moves towards the other side with the ball, then plays a diagonal pass into the path of the right central midfielder's (**RCM**) extensive movement.

14-15. **RCM** takes a touch forward and passes in behind for the run of the forward (**F**) in between the 2 centre back mannequins. Both wingers (**LW** and **RW**) and **LCM** make runs into the box to provide support and/or a possible final passing option.

Source: Roberto De Zerbi's Sassuolo Calcio preseason training session in Vipiteno, Italy - 20th July 2018

4. Possession Play on the Right Flank (5v2 Wide Zone) and Attack Through the Centre with Forward's Give & Go

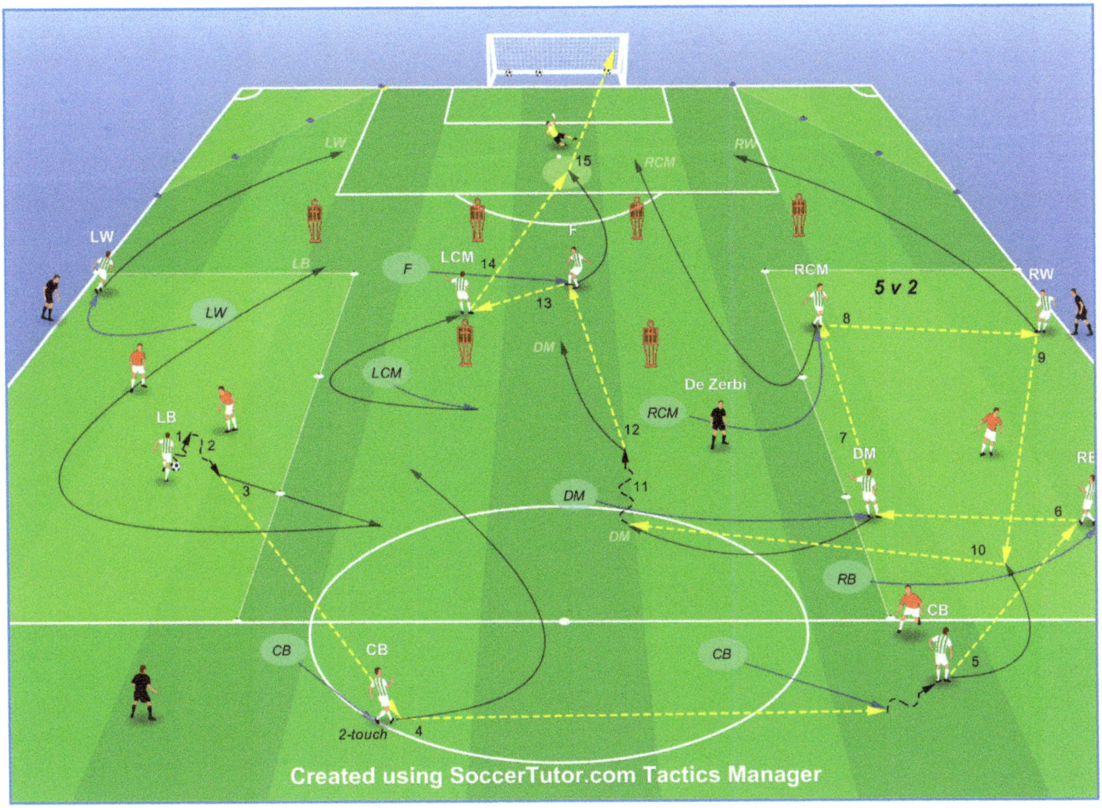

The blue circles show the starting positions.

Practice Description

1-4. The left back (**LB**) moves forward, back, and passes to the left centre back (**CB**). He passes to the right centre back, who receives and opens up.

5-9. **CB** passes to the right back (**RB**), and he passes inside to the **DM**, who shifts across to receive. **DM** passes to the right central midfielder (**RCM**). **RCM** passes to the right winger (**RW**), who passes back to the forward moving **CB**.

10-12. **DM** shifts again (into the centre) to receive the next pass from **CB**, carry the ball forward, and pass to the forward (**F**), who shifts across from the other side to receive with his back to goal.

13-15. **F** plays a give & go with the oncoming left central midfielder (**LCM**), spinning and making a run in between the 2 centre back mannequins and into the box to score. Both wingers (**LW** and **RW**) and **RCM** make forward runs to provide support to finish the attack.

Source: Roberto De Zerbi's Sassuolo Calcio preseason training session in Vipiteno, Italy - 20th July 2018

5. Possession Play on the Left Flank (5v2 Wide Zone) and Attack Through the Centre with Forward's Wall Pass

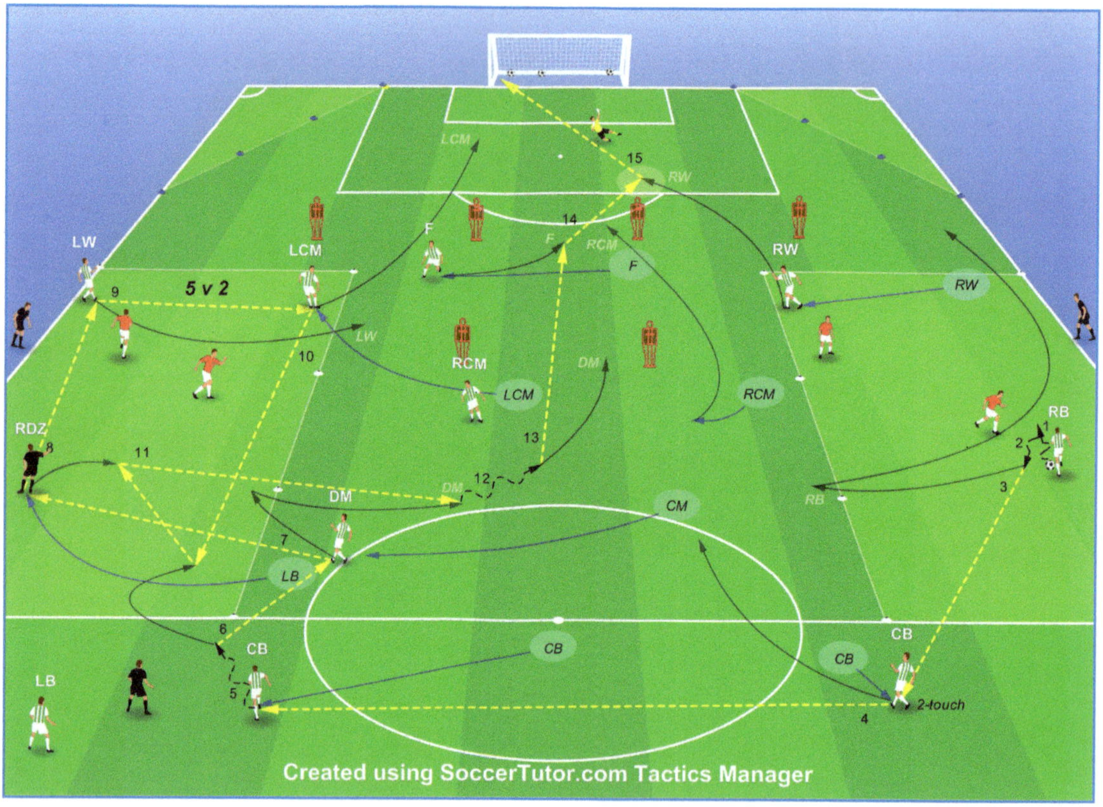

The blue circles show the starting positions.

Practice Description

1-4. The right back (**RB**) moves forward, back, and passes to the centre back (**CB**), who passes to the left centre back.

5-8. **CB** moves forward and passes to **DM**. He passes wide to **De Zerbi**, who is in the left back position. He passes to the left winger (**LW**) on the sideline.

9. **LW** passes inside to the left central midfielder (**LCM**), who has moved from the centre into the 5v2 wide zone.

10-11. **LCM** passes back to the oncoming **CB**, and he passes to **De Zerbi** (**LB**), who passes into the centre to the defensive midfielder **DM**.

12-15. **DM** has shifted to receive and opens up, then moves with the ball before playing a vertical pass to the forward (**F**), who moves to receive. **F** plays a wall pass in between the 2 centre back mannequins for the run of the right winger (**RW**) in behind - he tries to score. The **LCM** makes a run into the box to provide support for finishing the attack.

Source: Roberto De Zerbi's Sassuolo Calcio preseason training session in Vipiteno, Italy - 20th July 2018

6. Possession Play on the Left Flank (5v2 Wide Zone) and Switch Play for Right Back to Receive on Overlap

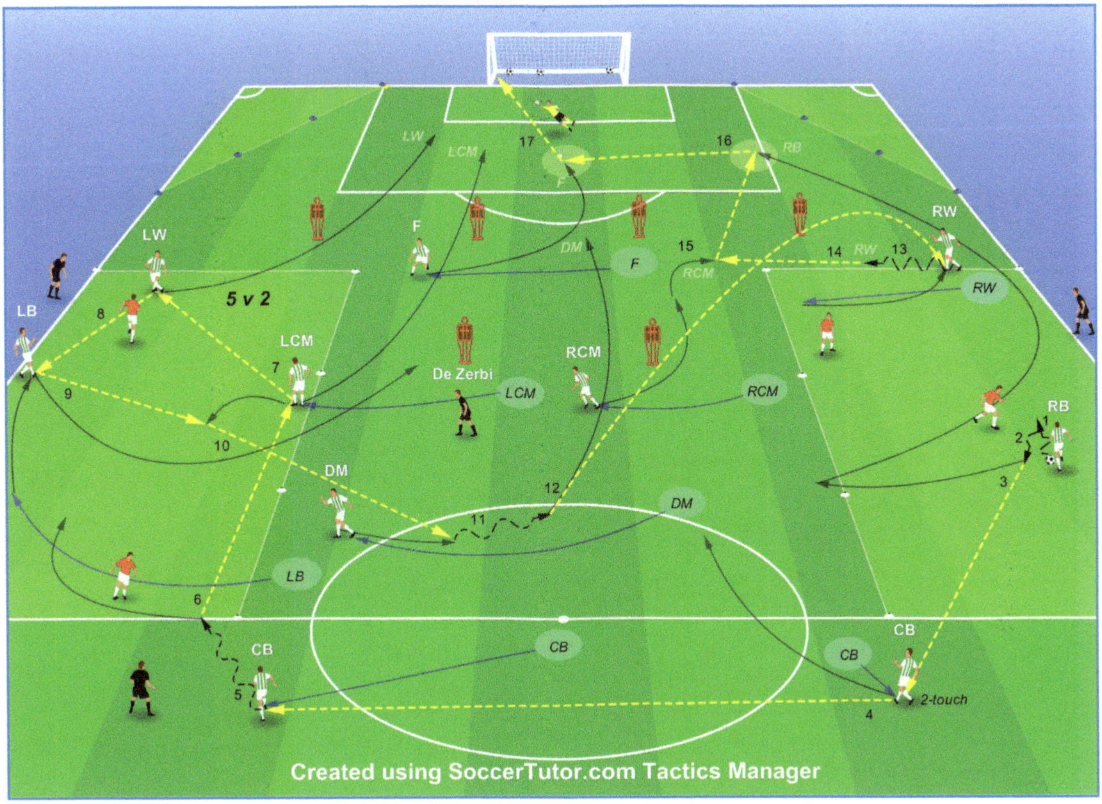

Created using SoccerTutor.com Tactics Manager

The blue circles show the starting positions.

Practice Description

1-4. The right back (**RB**) moves forward, back, and passes to the centre back (**CB**), who passes to the left centre back.

5-7. CB moves into the wide 5v2 zone and passes to the left central midfielder (**LCM**), who passes to the advanced left winger (**LW**).

8-10. LW passes back to the oncoming left back (**LB**). He passes inside to **LCM**, who passes back into the centre to **DM**.

11-12. DM opens up, moves inside, and switches play with an aerial pass to the right winger (**RW**).

13-17. RW moves inside and passes to the oncoming right central midfielder (**RCM**), who plays a through pass in between the full back and centre back mannequin for the deep overlapping run of the right back (**RB**). He cuts the ball back for the forward (**F**) to score in the centre. **LCM** and **LW** also make runs into the box to provide support.

Source: Roberto De Zerbi's Sassuolo Calcio preseason training session in Vipiteno, Italy - 20th July 2018

7. Passing Across the Back Line and Attacking Through the Centre with Inverted Forwards (3-4-3 Shape)

The blue circles show the starting positions.

Practice Description

1-5. The right wing back (**RWB**) passes back to the right centre back (**RCB**). **RCB** passes across to the middle centre back (**CB**), who passes to the left centre back (**LCB**). **LCB** moves forward with the ball and is pressed by the red opponent, so passes inside to the right central midfielder (**RCM**), who has moved extensively to the left side. The other 2 centre backs move past the halfway line.

6-7. **RCM** passes diagonally to the right forward (**RF**), who moves forward with the ball.

8-11. **RF** plays a give & go with the centre forward (**F**) to receive in behind and score. Both wing backs (**LWB** and **RWB**) and the left forward (**LF**) also make runs into the box to support the attack and provide alternative options.

Source: Roberto De Zerbi's Sassuolo Calcio preseason training session in Vipiteno, Italy - 20th July 2018

Attacking Combinations and Finishing

Direct from Roberto De Zerbi's Training Sessions

"He [De Zerbi] creates 20-25 chances on a game on average. He's better by far than all the opponents, he monopolises the ball in a way I haven't seen for a long, long time."

Pep Guardiola

1. 3 Player Combination on the Flank, Through Pass for Full Back's Third Man Run, Cut Back + Finish

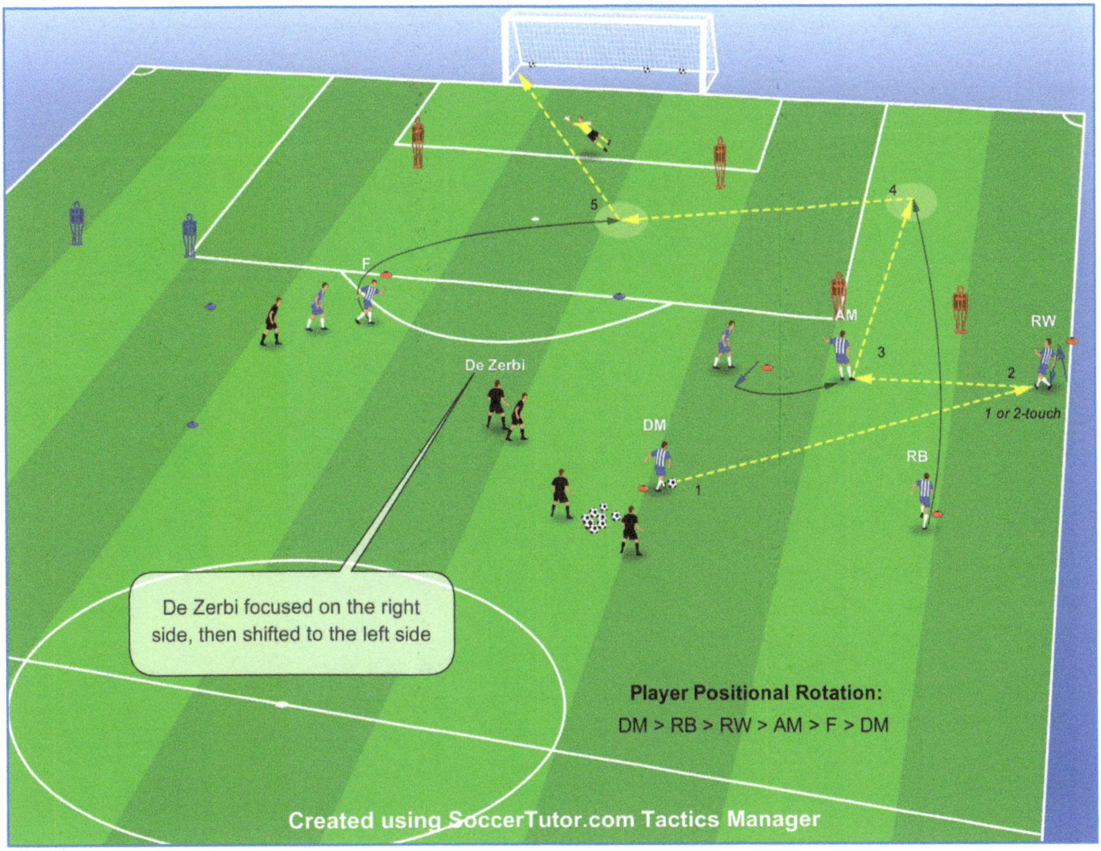

De Zerbi focused on the right side, then shifted to the left side

Player Positional Rotation:
DM > RB > RW > AM > F > DM

Created using SoccerTutor.com Tactics Manager

Practice Description

This was also practiced on the left side. The players rotate AM → RB → RW → AM → F → DM.

1. The defensive midfielder (**DM**) passes wide to the right winger (**RW**), who checks away from the cone before moving to receive.
2. **RW** uses 1 or 2 touches and moves the ball inside for the movement of the attacking midfielder (**AM**) off the cone.
3. **AM** plays a through pass for **RB's** deep run in between the 2 red mannequins.
4. **RB** cuts the ball back into the centre of the penalty area.
5. The forward (**F**) has run around the cone and times his movement well to score.

Source: Roberto De Zerbi's Brighton training session at Elite Football Performance Centre - 2

2. Wide Attacking Combination Play with Full Back's Overlap Run, Cut Back + Finish (1)

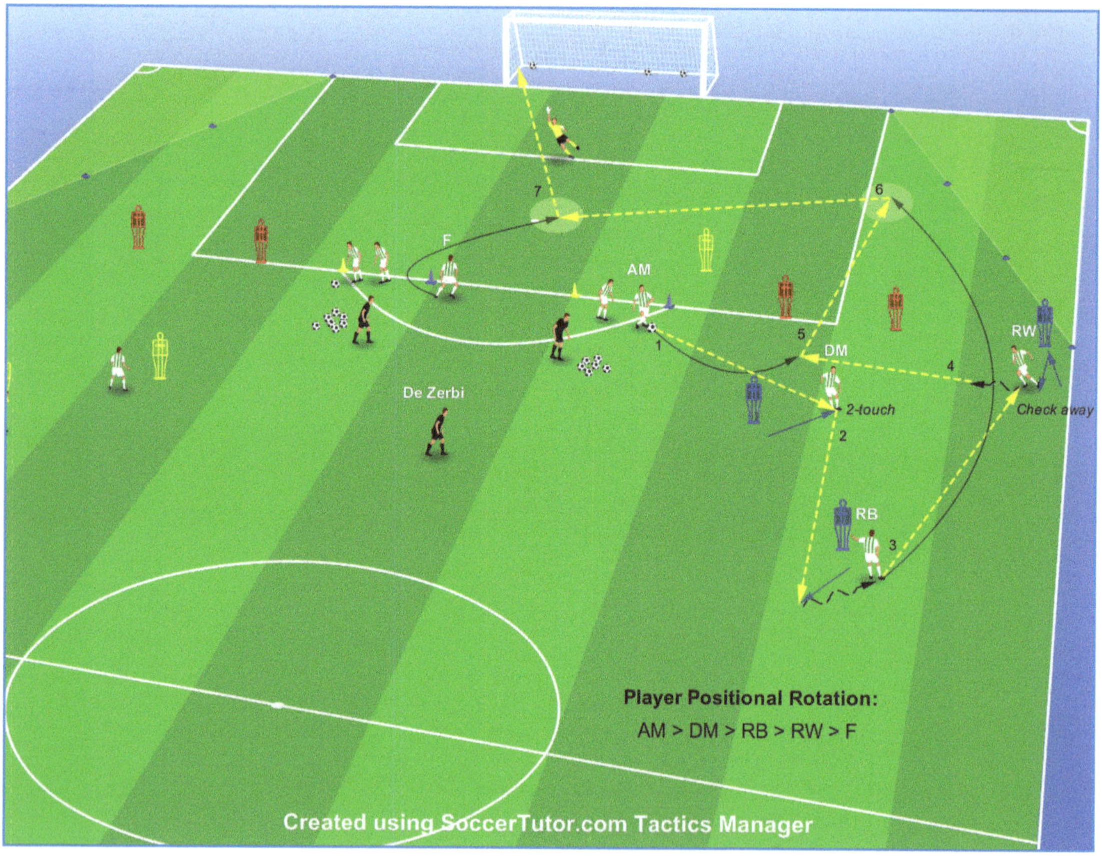

De Zerbi
AM
F
DM
RW
RB
2-touch
Check away
1
2
3
4
5
6
7

Player Positional Rotation:
AM > DM > RB > RW > F

Created using SoccerTutor.com Tactics Manager

Practice Description

This was also practiced on the left side. The players rotate AM → DM → RB → RW → F.

1. The attacking midfielder (**AM**) passes to the defensive midfielder (**DM**), who moves off the mannequin.
2. **DM** has opened up and passes back to the right back (**RB**), who drops back off the mannequin to receive.
3. **RB** takes a diagonal touch past the mannequin and passes wide to the right winger (**RW**), who checks away from the mannequin before moving to receive.
4. **RW** touches the ball inside and passes for the movement of **AM**.
5. **AM** plays a through pass for **RB's** deep overlapping run in behind.
6. **RB** cuts the ball back to the penalty spot.
7. The forward (**F**) has run around the cone and times his movement well to score.

Source: Roberto De Zerbi's Sassuolo Calcio preseason training session in Vipiteno, Italy - 19th July 2018

3. Wide Attacking Combination Play with Full Back's Overlap Run, Cut Back + Finish (2)

Player Positional Rotation:
AM > DM > RB > RW > F

Created using SoccerTutor.com Tactics Manager

Practice Description

This was also practiced on the left side. The players rotate AM → DM → RB → RW → F.

1. The attacking midfielder (**AM**) passes back to the defensive midfielder (**DM**), who moves inside off the mannequin.
2. **DM** passes back to the right back (**RB**), who drops back off the mannequin.
3. **RB** takes a diagonal touch past the mannequin and passes wide to the right winger (**RW**), who checks away from the mannequin before moving to receive.
4. **RW** touches the ball inside and passes for the movement of **AM**, who has checked away before moving to receive.
5. **AM** plays a through pass for **RB's** deep overlapping run in behind.
6. **RB** cuts the ball back to the penalty spot.
7. The forward (**F**) has run around the cone and times his movement well to score.

Source: Roberto De Zerbi's Sassuolo Calcio preseason training session in Vipiteno, Italy - 19th July 2018

4. Attacking Combination Play with One-Two, Full Back's Third Man Underlap Run in Behind, Cut Back + Finish

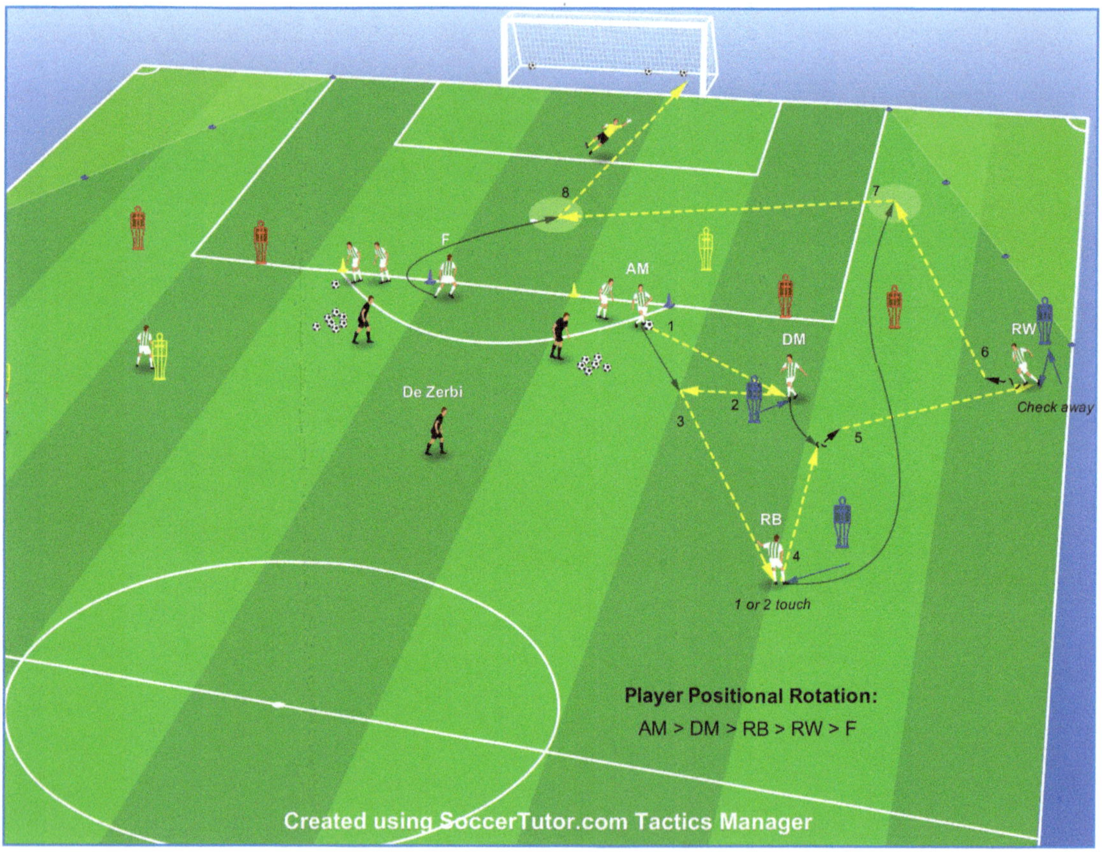

Practice Description

This was also practiced on the left side. The players rotate AM → DM → RB → RW → F.

1. The attacking midfielder (**AM**) passes to the defensive midfielder (**DM**).
2. **DM** plays the return for **AM** (one -two).
3. **AM** passes back to the right back (**RB**), who drops back off the mannequin.
4. **RB** passes to **DM**, who drops to receive and turn.
5. **DM** passes wide to the right winger (**RW**), who checks away from the mannequin before moving to receive.
6. **RW** takes a touch inside and passes in behind for the deep underlapping run of **RB** in between the 2 red mannequins.
7. **RB** cuts the ball back to the penalty spot.
8. The forward (**F**) has run around the cone and times his movement well to score.

Source: Roberto De Zerbi's Sassuolo Calcio preseason training session in Vipiteno, Italy - 19th July 2018

5. Pass Wide, Set the Ball, Pass in Behind for Full Back's Deep Third Man Run in Behind, Low Cross + Finish

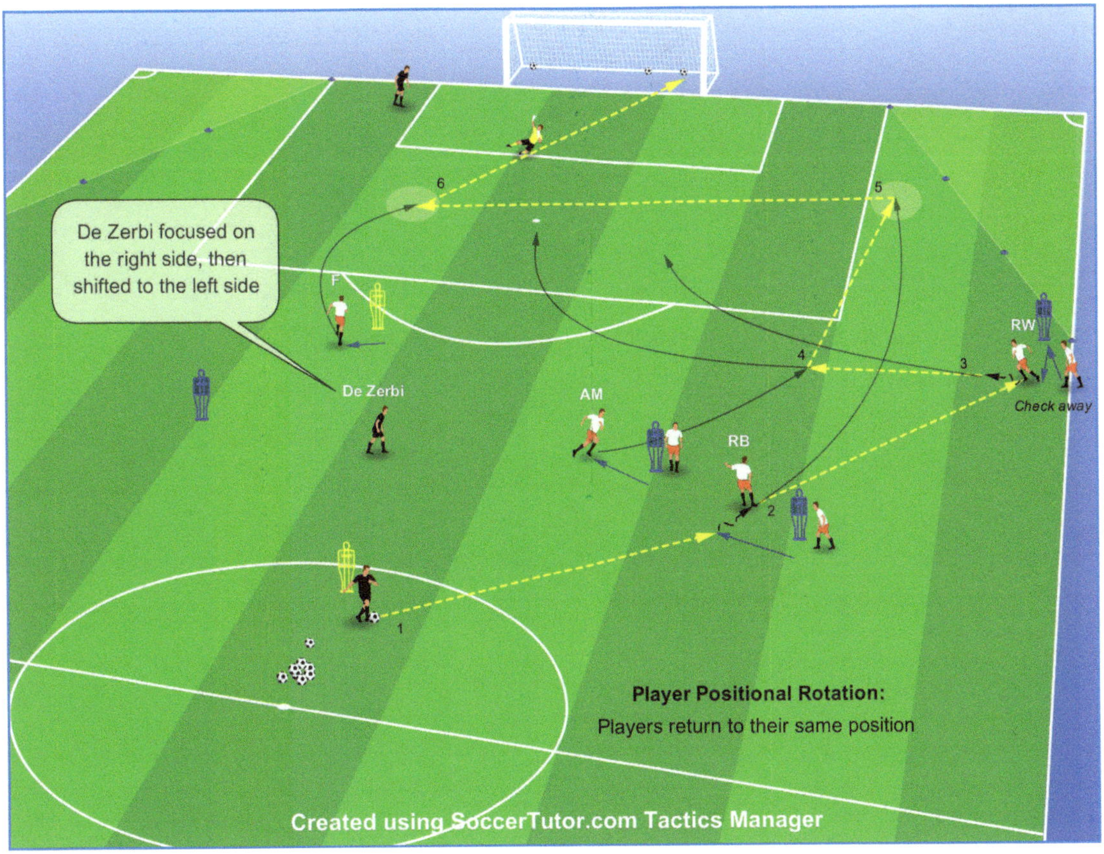

Practice Description

There is no player rotation. Each player returns to the same position to repeat the same sequence after each repetition.

1. The Coach starts with a pass to the right back (**RB**), who moves off the mannequin to receive.
2. **RB** opens up and passes wide to the right winger (**RW**), who checks away from the mannequin before moving to receive.
3. **RW** takes a touch inside and passes for the oncoming **AM** to receive on the run.
4. **AM** plays a through pass for **RB's** deep third man run in behind.
5. **RB** delivers a low cross across the box.
6. The forward (**F**) has made a run on the outside of the mannequin, aiming to time his run well to score from the cross.

→ After focusing on the right side, **De Zerbi** then coached the players on the left.

Source: Roberto De Zerbi's Benevento Calcio training session in Benevento, Campania - 2017

6. Play Through Centre with Forward's Back to Goal Support Play, Through Pass for Winger's Run, Cut Back + Finish

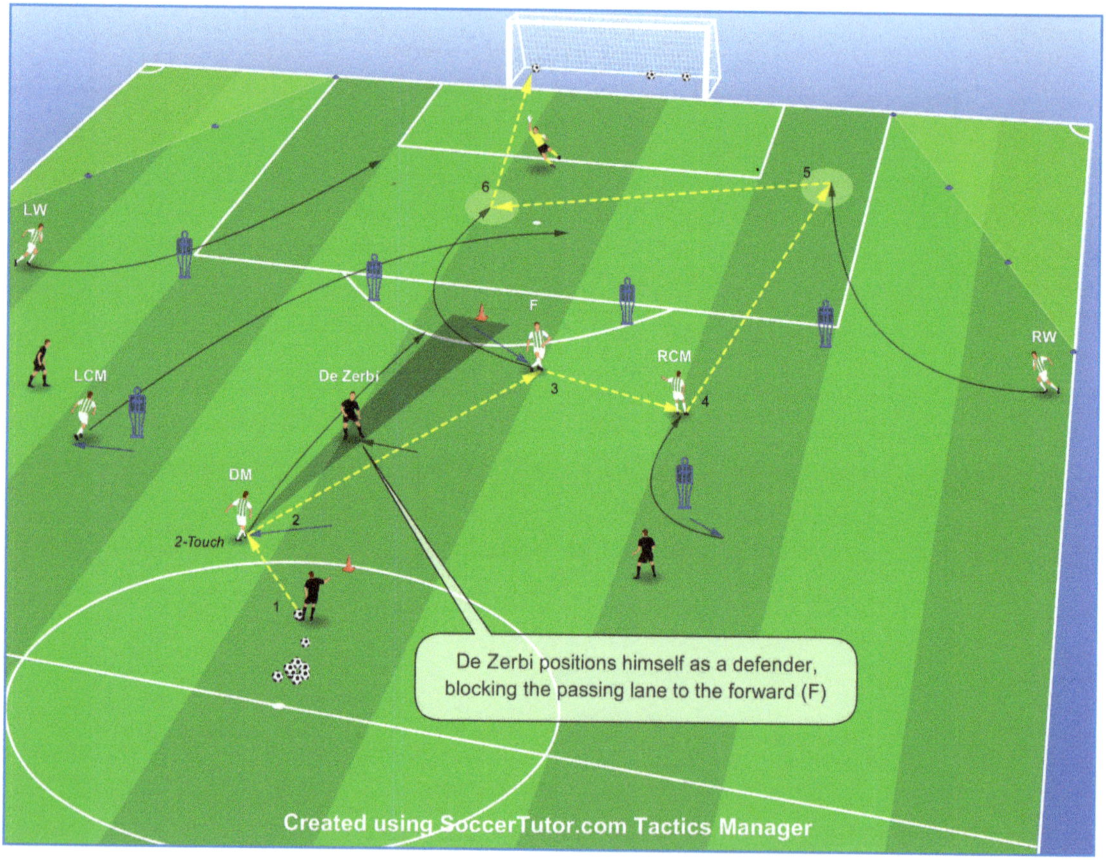

De Zerbi positions himself as a defender, blocking the passing lane to the forward (F)

Created using SoccerTutor.com Tactics Manager

Practice Description

1. The Coach passes to the defensive midfielder (**DM**), who drops and opens up to receive. **De Zerbi** positions himself as a defender to block **DM's** straight passing lane to the forward (**F**).
2. **F** drops off the cone to provide a passing angle and **DM** passes forward to him, evading **De Zerbi**.
3. **F** sets the ball for the oncoming right central midfielder (**RCM**), who initially checks away from the mannequin before making a curved run forward.
4. **RCM** plays a through pass in between the full back and centre back mannequin for the curved run of the right winger (**RW**) off the flank.
5. **RW** cuts the ball back across the box.
6. The forward (**F**) has run around the cone, and times his movement to score. The left central midfielder (**LCM**) and winger (**LW**) also make runs into the box.

Source: Roberto De Zerbi's Sassuolo Calcio preseason training session in Vipiteno, Italy - 18th July 2018

7. Play Through the Centre, Through Pass for Central Midfielder's Third Man Run + Finish

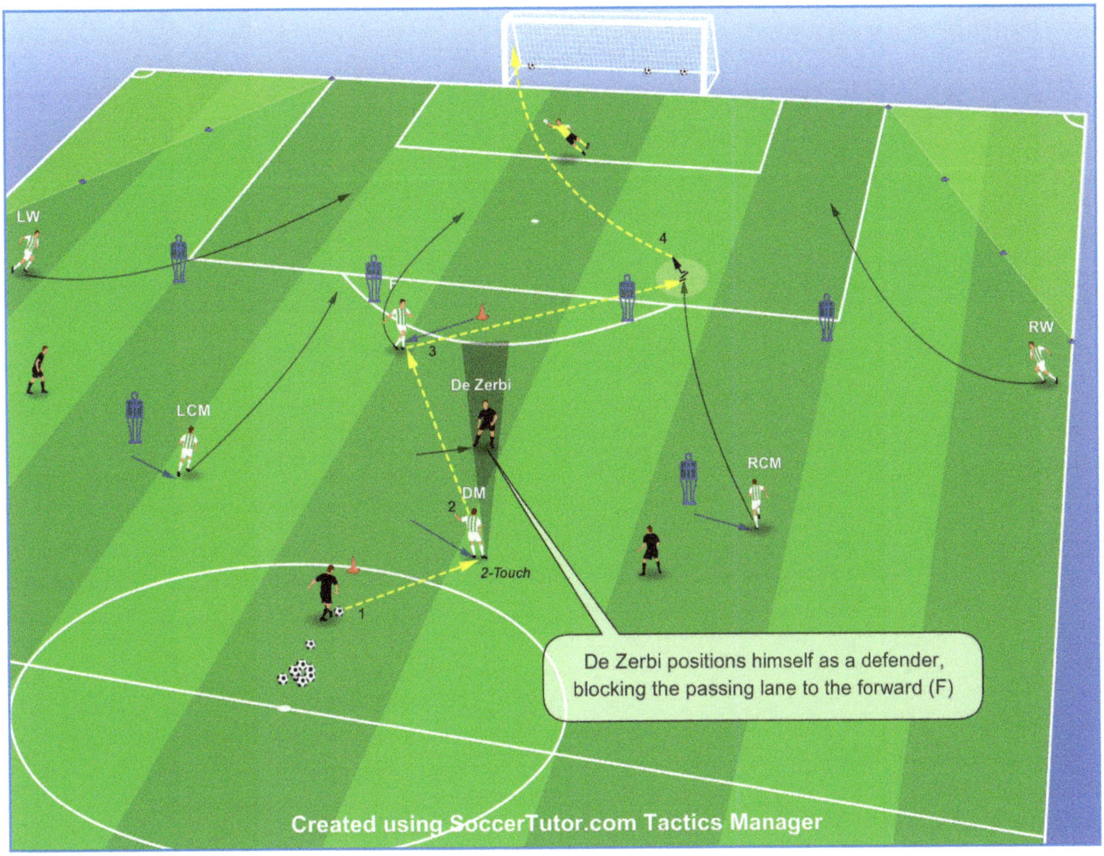

Practice Description

1. The Coach passes to the defensive midfielder (**DM**), who drops and opens up to receive. **De Zerbi** positions himself as a defender to block **DM's** initial passing lane to the forward (**F**).
2. **F** moves diagonally off the cone to provide a passing angle and **DM** passes to him, evading **De Zerbi**.
3. **F** plays a diagonal through pass in between the 2 centre back mannequins for the third man run of the right central midfielder (**RCM**) into the box.
4. **RCM** receives and tries to score past the GK. The left central midfielder (**LCM**), both wingers (**LW** & **RW**), and **F** also make runs into or towards the box to provide support for finishing the attack.

Source: Roberto De Zerbi's Sassuolo Calcio preseason training session in Vipiteno, Italy - 18th July 2018

8. Short Passing Combination Play and Finishing 3-Stations Circuit

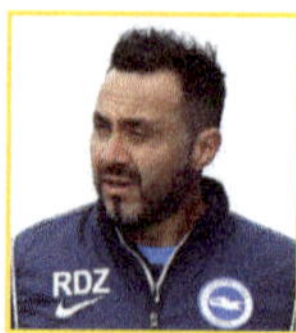

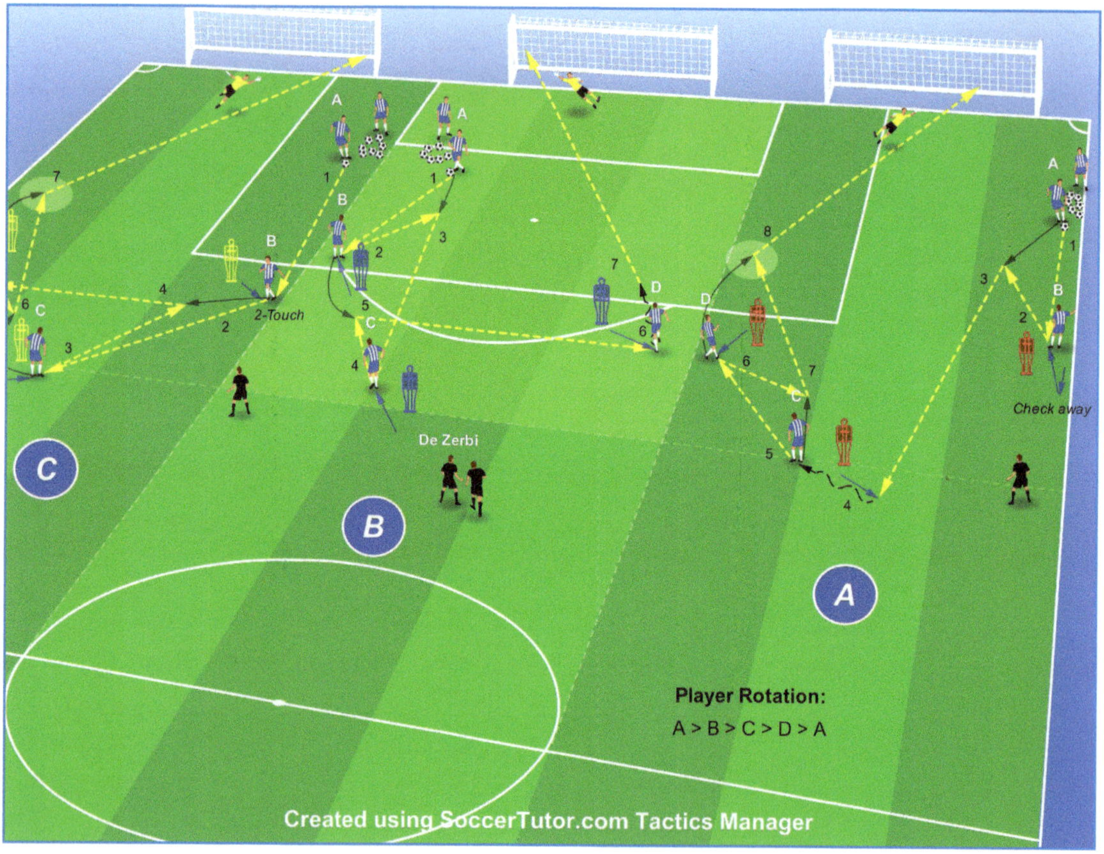

RDZ

2-Touch
Check away
De Zerbi
C
B
A
Player Rotation:
A > B > C > D > A
Created using SoccerTutor.com Tactics Manager

Practice Description

Players work in groups of 5 and move to the next station after a set period of time.

A. Player **A** plays a one-two with **B**, and then passes to **C**, who drops off the mannequin to receive. **C** takes the ball past the mannequin, plays a one-two with **D**, then plays a return pass which **D** receives on the other side of the mannequin. **D** shoots to try and score a goal.

B. Player **A** plays a one-two with **B**, and then passes to **C**, who moves forward off the mannequin to receive. **C** sets the ball for **B** to pass across to **D**. **D** receives, moves towards goal, and shoots.

C. Player **A** passes to **B**, who plays a one-two with **C**. **B** then passes across to **D**, who sets the ball back for **C**. **C** then plays a through pass for **D** ahead of the mannequin. **D** shoots and tries to score.

Source: Roberto De Zerbi's Brighton training session at Elite Football Performance Centre - 21st January 2023

www.ingramcontent.com/pod-product-compliance
Ingram Content Group UK Ltd.
Pitfield, Milton Keynes, MK11 3LW, UK
UKHW051337130225
4581UKWH00037B/448